upholstering methods

by
FRED W. ZIMMERMAN

Professor, Industrial Education
Technology, Western Illinois
University, Macomb

South Holland, Illinois
THE GOODHEART-WILLCOX COMPANY, INC.
Publishers

Library of Congress Cataloging in Publication Data

Zimmerman, Fred W
  Upholstering methods.

  Includes index.
  1. Upholstery.   I. Title
TT198.Z55   684.1'2   80—25308
ISBN 0—87006—313—8

INTRODUCTION

UPHOLSTERING METHODS is designed to provide a broad experience for the beginner who wants to master the basics of reupholstery. It will provide a solid foundation in all upholstery processes, through the use of tools, materials and techniques that are basic to this important area. Special attention has been given to the selection of the upholstery covering.

After the various processes have been mastered through the easy-to-follow step-by-step detailed instruction of the text, which are supplemented by numerous photographs and diagrams, the user will have the opportunity to try out newly acquired skills on a small scale. A section of UPHOLSTERING METHODS is devoted to the building and upholstering of a small furniture piece. Thus, if a larger project might seem overwhelming, the smaller one will provide a meaningful experience and assure success.

Fred W. Zimmerman

CONTENTS

Section 1
UPHOLSTERY MATERIALS
AND EQUIPMENT

As is true of any other occupation, upholstery or reupholstery requires certain tools which are especially designed for the job. Likewise, it depends on materials which have special qualities and characteristics. This section introduces you to the furniture frame and its parts; to adhesives and fasteners; to padding, springs and twine; to stains, sealers and varnishes. It also describes all the tools you will use from bolt cutters to upholstery pins. Finally, it explains about upholstery fabrics and their care.

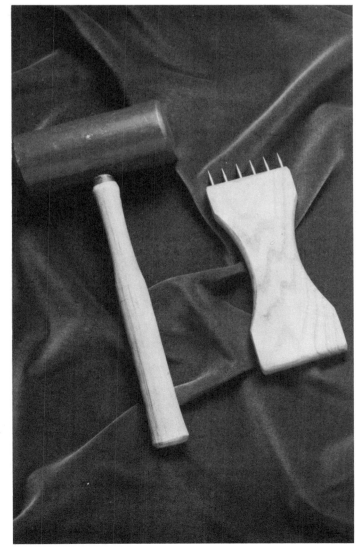

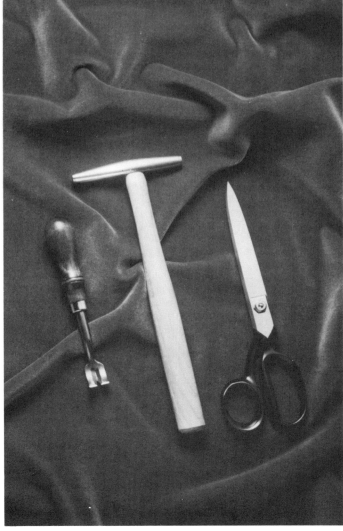

Examples of some of the upholstered furniture offered by an American manufacturer today. Skilled upholsterers are needed when such furniture is built. Their skills are also in demand to restore used furniture to its original beauty and usefulness.   (Kroehler Mfg. Co.)

Chapter 1
UPHOLSTERING MATERIALS

Upholstery materials come from all over the world. Wood for building or repairing furniture frames, cotton and moss for padding of seats and backs come from the United States. But many other materials are imported. For example:

1. Most jute and hemp fibers come from India.
2. Curled hair is brought from South America.
3. Kapok is produced in Java.
4. Needles are made in England.

In this chapter we will discuss the nature, uses and purposes of upholstery materials. Each will be described in the general order in which it is used during upholstering.

FRAME COMPONENTS

Frame components include materials of metal and wood which become a part of the structure of the frame itself. It also includes those parts whose function is to attach or reinforce the structural parts.

DOWELS, PEGS AND BLOCKS

Dowels are round wood pieces usually made of birch. They are made in diameters of 1/8 to 1 in. (3 mm to 2.5 cm) and in 3 ft. (91 cm) length. Dowels are frequently used to reinforce wood parts fastened together with glue. Short dowel pegs with spiral grooves are specially made for wood joints. The grooves allow air and excess glue to escape during assembly and the clamping process. See Fig. 1-1.

Glue blocks are small pieces of wood attached to the frame with glue or metal fasteners to strengthen or brace joints. See Fig. 1-2. Glue blocks also serve as supports for attaching feet or legs under upholstery frame seats. Sometimes they anchor a slip seat to an upholstery frame.

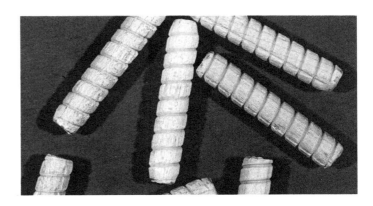

Fig. 1-1. Hardwood dowels and glue make strong butt joints.

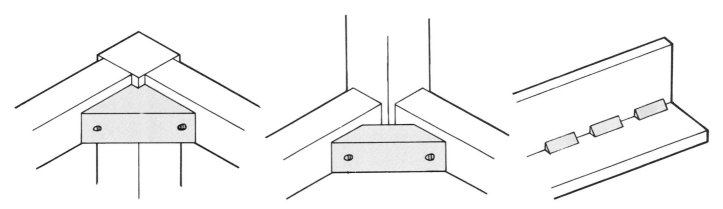

Fig. 1.2 Glue blocks are another device used to reinforce corner joints. On slip-seated chair, they reinforce the joint, hold the legs against rails and provide a base to which the slip seat is fastened.

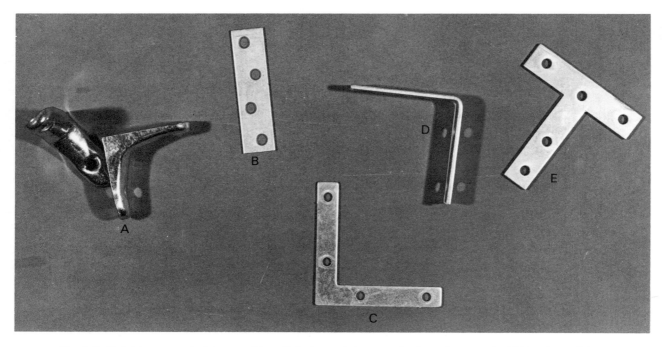

Fig. 1-3. Metal braces and plates provide satisfactory reinforcement where they can be hidden from sight.
A—Chair brace. B—Flat plate. C—Flat corner. D—Bent corner. E—T plate.

METAL STRAPPING AND BRACES

Chair braces, being strong and rigid, are used to strengthen chair joints, particularly near the seat. Chair braces are also useful for attaching furniture frames to tops. Repair strap metal plates are available in a variety of shapes, Fig. 1-3. They can be used on chairs, couches, tables and other furniture.

ATTACHING PLATE AND HANGER BOLTS

Legs are more easily installed with attaching plates and hanger bolts, Fig. 1-4. The hanger bolt has a wood screw thread on one end and a machine screw thread on the other end. The wood screw thread is turned into a hole drilled in the leg and the machine screw thread is fitted into a nut joined to the attaching plate.

GLIDES

Either tilt-base or stationary glides, Fig. 1-5, can be used beneath furniture legs and feet. Glides protect the legs, stabilize furniture, and help in moving it about. Glides also protect the floor.

ADHESIVES AND FASTENERS

Adhesives stick to the surfaces of the materials they are holding together. Fasteners grip the materials mechanically, usually by friction, after the fastener is embedded in the material. Each has its special uses in furniture construction, as we will see.

Fig. 1-4. Legs can be easily detached when attaching bolts and hangers are used. Hangers have threaded holes to receive bolts.

Fig. 1-5. Glides protect bottoms of chair legs. Left. Tilt-base glide. Right. Stationary glide.

Fig. 1-6. Typical cements. Some can be used directly from the container; others must be mixed before use. Contact cement offers instant bonding.

Fig. 1-7. All of these glues are satisfactory for bonding of woods and other furniture materials.

Many adhesives have been developed with special purposes and properties. A variety is shown in Fig. 1-6 and Fig. 1-7.

Method of application differs with type of product. Always read the manufacturer's directions carefully before using any cement or glue.

RUBBER CEMENT

Rubber cement bonds paper, cardboard, felt, and other light, porous materials. Especially useful in preparing patterns, it is available in ready-mixed, liquid form. Rubber cement is brushed on to the surfaces of both pieces to be attached. When the cement has dried to a dull appearance, the two pieces can be carefully pressed together.

FOAM CEMENT

Foam cement is specially made to adhere foam cushion material to other seat material. It is available in brush or spray form.

CONTACT CEMENT

Contact cement is frequently used to fasten veneer or laminated plastic to other surfaces. It is sold in liquid form and may be applied with a brush, roller, or spray gun. One or more thin coats are applied to the bonding surfaces of both pieces. When dried (usually after 30 minutes) to a dull appearance, the surfaces are carefully brought together.

As the name implies, this cement bonds instantly on

contact of two coated surfaces. Keep the pieces separated with wrapping paper or dowel rods until properly positioned. Once in contact, parts cannot be shifted. Then, working from one end, begin removing the dowels or paper and press the two parts together. Move toward the other end, pressing from the center outward, and removing the separating materials a piece at a time. Roll the surface with a large dowel or rubber roller to remove air pockets. Tapping the surface with a block of wood and a mallet will also help bond the surfaces together.

PLASTICS CEMENTS

Plastics cements are useful for repair jobs on a variety of materials. These cements usually come in tubes.

Airplane cement, a common plastics adhesive, sets quickly and hardens overnight to form a waterproof bond. It can be used to fasten porous or impervious materials.

One of our strongest adhesives is epoxy cement. It is usually packed in two separate parts, a resin and a catalyst. These are mixed in small amounts as the cement is used. Epoxy cement usually requires six to eight hours curing time. It dries to a hard, waterproof consistency.

ALIPHATIC RESIN GLUE

Aliphatic resin glue is a cream-colored, nonstaining liquid adhesive which comes in ready-to-use form. A very strong glue, it produces a joint, if properly made, that is stronger than the wood itself. It is highly resistant to heat and chemicals. When dry, aliphatic resin glue sands easily without clogging sandpaper.

This glue sets quickly, requiring only about 45 minutes curing time at temperatures above 70 °F (21 °C). It can be used at temperatures as low as 40 °F (4 °C). Aliphatic resin glue is excellent for use on upholstery frames and furniture. Its chief disadvantage is its inability to resist moisture. However, it is a good choice for interior work.

WHITE LIQUID RESIN GLUE

White liquid resin glue (polyvinyl acetate) comes in convenient squeeze bottles. It spreads easily at temperatures above 60 °F (16 °C). White glue is strong and has good gap-filling qualities. It sets and dries quickly, usually requiring only about 30 minutes of clamping time. Only enough pressure is required to pull the joints tightly together. Twenty five psi or 172 kPa of clamping pressure should be sufficient.

Polyvinyl glue dries by moisture absorption and evaporation. When dry it is flexible and colorless making it ideal for furniture and cabinetwork. A disadvantage is its lack of resistance to heat and moisture.

Remove excess glue before sanding to prevent clogging the sandpaper.

ANIMAL GLUE

Animal (hide) glue, made from hides and hooves, is one of the oldest wood glues. A liquid form is packaged in plastic squeeze bottles for easy application and storage. Being difficult to prepare, the dry form is seldom used, except by expert gluers on production jobs. It must be dissolved in water, heated to about 140 °F (60 °C) and applied hot.

Hide glue is excellent for furniture and cabinetwork. Since it is not waterproof, it should be used only for interior work. Hide glues should be clamped 3 to 4 hours at temperatures above 70 °F (21 °C).

PLASTIC RESIN GLUE

Plastic resin glue (urea-formaldehyde) is highly moisture resistant and very strong when used properly. It is most suitable where it will be subjected to large amounts of moisture for a short time. However, plastic resin glue should be used only with non-oily woods.

A powder, it is mixed with water to a creamy consistency. It is easy to use, becoming hard and brittle when dry. Drying, a chemical process, takes place slowly. Thus, there is plenty of time for clamping.

Plastic resin glue should be used only on stock with well-fitted joints. The joint should be clamped securely for six to eight hours or longer at temperatures above 70 °F (21 °C). Additional heat is desirable since it helps set the glue. Certain compounds of this glue are used with electronic gluing equipment.

RESORCINOL RESIN GLUE

Packaged in powdered form, this glue is mixed to a creamy consistency with a liquid catalyst and water immediately before use. Being a very strong, waterproof glue, it can be used with materials subjected to large amounts of moisture. Resorcinol glue, however, creates an unwanted dark glue line and requires 12 to 16 hours of clamping time at temperatures above 70 °F (21 °C).

CASEIN GLUE

Casein glue is made in powder form primarily from milk curd. Before use, it is mixed with cold water and allowed to stand a few minutes. Then it is further mixed to a creamy consistency. It is a strong glue requiring moderate clamping time. Casein glue can be used at temperatures just above freezing, but it works better at warmer temperatures. It is water resistant and especially useful with oily wood, such as cypress. Casein glue has a tendency to stain some woods, like maple and oak.

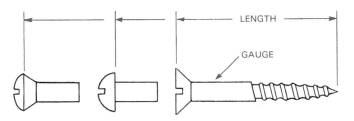

Fig. 1-8. Screw length is measured from its tip to point on head which is at surface of material it is holding. Left. Oval head screw. Center. Round head screw. Right. Flat head screw.

SCREWS

Screws fasten hardware and pieces of wood which may need to be disassembled later.

Many kinds and sizes of screws are made from mild steel, brass, aluminum and other metals. Finishes include bright, blued, zinc chromate, brass, copper, nickel, and chromium. Diameters are given by gage numbers from 0, the smallest, to 24. Lengths are marked in inches from 1/4 to 6 in.

Flat head screws are designed so the heads rest flush with the surface of the wood or slightly below it. The entire screw, head to point, is measured to determine its length. Since heads of round head screws fit on top of the wood surface, the length is measured from under the head to the tip. Heads of oval head screws are partially recessed into the wood surface. The length is determined by measuring from the point of recess to the tip of the screw point. See Fig. 1-8. Heads of screws may be slotted to take a regular screwdriver or recessed to take a Phillips screwdriver.

UPHOLSTERY MATERIAL

Attached to the furniture frame are the materials which provide the comfort built into upholstered furniture. Included are not only the padding and the covers but the materials which provide support, such as tacks, springs and webbing.

Fig. 1-9. Jute webbing is sold in rolls.

Fig. 1-10. Burlap is a coarse-woven jute or hemp fabric. Heavier weights—12 oz. and above—are recommended for upholstery use.

WEBBING

Webbing provides support for padding materials or springs. Jute webbing, a closely woven strap or tape, is made from jute fibers. It is very strong and comes in widths of 3, 3 1/2 or 4 in. (7.5, 9 or 10 cm) by 72 yd. (66 m) or more long. Jute webbing, generally khaki colored, is available in three quality grades. Grades are indicated by colored stripes running the length of the webbing. Red stripes indicate the highest grade and black the lowest. See Fig. 1-9. Webbing is also made of rubber, plastic, wood and steel.

BURLAP

Burlap is a coarse, strong fabric loosely woven from jute or hemp. Widths range from 36 to 100 in. (91 to 254 cm) but a 40 in. (102 cm) width is most common in upholstery. Weights usually range from 8 to 16 oz. (0.23 to 0.45 kg). Burlap is generally used to cover springs before installing padding materials. It is also used for edge rolls and as a foundation base over webbing, Fig. 1-10.

MUSLIN

A lightweight, cotton cloth, muslin is sold unbleached or bleached. It is an open-textured fabric often used as the first covering over padding materials. This covering helps produce the right density of padding, eases installation of the final covering and gives it a smoother appearance. See Fig. 1-11.

Fig. 1-11. Muslin is often used to encase padding materials—especially if they are loose—before final covers are installed.

Fig. 1-12. Denim is a strong, usually inexpensive fabric used as covering material where it will not show.

DENIM

Denim is a strong, twilled cotton fabric, Fig. 1-12. It comes in plain colors or has a small pattern woven into it. Plain denim is sometimes used for upholstering under loose cushions. Figured denim is used for upholstering furniture and for mattress covers.

CAMBRIC

Cambric is a lightweight fabric, generally made of cotton. It is sized and glazed during manufacture to render it dust resistant. White cambric is often used for cushion and pillow casings. Black cambric, Fig. 1-13, being less conspicuous, is used on the bases of upholstered furniture to catch loosened stuffing materials and to keep out dust.

Fig. 1-13. Light and inexpensive, cambric is chiefly used as a covering for undersides of furniture. White cambric is sometimes used to encase stuffing for pillows.

UPHOLSTERY FASTENERS

Upholstery tacks have flat heads and are made of steel with blued finish. Tacks fasten upholstery fabrics to frames in unexposed areas or in areas where they can be hidden with more decorative materials. Sizes range from No. 1 to No. 24. Numbers 3 to 14 are generally used in upholstery. The best size is determined by strength needed, thickness of materials being fastened, and quality of frame. Tacks are packaged in 1/4 lb. containers and larger. See Fig. 1-14.

Gimp tacks are designed to fasten cloth gimp (narrow decorative edging) and other outside covering materials to exposed portions of furniture frames. The small round heads are easily concealed in the nap of the fabric.

Gimp tacks, though considered obsolete for modern upholstery methods, are still useful to have. They are made of steel which is coated for rust protection. See Fig. 1-15.

Fig. 1-14. No. 12 upholstery tacks are quite large. The larger the number the larger the tack.

Fig. 1-15. Gimp tacks are packaged in 1/4 lb. and larger containers. Sizes range from No. 2 (5/16 in.) to No. 8 (10/16 in.).

Fig. 1-16. Metalene tacks are used to attach vinyl plastic gimp. They are decorative and come in several colors.

Metalene nails, generally made of steel, have large, rounded heads 1/4 to 1/2 in. in diameter. See Fig. 1-16. They are available in several colors in packages of 1000. Their most frequent use is for attaching and decorating vinyl gimp trim.

Furniture nails are made of either brass or steel. Heads are large, measuring 1/4 to 1/2 in. (6 mm to 1.2 cm) in diameter. Made in several designs, shapes and finishes, these fasteners are color coordinated to a variety of furniture coverings.

They may be used for:
1. Decorative purposes.
2. Attaching gimp to furniture.
3. Attaching coverings to furniture.

Like metalene nails, furniture nails are packaged in quantities of 1000. See Fig. 1-17.

Fig. 1-17. Furniture nails also have decorative heads. Top. Smooth finish. Bottom. Hammer finish.

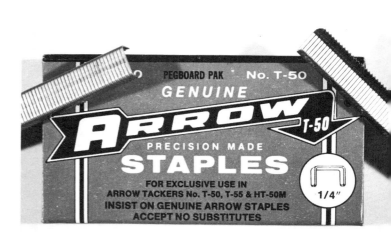

Fig. 1-18. Staples, such as these, are meant to be used in tack guns. Single bars are loaded into the gun. Spring action feeds staples to the driving head one at a time.

Staples are pieces of wire bent to a "U" shape. They have a sharp point at either end to make driving easier. Lengths range from 1/4 to 9/16 in. (6 mm to 1.4 cm). They are made up in bars by temporarily attaching the staples to one another horizontally. See Fig. 1-18. The bars, of uniform length, are inserted into a gun which drives the staples one by one. The gun is powered by electricity, air pressure or by a strong spring. Usually the staples are packaged in quantities of 5000. They are useful for attaching a variety of materials to furniture frames.

Sinuous (no sag or zig-zag) nails are made of hardened steel, 14 gage or heavier and in lengths of 3/4 to 1 in. They are usually barbed or cement coated for greater holding strength and are used to fasten spring clips to furniture frames. Sinuous nails are sold in 1 lb. packages or in larger quantities, Fig. 1-19.

Upholstery-covered buttons are used as decoration and to shape final covering and padding materials. Buttons are covered by hand or machine to match the final covering material used. You can generally purchase covered buttons from upholstery supply companies.

Fig. 1-19. Heavy nails are needed to secure clips for sinuous springs.

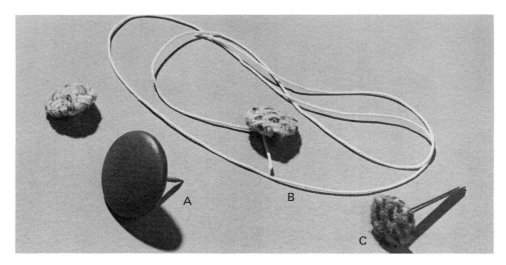

Fig. 1-20. Upholstery-covered nails add interesting detail to upholstery seats and backs. A—Nail type. B— Eyelet and string type. C—Clasp type.

Three methods are used to fasten buttons:
1. Clasp.
2. Eyelet and string.
3. Nail. See Fig. 1-20.

Hog rings, so called because they resemble the rings placed in the snouts of pigs, are popular as fasteners because they are quickly and easily used. They are made of 14 or 15 gage steel wire bent into "U" shaped grippers. See Fig. 1-21.

Available in lengths of 1/2 to 3/4 in. (1.2 to 2 cm), the rings are sold by the pound. A specially designed pliers installs them by a crimping action that closes the points across each other forming a somewhat irregular circle. Hog rings are used to attach burlap, sisal pads, seat covers and other materials to springs.

Edge wire clips, used to fasten edge wire to springs, are stamped from strip steel. They are made in lengths from 3/4 to 1 3/8 in. (2 to 3.5 cm) and in inside widths of 9/32 to 3/8 in. (7 to 9 mm). They are made in various shapes and must be installed with a special pliers. See. Fig. 1-22.

Metal spring clips are designed to fasten sinuous springs to furniture frames. They may be purchased in quantities of 100 or 1000, Fig. 1-23.

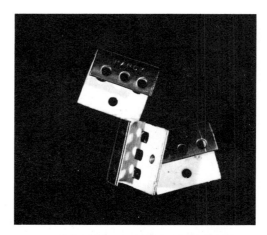

Fig. 1-21. Hog rings have pointed ends to pierce material as they are closed with a pliers.

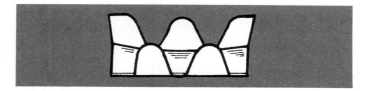

Fig. 1-22. Edge-wire clip is designed to wrap around top spiral of coil spring and spring edge when building seat and back spring units. Special pliers are needed to close it.

1-23. Sinuous spring clip must be strongly made to hold spring under constant tension.

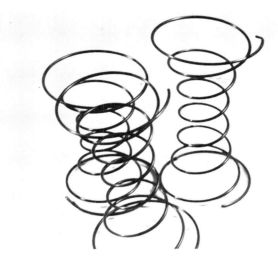

Fig. 1-24. Coil springs with widening spirals at each end are called "double coil" springs.

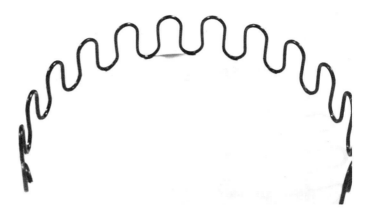

Fig. 1-26. Slimline furniture often uses the sinuous spring pictured. Curves give it spring action.

SPRINGS

Springs are made of steel wire in several sizes, gages and shapes to serve a variety of purposes.

Upholstery springs are made with single or double coils and are used for seats. Seat springs are made of heavy wire, 9 to 11 gage, and range from 4 to 14 in. high. These are available in hard, medium and soft firmness, Fig. 1-24.

Innerspring (Marshall) units are coil springs individually sewn in muslin or burlap pockets. These pockets are fastened together in strips or ready-made units. Innerspring units are used in seats of overstuffed furniture, furniture backs, cushions, and sometimes arms. Spring wire is generally 15 gage and coils are 3 in. in diameter by 3 1/2 to 6 in. high, Fig. 1-25.

Sinuous (sagless, no-sag, or zig-zag) springs, Fig. 1-26, are made from a continuous length of wire which is bent into a zig-zag shape and rolled into a coil. They are used for furniture seats (usually 7 to 9 gage) and backs (generally 10 to 12 gage). Special metal

Fig. 1-27. Helical springs act as fasteners to distribute weight of other springs they are fastened to. They are 1 3/8 to 6 in. long and are 15 to 17 gage.

clips, as shown in Fig. 1-23, are used to attach the spring sections to furniture frames.

Helical springs are short, lightweight springs with a hook at either end. They are often used to anchor sinuous springs, particularly outside rows, to furniture frames. See Fig. 1-27.

Fig. 1-25. Innerspring or Marshall units are small coil springs individually encased in muslin pockets.

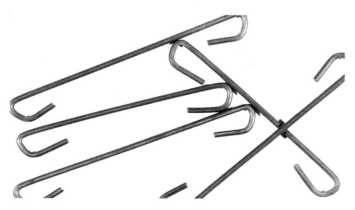

Fig. 1-28. Metal connecting links are used to distribute weight between sinuous springs.

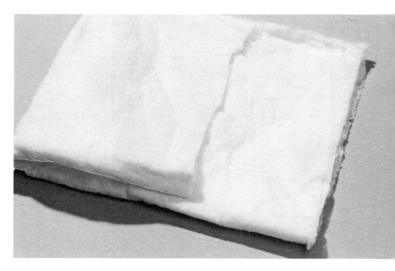

Fig. 1-30. White wadding provides thin layer of very soft padding.

Metal connecting links are generally used to interconnect sinuous spring rows providing even distribution of the seating load. These links are usually available in 2 to 4 in. (5 to 10 cm) lengths, Fig. 1-28.

PADDING

Fiber mat, a coarse, resilient material made from fibers of the sisal plant, is used for platform foundation padding, and to pad arms and backs of furniture. It usually comes in 50 ft. (15 mm) rolls, 24 in. (61 cm) wide, Fig. 1-29.

White wadding is a thin cotton padding usually sold in rolls 12 yd. (11 m) or more in length and 32 in. (81 cm) wide. See Fig. 1-30.

Curled hair, made of refined hair from hogs and other animals, is available loose by the pound or in rubberized pads 24 .n. (61 cm) wide by 1 to 3 in. (2.5 to 7.5 cm) thick. Rubberized hair is ideal for foundation padding or as padding over springs, Fig. 1-31.

Foam rubber, Fig. 1-32, is manufactured in flat solid sheets 1/4 to 1 1/2 in. (6 mm to 3.7 cm) thick. Its resistance to compression ranges from medium to firm.

Fig. 1-31. Rubberized curled hair is sold in mats of uniform thickness.

Fig. 1-29. Sisal matting provides a firm foundation for additional platform padding.

Fig. 1-32. Foam rubber is popular as padding for chairs, benches and stools.

Fig. 1-33. Foam plastic comes in both medium and firm compression. It provides firm support with great comfort.

Fig. 1-35. Dacron polyester fiberfill padding, like cotton mat, is used to provide extra softness over other padding material. It also is used as pillow stuffing.

Foam plastic, Fig. 1-33, is often substituted for foam rubber. Sheet thicknesses range from 1/2 to 5 in. (1.2 to 13 cm).

Cotton mat is sold in 15 lb. rolls, 27 in. (68.5 cm) wide or by the bale. It is available in several grades and is generally used over other foundation padding for greater softness, Fig. 1-34.

Dacron polyester fiberfill, Fig. 1-35, is often used over other padding as a substitute for cotton mat. It is sold in rolls 27 in. wide and produces a soft, resilient surface.

Moss, sometimes called Spanish Moss, is refined from an air plant that lodges on trees in the southern United States. See Fig. 1-36. In recent years, it has lost its popularity to other padding materials.

Kapok (silk floss) is refined from the seed pods of the "ceiba pentandra" tree which grows best in Java. Kapok, Fig. 1-37, is a soft, silky, resilient material highly resistant to moisture. It is sold loose by the pound or in bales.

Fig. 1-36. Moss was once used widely as a loose stuffing. It is sold loose by the pound or bale.

Fig. 1-34. Cotton mat is usually added over other coarser padding for extra comfort.

Fig. 1-37. Kapok is used as a loose stuffing for pillows, cushions and mattresses.

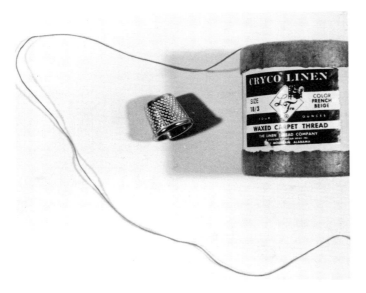

Fig. 1-38. Spring twine must be strong to withstand the stress of holding springs under constant tension. Best grades should be used for longer life.

TWINE AND THREAD

Spring twine, Fig. 1-38, is used to fasten seat and back springs and hold them in position on the frame. It has a waxed or polished finish and is available in 1 lb. (0.5 kg) balls, six balls to the package; 5 lb. (2.3 kg) tubes and 50 lb. (23 kg) reels.

Stitching twine is made of flax or linen that has been waxed. It is used to stitch springs to webbing, burlap to springs and padding to burlap. It comes in 4 oz. (113 g), and larger, packages. See Fig. 1-39.

Tufting twine is needed to attach covered buttons to other upholstery materials. It is available in 4 oz. and larger rolls, Fig. 1-40.

Sewing thread is needed to sew welt strips, cushion seams, corner folds and upholstered backs. Cotton and nylon thread are available in a variety of colors and quantities, Fig. 1-41.

Fig. 1-39. Linen stitching twine is a heavy duty cord intended to fasten down springs and padding.

Fig. 1-41. Sewing thread. Either cotton or nylon is suitable.

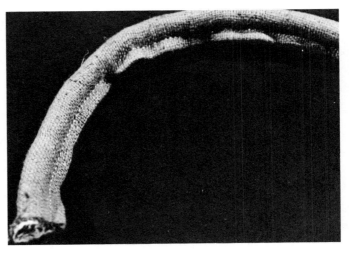

Fig. 1-42. Prefabricated spring or edge roll. Core is often made of paper. Covering is burlap.

Fig. 1-40. Tufting twine. Nylon is recommended.

Fig. 1-43. Blind tacking is packaged in rolls 600 ft. long.

EDGING MATERIALS

Ready-made spring and roll edging is prepared in diameters of 1/2 and 1 in. (1.2 and 2.5 cm). It is sold in lengths of 50 ft. (15 m) or more. Roll edging is fastened to furniture frames to smooth sharp edges along springs and around seats or arms. See Fig. 1-42.

Blind tacking strip is a narrow band of stiff paper, 1/2 in. (1.2 cm) wide and 1/32 in. (0.8 mm) thick, Fig. 1-43. It is used for blind tacking outside arms, sides and backs.

COVERINGS

Truly fine upholstery is made from leather. Top grain cattle hides are sold by the square foot in full and half hides. For 36 in. material, 12 sq. ft. is usually allowed for a yard. For 50 to 54 in. material, 15 to 17 sq. ft. is generally allowed for one yard, depending upon the variety of shapes and patterns.

Whole hides average 45 sq. ft. This is equivalent to about 3 yards of 50 to 54 in. material. Imperfections on the top grain (hair) side of leather, such as briar marks or scratches, are natural defects often considered marks of distinction. Excellent top grain leather is available from upholstery supply companies. See Chapter 3 for more information.

Vinyl plastic Naugahyde materials have remarkable resemblance to genuine leather or fabrics. Their tough, resilient surfaces render years of enjoyable service with considerable saving in cost. Vinyl plastic material is usually manufactured with a width of 54 in. (137 cm) and is sold by the lineal yard. Samples of the finest vinyl upholstery materials are available from upholstery supply companies. Refer to Chapter 3 for additional information.

Their warm appeal and comfort keep cloth fabrics in great demand. Variety in design, weave, texture and color of cloth fabrics is almost unlimited. Cloth fabric upholstery material is generally manufactured with a width of 54 in. (137 cm) and is sold by the lineal yard. Samples of fine cloth fabrics are available through upholstery supply companies. See Chapter 3 for a description of fibers and weaves suitable for upholstery.

Gimp is a thin, narrow tape of material 1/2 in. (1.2 cm) wide, Fig. 1-44. Often used to cover upholstery tacks or staples around the edges of covering material, it is sold by the yard.

Plastic gimp is made of vinyl plastic and is fastened to furniture frames with metalene nails. It is made in several colors to match covering materials.

Fabric gimp is made with decorative fabric in a variety of colors to match covering materials. It is fastened to furniture frames with gimp tacks.

Welt cord is the rope-like core material sewn inside fabric covering strips. When fabricated, it is used to form decorative seams in the final upholstery covering material. See Fig. 1-45.

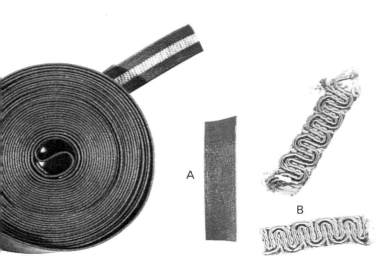

Fig. 1-44. Gimp is supplied in large rolls. Pieces are cut to length as needed. A—Plastic gimp. B—Cloth gimp.

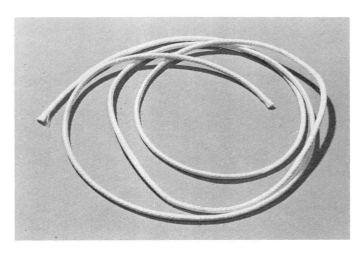

Fig. 1-45. Fiber flex welt cord is packaged in spools of 500 yards. Cord sizes range from 4/32 in. to 7/32 in. diameter.

FINISHING AND REFINISHING PRODUCTS

A special aspect of upholstering is the finishing and refinishing of wood parts that are exposed. A number of products are required for preparation of the wood, coloring or staining and, then, recoating of the wood with a final finish.

PAINT AND VARNISH REMOVERS

Ready-to-use preparations for effectively removing paint and varnish from wood surfaces are readily available from paint and hardware stores. These preparations are formulated in various ways so that different needs are met by different products. Some are liquid for quick action; others are in semi-paste form so they will cling to vertical surfaces long enough to lift the finish. Some are intended to be washed off with liberal application of water; others, for indoor use, are meant to be scraped off with putty knife or steel wool. Nonflammable types are formulated for safe use where flames may be present. Different types are shown in Fig. 1-46.

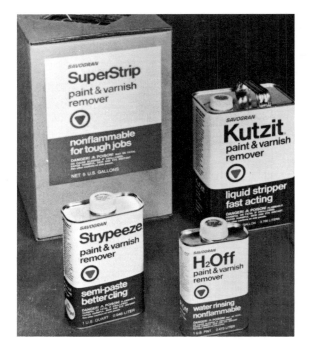

Fig. 1-46. Paint and varnish removers are formulated to handle a variety of different finish-removing situations. (Savogran Co.)

SANDING AND SMOOTHING MATERIALS

Coated abrasives (sandpapers) are manufactured in a variety of grit sizes, in several types and weights of backing and in a choice of four or more types of abrasive particle. There are two systems which classify the abrasives for their degree of roughness or smoothness:
1. A numbering system corresponding to mesh size of screening used to sift the abrasive particles.
2. An older symbol system of zeroes and numbers referring directly to the grit particle.

The numbering system ranges from 400 which is very fine to 20, very coarse. The number corresponds to the number of holes in a linear inch of the screen used to separate the grit. Sandpaper classified as 400 is covered with abrasive particles small enough to fall through the holes of a 400-mesh screen.

In the symbol system, coarse abrasives are classified with numbers and fractions. Finer abrasives are classified with zeroes preceded by another number. The higher the preceding number, the finer the abrasive.

The chart in Fig. 1-47 lists mesh sizes available and gives corresponding symbols. Coarse sizes are intended for fast cutting; fine grits are for smoothing the surface in preparation for finishing.

Coated abrasives are made in sheets, belts, disks and drums. Sheet sizes are usually 9 by 11 in. (23 by 28 cm). The grit materials (manufactured or natural) include:
1. FLINT, a rock material known as quartz. Low in cost, it is neither as tough nor as durable as other abrasives.
2. GARNET, a natural red silicated mineral which is tough and durable.

CLASS	MESH SIZE	SYMBOL	CLASS	MESH SIZE	SYMBOL
	400	10/0		100	2/0
	360	--	Medium	80	1/0
Very	320	9/0		60	1/2
Fine	280	8/0		50	1
	240	7/0	Coarse	40	1 1/2
	220	6/0		36	2
	180	5/0	Very	30	2 1/2
Fine	150	4/0	Coarse	24	3
	120	3/0		20	3 1/2

Fig. 1-47. Abrasive materials are manufactured in a number of degrees of fineness and coarseness. Chart lists mesh sizes which are replacing the symbols.

Fig. 1-48. Wood defects—gouges, holes and cracks are repaired with these products.

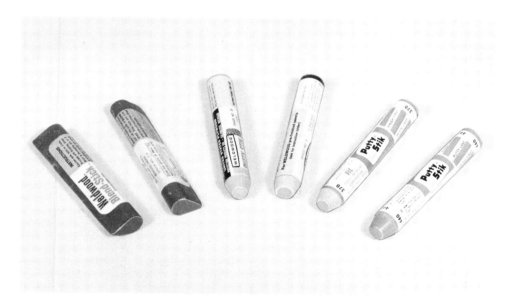

Fig. 1-49. Putty and blend sticks are crayon-like products used to repair defects after finish has been applied.

3. ALUMINUM OXIDE, synthetic grit made by heating aluminum ore (bauxite) in an electric furnace. It is tough and durable with sharp cutting edges.
4. SILICON CARBIDE, a synthetic green-black material made from silica, petroleum coke, salt and wood sawdust. It is sharp, brittle and nearly as hard as diamonds. Its main use is in production work.

Steel wool

Steel wool is made of thin shavings of steel which are packaged in pads and rolls. Grades vary from very fine (4/0) to coarse (3). Steel wool is used to smooth intricate and curved surfaces, and for smoothing finished surfaces.

Polishing compounds

Still finer abrasives are used as polishing compounds. PUMICE, a finely ground lava, is used for rubbing down varnishes and other clear finishes. Grades FF and FFF are most common. ROTTENSTONE, an iron oxide produced from shale, has a red-brown color. It is finer than pumice and is usually used for a final fine polishing when a high luster is desired.

Fillers

Fillers are soft, doughlike materials designed to repair holes, cracks and other defects in wood. They include plastic wood, wood putty, water putty and stick shellac. See Fig. 1-48 and Fig. 1-49.

Fig. 1-50. Finishing products such as these put a protective and sometimes penetrating finish on woods.

Fig. 1-51. These solvents are used as thinning mediums for shellac, lacquer and varnish.

Wood and water putties are powdered and must be mixed with water. Putty sticks are designed to correct wood defects after finishes have been applied. Stick shellac is melted with a heated knife and worked into the hole or defect.

STAINS, FINISHES AND THINNERS

Stains, finishes and thinners are products designed to beautify the natural grain and markings of wood. Thinners are solvents for the pigments and vehicle (fluids) making up the finishes. See Figs. 1-50 and 1-51. Refer to Chapter 5 for more information on these products and how to use them.

REVIEW QUESTIONS — CHAPTER 1

1. What is the most frequent use of doweling in furniture building and repair?
2. Indicate a use for each of the following adhesives:
   a. Rubber cement.
   b. Foam cement.
   c. Contact cement.
   d. Animal glues.
3. What is webbing and how is it used?
4. _____ is a lightweight cotton material often used as the first covering over padding material.
5. What is a gimp tack? How is it used?
6. _____ is a plastic covering material which resembles leather.
7. The roughness or fineness of sandpaper is classified by a _____ system which corresponds to the _____ size of screening used to sift the abrasive particles.
8. What are pumice and rottenstone? How are they used?
9. _____ are soft, doughlike materials for repairing defects in wood.
10. Match items in the left column with descriptions in the right column. (Do not write in the book. Use a separate answer sheet.)
    a. Upholstery springs.
    b. Innersprings.
    c. Sinuous springs.
    d. Helical springs.
    e. Spring twine.
    f. Tufting twine.
    g. Spring and roll edging.
    h. White wadding.

    1. Thin cotton padding.
    2. Single or double coils with large spirals at top tapering to narrow center or bottom depending on type.
    3. Small resilient, roll of padding contained in narrow band of fabric; used to smooth sharp edges of springs and frames under padding materials.
    4. Coil springs contained in cloth pockets and used to cushion backs and seats of upholstered furniture.
    5. Heavy cord used to attach buttons to upholstery.
    6. Flat springs used in backs or seats.
    7. Small, tightly coiled springs with hooks at each end.
    8. Strong cord used to tie back and seat springing materials.

Chapter 2
TOOLS AND EQUIPMENT

Nothing is more frustrating to the beginner in upholstering than attempting to work without proper equipment. This chapter will describe the basic hand tools and the minimum amount of equipment needed. Some of the tools might be unfamiliar. In such cases, their proper use will also be discussed.

As with any type of craft, quality is important and, if tools must be purchased, this should be kept in mind. The satisfaction derived from using a good, well designed tool will continue long after its cost is forgotten.

WEBBING STRETCHER

This tool, Fig. 2-1, stretches webbing tightly across furniture frames. A series of small spikes about 1/2 in. long catch the material and hold it while the handle acts as a lever to apply pressure downward. The edge opposite the spikes is covered with rubber so the tool cannot slip or mar the exposed furniture parts, Fig. 2-2.

Fig. 2-1. Webbing stretcher has metal handle to increase leverage. (George W. Mount, Inc.)

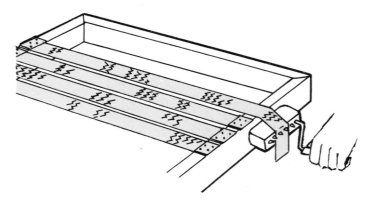

Fig. 2-2. Using long handled webbing stretcher. Pressure is applied with one hand while other hand is free for tacking.

Another kind of webbing stretcher is shown in Fig. 2-3, view A. Its design is similar except that it has no separate handle. Fig. 2-3, view B, shows how to use it.

Steel webbing, sometimes used to repair sagging seat webbing, requires a special tensioning tool. Fig. 2-4 shows a steel webbing tensioner and how to use it.

SPECIAL PLIERS

Also called the "sagless webbing stretcher," the stretching pliers, Fig. 2-5, is used for stretching short pieces of webbing and restretching sagging webbing. Its wide, ribbed jaws also make it a useful tool for stretching burlap, leather and other materials. To use it, squeeze down on the grips to close the jaws. Push downward on the handle to stretch the material. The short protruding section on the lower jaw rests against the frame and acts like a lever.

The hog ring pliers, Fig. 2-6, holds and closes the metal clips which resemble hog rings. It is generally used in production work to install burlap over springs or to fasten covers and other upholstery materials.

Spring clip pliers, Fig. 2-7, are designed to close the special steel clips which fasten metal edge wire or spring edge wire and the top edges of coil springs. Fig. 2-8 shows how the clips are attached.

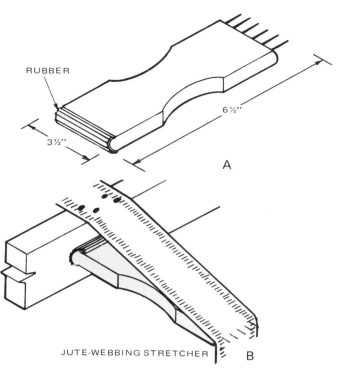

Fig. 2-3. Another kind of webbing stretcher has handle which is part of stretcher body. A—Dimensions of stretcher. B—How the stretcher is used.

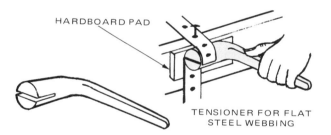

Fig. 2-4. Webbing tensioner has a slotted end which grasps metal webbing firmly without danger of slipping. Block or pad will protect show wood.

Fig. 2-5. Stretching pliers is designed to grasp short ends of webbing and hold them under tension.   (George W. Mount, Inc.)

Fig. 2-6. Straight nose hog ring pliers. Head is shaped to hold hog rings securely as they are closed.

Fig. 2-7. Spring clip pliers is designed to close three-prong spring clips.

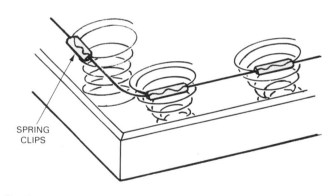

Fig. 2-8. Spring clips are employed to fasten coil springs to spring edging.

RIPPING TOOLS

The ripping chisel, Fig. 2-9, is helpful in removing used upholstery materials from furniture frames (stripping). Its wedge shaped working end is designed to slide under tack heads. The shank has a double bend which allows you to elevate your hand to a comfortable

Fig. 2-9. Ripping chisel. Durable handle is designed to withstand pounding from hardwood mallet. It is 7 to 8 in. long.

Fig. 2-10. Staple lifter has slotted edge which gets under staples of various sizes. (George W. Mount, Inc.)

Fig. 2-11. Claw tool works like claw on carpenters' hammer.

angle above the frame during use. The handle is made of break resistant plastic, or wood with a metal ferrule to prevent its splitting when struck with a mallet.

The staple lifter, Fig. 2-10, prys out staples as you remove upholstery materials from furniture frames.

The claw tool is similar to the ripping chisel. It has a fine, notched point which easily slides under the tack heads. This design allows the claw tool to lift tacks or nails all the way out with a downward motion of the handle. It will generally lift bent or poorly driven fasteners without damaging upholstery materials. See Fig. 2-11.

Beginners usually prefer the claw tool to the ripping chisel for ripping. As they grow more skilled, they discover that the ripping chisel is faster for most work.

HAMMERS

Upholsterers' hammers, Fig. 2-12, are made in several sizes and styles. Each style is suited to a certain job. The nylon tipped hammer head is designed for driving fancy furniture nails without marring their finish. Metal tipped heads are designed for driving assorted fasteners.

Tips are of different sizes and designs. The large tip, 1/2 in. in diameter is meant for driving tacks and nails. The smaller tip is slotted and magnetic. It allows you to pick up tacks and start them into the wood one-handed. The head is small in diameter, curved and quite long. This makes it possible to tack deep into corners without damaging upholstery materials or furniture frames.

MALLET

Mallets, Fig. 2-13, may be made of rawhide, wood or rubber. They are needed primarily for striking the handles of the ripping chisel, staple lifter and claw tool. A rubber or rawhide mallet is best for knocking apart frames that are in need of regluing. The softer material will not mar the wood.

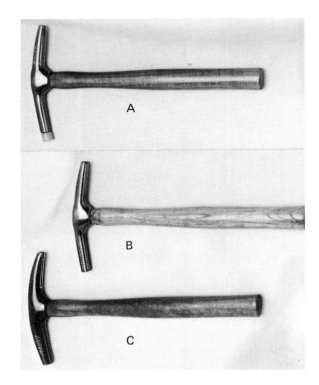

Fig. 2-12. Upholsterers' hammers. A—Nylon tip, 7 oz. head. B—Magnetic 7 oz. head. C—Magnetic split-end with 9 oz. head. (George W. Mount, Inc.)

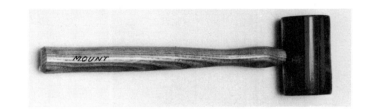

Fig. 2-13. Mallet is usually used along with one of the tools for lifting out fasteners. (George W. Mount, Inc.)

UPHOLSTERERS' SHEARS

Ten-inch, heavy duty shears are preferred for cutting webbing, burlap, rubberized hair pads and covering materials. See Fig. 2-14. Those with offset (bent) handles are easier to use on a cutting table. Having to lift covering materials too high off the table could cause

Fig. 2-14. Upholsterers' shears. Heavy duty kind work best.

Fig. 2-15. Cloth measuring tape is needed for accurate measurement of curved surfaces.

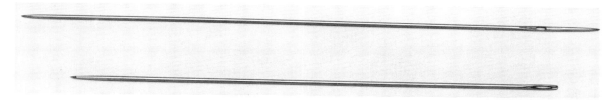

Fig. 2-16. Metal straight edge rule is used for marking straight cutting lines.   (George W. Mount, Inc.)

Fig. 2-17. Straight double-pointed needle is favored for sewing springs and padding to webbing.

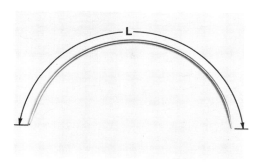

Fig. 2-18. Curved upholstering needle. Size is measured along the curve.   (George W. Mount, Inc.)

a crooked cut. Keep the shears well oiled and sharp. Be sure to wipe away excess oil before use.

MEASURING AND LAYOUT TOOLS

Several tools should be on hand for measuring and marking such materials as padding, casing and final covers. Cloth or tape rules are needed for measuring dimensions especially on rounded and irregular surfaces. See Fig. 2-15. For measuring and marking pieces of fabric, metal or wood straightedges are used, Fig. 2-16. Marking of fabrics requires dressmakers' chalk or tailors' wax.

UPHOLSTERING NEEDLES

Straight needles are either single or double pointed and may have rounded or triangular points. Lengths range from 4 to 20 in. (10 to 50 cm).

The double-pointed needle, Fig. 2-17, is often preferred since it may be pushed through the material and returned without being reversed. This saves time, especially when sewing springs to webbing.

The curved needle, Fig. 2-18, allows the upholsterer to sew back and forth through materials without having to reach behind the work. Curved needles vary in length from 2 to 10 in. (5 to 25 cm) and, like the straight needle, have either round or triangular points. They are available in light or heavy weights. Lightweight needles are used with thin materials.

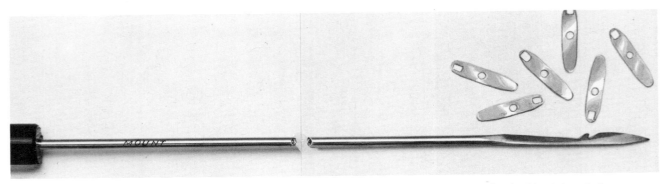

Fig. 2-19. Button tufter. Patented metal clip allows attaching buttons to back or seat after backing is installed.

Fig. 2-20. Stuffing regulator can be inserted through muslin casing to adjust padding.

Fig. 2-21. Stuffing iron pushes stuffing into hard-to-reach corners. Toothed edge grips stuffing material.

Fig. 2-22. Channel tins or channel stuffing tins compress padding for easier stuffing of channel pockets.

Tufting needles are made in several designs usually ranging from 12 to 14 in. (30 to 36 cm) long. Usually made of surgical steel, they are well adapted to the rugged task of installing buttons. Often, such needles must carry strong thread through several thick layers of stuffing and webbing materials.

Fig. 2-19 illustrates a tufting needle designed to carry a metal clip through the material without need to have access to the exposed springs or webbing. To use this tufter:

1. Thread twine through the round hole in the clip and tie it.
2. Hook the clip onto the needle through the square hole and push the needle through the material.
3. Withdraw the needle. The clip will fall off and lodge behind the webbing acting as an anchor for the twine.
4. Fasten the loose end of the twine to the underside of the button with a slip knot.
5. Slide the knot until the button is at the right compression against the cover. Cut off the excess twine. Buttons used in tufting are shown in Chapter 1. See Fig. 1-20.

STUFFING TOOLS

The stuffing regulator, Fig. 2-20, is used to smooth irregularities in stuffing materials underneath muslin or other coverings beneath the final cover. Though shaped much like a needle it is much heavier. Both a light and a heavy gage are available. Sizes range from 6 to 12 in. (15 to 30 cm) long.

The stuffing iron or stuffing rod is a narrow, rigid piece of steel usually about 18 in. (46 cm) long. It is used to stuff loose padding materials in the corners and other hard-to-reach areas. One end has a toothed edge which grips the stuffing materials. See Fig. 2-21.

Channel tins usually come in pairs. They are used to compress resilient materials being used to stuff channels (pipes or flutes). They are made of light metal in widths of 2 to 4 in. (5 to 10 cm) and are about 36 in. (91 cm) long. See Fig. 2-22.

UPHOLSTERY PINS

The upholsterers' pin or skewer holds fabric in place while it is sewed, tacked or stapled. It is a short length

Fig. 2-23. Upholsterers' pin or skewer is made heavy to hold heavy coverings in place during blind stitching. (George W. Mount, Inc.)

Fig. 2-24. Lighter weight T pin is used in same way as upholsterers' pin.

Fig. 2-25. Hand operated, spring loaded stapler is used with one hand. It often replaces tack hammer. (Arrow Fastener, Inc.)

of wire, 3 to 3 1/2 in. (8 to 9 cm) long. It has a sharp point at one end for piercing fabric. The other end has a loop, Fig. 2-23.

The T pin, Fig. 2-24, is smaller. Though only 1 to 2 in. (2.5 to 5 cm) long it is used in the same way as an upholsterers' pin.

STAPLERS

Though not essential to upholstering, staplers speed up the installation of upholstery materials. One hand can manipulate the stapler while the other stretches and holds the material. For hand work, the spring loaded stapler, Fig. 2-25, or a stapler hammer is generally used. Electric or pneumatic staplers are frequently used commercially. See Fig. 2-26.

BOLT CUTTER

While a sidecutting pliers or a hacksaw will cut most wire used in upholstering, a bolt cutter is a helpful tool for cutting tempered metals like edge wire and sagless (sinuous) springs. See Fig. 2-27.

Fig. 2-26. Electric stapling gun is preferred by commercial upholsterers because of its speed. (Duo Fast Corp.)

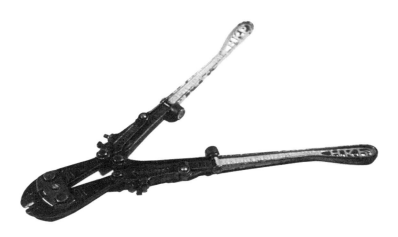

Fig. 2-27. Bolt cutter. This is handy, though not indispensable tool for upholsterer. It speeds up cutting of spring wire and sinuous spring material.

Fig. 2-28. Driving common slotted screw with screwdriver. Holes should be predrilled.

Fig. 2-29. Variable speed electric drill is fitted with Phillips screwdriver to speed up driving of screws.

SCREWDRIVERS AND BORING TOOLS

Screws with slotted heads are driven with a regular screwdriver. A variety of sizes should be on hand to fit different sizes of screws. The tip of the screwdriver should fit the screw slot. A screwdriver too large for the screw may damage the screw slot and tear the wood. One that is too small is inefficient and may break. Screws with Phillips heads are driven with a Phillips screwdriver. With speed control, screwdriver tips can be used effectively in an electric or pneumatic drill. See Fig. 2-28 and Fig. 2-29.

Drilling or boring of holes for dowels and screws will require hand or power drills and drill bits. Holes larger than 1/4 in. are bored with an auger bit, expansion or forstner bit. They are held in a brace like the one shown in Fig. 2-30. The brace will hold either round or square bit shanks. A suitable power tool is the electric drill pictured in Fig. 2-29. Fig. 2-31 illustrates a variety of

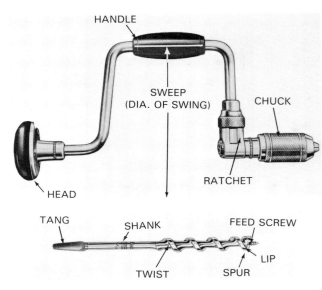

Fig. 2-30. Large holes can be drilled with brace and auger bit. Top. Brace with parts named. Bottom. Parts of an auger.

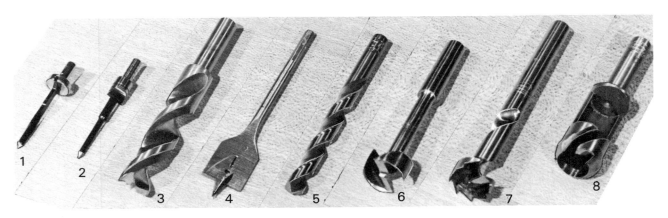

Fig. 2-31. Power operated drill will use any of these machine drill bits. 1—Screwmate. 2—Screwmate counterbore. 3—Spur machine bit. 4—Speed or spade bit. 5—Twist drill. 6—Forstner. 7—Multi-spur bit. 8—Plug cutter.

machine drill bits which can be used with either a drill press or the hand electric drill. Drilling screw holes with the screwmate bit is shown in Fig. 2-32.

CLAMPING DEVICES

Clamping devices are available in many sizes and types. They are necessary in furniture repair whenever glues are used to fasten joints or repair split and broken wood. Some clamps must be capable of exerting and maintaining great pressure while the glue cures. In using any clamp, especially a metal one, use great care not to mar the wood, Fig. 2-33.

HANDSCREWS

Handscrews (parallel clamps) have two adjustable wood jaws which should be carefully set before use. See Fig. 2-34.

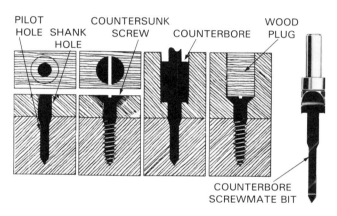

Fig. 2-32. Operation of counterbore screwmate. One drill operation makes hole to hold recessed screw and wooden plug.

Fig. 2-33. How to protect lumber facings. Scrap lumber top and bottom protects wood surfaces from clamp anvils.

To adjust the handscrew, grasp the "end" spindle, Fig. 2-35, with your right hand so that the direction for rotating the handscrew for adjustment will always be the same to open or close the jaws. Rapid adjustment of the handscrew is obtained by proper "swinging." Hold handles firmly, arms extended, and, by motion of the wrist only, make the jaws revolve. When the jaw opening is about right, adjust either or both handles so that the jaws grip the work easily and are slightly more open at the end.

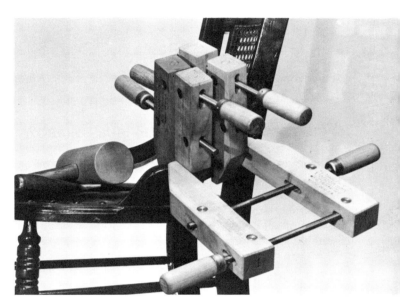

Fig. 2-34. Used alone or in combinations, handscrews perform a variety of clamping tasks.   (Adjustable Clamp Co.)

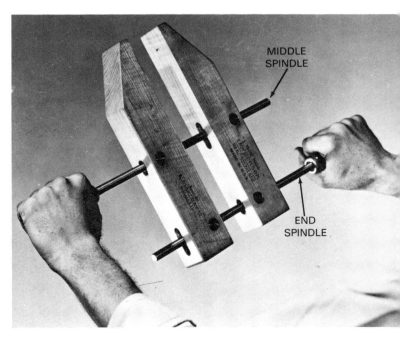

Fig. 2-35. Adjusting jaws of handscrew. With left hand on middle spindle and right hand on end spindle, rotate jaws in action similar to "pumping" a bicycle.

Fig. 2-43. Heavy duty sewing machine is designed especially to handle thick stitching jobs.   (Singer Co.)

upholstery seams. For extensive sewing, it is recommended that a heavy duty machine be used, Fig. 2-43.

CUSHION FILLERS

Cushion fillers compress cushion padding materials and make it easier to install final coverings. Hand sets are economical and are generally suitable for small shops and training centers. They come in three sizes: 24, 36 and 48 in. The smallest size is adjustable in

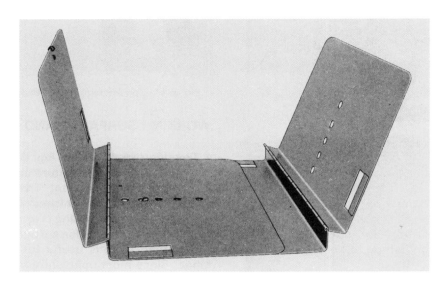

Fig. 2-44. Hand set cushion filler is adjustable to several sizes.
(Lochner Mfg. Co. and Charles W. Meline, WIU.)

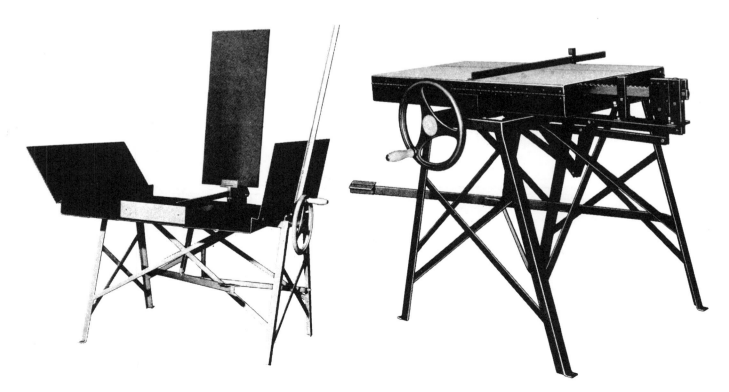

Fig. 2-45.   Foot operated machine set cushion fillers. Left. Open position. Right. Closed position.

width from 15 to 22 in. (38 to 56 cm). Hand sets are made of two sheet metal halves which are fastened with a hook and eye closure. See Fig. 2-44.

To use the hand filler, place the two halves together on a bench to form a box shape. Open the top and place the cushion in the box. Close the top and hold the filler case crosswise against the body. Pull the halves together to compress the cushion. Slip the cushion cover over it. After cover is on, unlock the filler halves by applying sharp pressure to the cushion. Remove the filler halves.

Foot operated cushion fillers are made in several sizes. These units, Fig. 2-45, are used in industrial production.

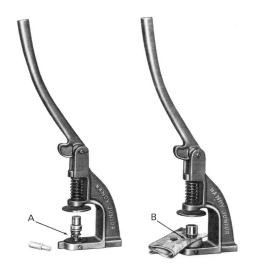

Fig. 2-46. Button covering machine used in upholstering field. A—Button assembly anvil. B—Fabric cutter. (Handy Button Machine Co.)

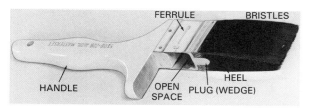

Fig. 2-47. Cutaway shows construction details of a good brush.

BUTTON COVERING MACHINE

Button machines are manufactured for both hand and power (electricity or air) operation. The machines, Fig. 2-46, cut the fabric and force it into position around the button. Upholstery supply companies usually offer this service for a nominal charge.

BRUSHES

Occasionally, refinishing of exposed parts of a wooden frame will require brushes for staining and applying clear finishes. Brushes are manufactured in many sizes, shapes and grades. Only good quality brushes should be used in handling stains and varnishes.

Bristles may be natural animal hair or a synthetic material. Usually nylon is used. The bristles are generally set in rubber. A metal ferrule is used to attach the bristles to the handle. See Fig. 2-47.

REVIEW QUESTIONS — CHAPTER 2

1. Name the several tools used to stretch or tension webbing and explain for what materials each is suited.
2. Upholsterers may use the following hammers or striking tools (select the correct ones):
   a. Nylon tipped upholsterers' hammer.
   b. Magnetic tack hammer.
   c. Wood mallet.
   d. Magnetic split end tack hammer.
   e. Ball peen hammer.
   f. Claw tool.
   g. All of the above.
3. Explain the difference between a ripping chisel, a claw tool and a staple lifter.
4. Explain the advantage of a curved needle over a straight needle.
5. Name the stuffing tools used in upholstery.
6. List at least three clamping tools used by upholsterers.
7. A _____ _____ compresses cushion padding materials, making them easier to slip inside final coverings.
8. Brushes for applying finishes are available in two types of bristles, _____ and _____.

Chapter 3
SELECTING UPHOLSTERY FABRICS

The upholsterer has a wide variety of coverings from which to choose. Perhaps it is the most important choice that must be made. A wisely chosen fabric has much to do with the pleasing appearance and durability of the upholstered unit.

The covering should be suited to the type and style of furniture being covered. In general, material of modern design looks best on modern units. Traditional designs look best on traditional and period furniture.

FABRIC SUITABILITY

In the same way, size suggests the kind of covering to use. Large, sturdy pieces require coarse weaves, leather or solid plastic material with a coarsely textured surface. Velvets, silks and other finely textured weaves look best on small, light furniture. Plain and brightly colored weaves make large pieces appear larger. Vertical stripes appear to lend height and make pieces appear narrower; horizontals have the opposite effect. Avoid scenic patterns and large figures on channeled surfaces. Wide vertical stripes, large designs and scenic patterns can rarely be used successfully on tufted or small surfaces. See Fig. 3-1.

Consider also the use to which the finished upholstered piece is put:

1. If wearability is important, choose plastic, leather or a durable fiber in a tight, hard weave, Fig. 3-2.

Fig. 3-1. Upholstery material with large pattern looks well on large furniture pieces. Smaller pieces, as above, are best upholstered in small-figure patterns or solid colors.   (American of Martinsville)

Fig. 3-2. Furniture which will receive hard usage should be upholstered in durable materials.

Fig. 3-3. More delicate fabrics suit the more delicate lines of this chair. (American of Martinsville)

Show pieces can be covered in more delicate fabrics, Fig. 3-3.

2. Some finishes resist soiling better than others. A fiber may have this property naturally or a special coating may have given it this quality.

3. If the finished piece will be used where there is considerable sunlight, choose fabrics which resist damage and fading from ultraviolet rays. Many synthetics have this quality.

4. If the furniture will be subjected to heavy use and soiling, choose a fabric which will clean easily.

5. Covers that tear easily, stretch too readily or have loose surface threads will not last long under heavy usage. Better to choose longer lasting goods such as mohair, synthetics or leather.

The room in which the furniture will be used will have a certain character which will also help you decide color and texture of upholstery material, Fig. 3-4. If a room is small, using different shades of the same color will make it appear larger. Likewise, combinations of neutral colors used with bright accessories will expand the small room.

Fig. 3-4. Color and texture of upholstery material is carefully planned to fit these surroundings.

If you wish to add excitement to a room use complementary colors. These are the opposites on the color wheel, for example, red and green. By far, the most popular color schemes are those which combine related colors such as blue and green or red, orange and yellow. Color, texture and pattern of upholstery must harmonize with surroundings.

KINDS OF UPHOLSTERY MATERIALS

Upholstery materials are of two basic kinds. There is cloth made by weaving or knitting natural or synthetic fibers into a fabric. There is solid material such as leather and plastic. The latter is usually bonded to a woven or knitted backing cloth.

In recent years, the variety of plastic materials for upholstering has grown greatly. Even so, the greater variety of fabrics is still in woven materials. The durability, appearance and desirability of a woven cloth is affected by four things:

1. Type of fiber.
2. Type of weave. In general, tight weaves are more durable than loose ones.
3. Weight of the fabric. This is determined by the weight (thickness) and density of the yarn used in weaving.
4. Processing. This refers to special treatment of the yarn or cloth to improve one or more of its characteristics. For example, cotton can be mercerized to give it sheen and better wearing qualities and many fibers are treated to make them repel dirt.

FIBERS

The basic material of woven upholstery is, of course, fibers. Cotton, linen (flax), wool, mohair and silk are natural fibers. Among the manufactured fibers suited for upholstery, are rayon, acetate, triacetates, nylon, acrylic and olefin. Each has its own characteristics which make it desirable.

Natural fibers

Cotton, classified as a seed hair, is the most widely used of all textile fibers. It is quite strong and becomes even stronger when wet. Cotton fabrics are noted for their durability, ease of care and economy. These qualities make it a popular covering for all kinds of upholstered furniture.

Linen, made from the fibers of flax, is noted for its strength, coolness and luster. There is little deterioration of fibers due to aging. Sunlight has only a slight affect on fiber strength over a long period of exposure. It is a durable fabric and withstands drycleaning chemicals well. Linen is more expensive than cotton fabrics.

Wool, a protein-base fiber, is somewhat weak and relatively expensive. While it accepts dyes well it tends to shed liquid. Solvents used in drycleaning or to remove stains are not harmful to wool. Prolonged exposure to sun can eventually destroy it. In general, wool fabrics demand a great deal of care and are susceptible to moth damage.

Like wool, mohair is a protein fiber. It is obtained from shearing the long, silky hair of goats. It has remarkable resistance to wear, a high luster, resilience and easily adapts to complex yarns. Mohair is very expensive and has been largely replaced by synthetics. It is noted for its strength, durability, elasticity and luxurious appearance.

Manufactured fiber

The synthetic fibers are classified either as cellulose based or polymer based. Cellulosic fibers include rayon, acetate and triacetate. Polymeric fibers include nylon, acrylic, olefin and saran. There are others but these are the most commonly used.

Rayon is made from wood pulp treated to break down the material so that it can be spun in endless filaments. These filaments are twisted together to form threads.

Rayon, nearly as inexpensive as cotton, has good resistance to drycleaning fluids and stain removers. Ultraviolet rays from the sun can cause deterioration. Combinations of rayon and other fibers such as polyester, acrylic, nylon, silk, acetate, cotton and linen are often found.

Acetate, another of the cellulosic fibers, is closely related to rayon. The cellulosic materials are combined with acetic acid, acetic anhydride and sulfuric acid.

Though relatively weak, acetate fibers are not likely to shrink under normal care and usage. An inexpensive material, acetate can be made into fabric of varying weight, thickness and softness. Prolonged exposure to sunlight will weaken the fiber.

Since they are made from the same raw materials as acetate, triacetate fibers are relatively low in strength. The stable fibers resist aging and are less affected by the sun than silk or nylon. Triacetate fabrics are more expensive than acetate.

Nylon fibers are very strong, elastic, abrasion resistant and absorb little moisture. They are not subject to damage from insects, or mildew and bacteria have no affect on them. Much used in upholstery, they wear well, are easy to clean and do not require protection against moths and carpet beetles.

Acrylic fibers are better known by trade names such as Orlon, Zefran, Creslan and Acrilan. Though more often used in other home furnishings, they are well suited to upholstery because of the fiber's light weight, ease of maintenance and rapid recovery from stretching.

Olefin fibers are a synthetic polymer. There are two types:

1. Polyethylene.
2. Polypropylene.

Selecting Upholstery Fabrics

Since the polyethylenes do not readily accept dyes they are not popular for home furnishings. However, polyethylene is used for carpeting, draperies and upholstering. The fibers are strong, resist weather and mildew and can be cleaned with laundry detergents.

Polypropylene fibers, which have the feel of wool, are low in cost. They are sold under more than a half dozen trade names but Herculon is the one most popular for upholstery.

Also of polymeric origin, saran is only infrequently used as an upholstery material because of its high cost. It is excellent for this purpose because of its dense fiber and cleanability. Soil may be removed with a detergent and lukewarm water. Being very expensive, it is most generally used only for automobile upholstering. The olefin fibers have largely replaced it in common usage.

Fiber glass, a mineral fiber produced mainly from silica sand and limestone, is strong, fireproof, launders easily and resists wrinkling. Beta, a glass fiber produced by Owens-Corning, has been recommended for upholstery fabrics. However, it has not been widely used for that purpose and may be hard to find from suppliers.

Kynol is a flame resistant fiber also recommended for upholstery fabric where fireproof qualities are desired. It is a phenolic fiber and is produced by the Carborundum Company.

The upholsterer must bear in mind the suitability and cost of the many fibers used in upholstery coverings. Fig. 3-5 should be consulted.

COMPARISON OF FIBERS SUITABLE FOR UPHOLSTERY FABRICS

FIBER	COST COMPARISON	STRENGTH	ABRASION RESISTANCE	FEEL	MAIN ADVANTAGE	MAIN DISADVANTAGE
Cotton	low cost	strong	good	soft, cool	can be used many applications	burns and wrinkles easily
Linen	expensive	very strong	very good	much like cotton	durable, has natural luster	wrinkles easily, needs special care
Wool	moderately expensive	moderate	moderate	warm, soft, resilient	easy to sew and shape	needs careful handling, cleaning
Silk	very expensive	strong	good	very soft, warm	beautiful luster, easy to work	high cost, needs careful treatment
Mohair	expensive	moderate	moderate	quite soft, warm, very resilient	lustrous and resilient	difficult to spin evenly
Viscose rayon	low	fairly strong	moderate	soft, limp fiber, cool	has many uses	weak if wet, wrinkles easily
Modified rayon	low	fairly strong	moderate	warmer than oridnary rayon	warmer, deeper texture	weak when wet, wrinkles easily
Acetate	moderately low	moderate	fair	soft, not very resilient	easily worked	heat sensitive, moderately durable
Triacetate	moderate	moderate	fair	like acetate	like acetate but can be heat set and is drip dry	only moderately durable
Polyamides (nylon)	moderately expensive	very strong	excellent	glassy or slippery	strong and tough; can be heat set; drip dry	nonabsorbent; uncomfortable feel in tight weaves .
Acrylics (Orlon, Acrilan, Creslan and Zefran)	moderately expensive	fairly strong	fairly good	soft, warm, resilient	like wool in texture	sensitive to heat and moisture
Olefin						
Polyethylene	relatively low	moderately strong	good	like wool	dense fiber, easy to clean with detergents	does not accept dyes easily
Polypropylene	relatively low	strong	good	like wool	dense fiber, easy to clean with detergents	does not accept dyes readily
Saran	very expensive	strong	good	silky	dense fiber, easy to clean	high cost

Fig. 3-5. Many fibers are suited to upholstery use. Each has characteristics which make it suitable under certain conditions.

TERMS USED IN WEAVING

Special terms are used in describing woven materials:

1. WARP or warp yarn is the yarn which runs the long way of the fabric (in the same direction as the selvage).
2. SELVAGE is the border woven along either side of a piece of fabric to keep it from unraveling. It usually consists of extra warp yarns.
3. FILLING or filling yarn is that yarn which is woven across the width of the fabric at right angles to the warp. Also called WEFT.
4. WEAVE is the pattern or sequence in which the fillers and warp yarns are interwoven.
5. NAP is the hairy or downy surface of a fabric. It is created by brushing the material to raise the individual fibers of the yarn.
6. PILE is the surface created by the ends of yarn or loops fastened to a backing material. (The terms pile and nap are often confused.)

TYPES OF WEAVES

Upholstery fabrics are produced in such variety that it is difficult to classify them. However, there are certain basic weaves such as:

1. Plain weave. Weft and warp yarns or threads are woven over and under, alternating every other thread, Fig. 3-6.
2. Twill. This weave, Fig. 3-7, has a diagonal pattern of ribs formed by passing the filling yarn under one and over two warp yarns. This pattern is staggered

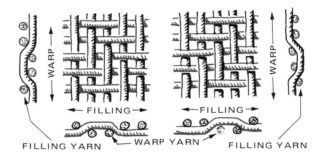

Fig. 3-7. Each filling yarn passes over, then under, two or more warp yarns in twill weave. Pattern of interweaving moves left or right one yarn for each row. This variation forms familiar pattern of diagonal ridges.

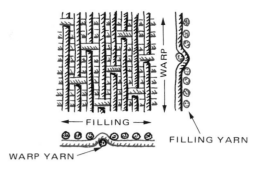

Fig. 3-8. Satin weave is formed when one yarn passes over several yarns and then under one. Pattern moves to left or right by two yarns. This gives fabric its smooth surface.

in each row to form the diagonal rib.

3. Satin. In this weave, warp yarns are passed over the filling yarns at widely spaced and irregular intervals. See Fig. 3-8.

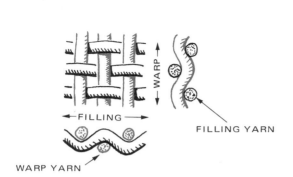

Fig. 3-6. Left. In plain weave, filling (or weft) yarns pass over and under single warp yarns in a regular pattern. Right. Example of a plain woven nylon fabric on which a design has been printed. (John K. Burch Co.)

PLAIN WEAVE   LOOP-PILE WEAVE   CUT-PILE WEAVE

Fig. 3-9. Pile weave is built upon base of plain weave. Additional yarns are woven into the fabric to produce characteristic fabric surface. Top. Samples of two types of pile-woven upholstery fabric. Bottom. Diagram showing how pile weave is constructed.

4. Decorative weaves. Also called fancy, figure and design weaves, they are formed by predetermined changes in the interlacing of the warp and weft yarns. Jacquard, pile and dobby weaves are in this classification.

A variation of the plain weave, often found in upholstery material, is the pile weave. Some of its patterns are shown in Fig. 3-9.

FABRIC CHOICES

Following are a few of the fabrics from which the upholsterer may choose. The list is by no means complete but indicates the variety available.

BROCADE. This is a jacquard weave in which colored threads are floated on the back of the fabric and brought to the surface to create brilliant designs. The designs are prominent and rise above the background fabric. This background is often a satin or twill weave, Fig. 3-10. (A jacquard weave is one which has an intricate pattern of colored yarns woven by a special loom.)

BROCATELLE. Like brocade but heavier, brocatelle designs are raised supposedly in imitation of Italian tooled leather, Fig. 3-11. It is produced in mixtures of cotton, silk or rayon fibers. Both figures and background are tightly woven. It is a firm and long-wearing material.

Fig. 3-10. This brocade fabric is 66 percent cotton and 34 percent rayon. The rayon fibers are in the yarns forming the design. These yarns are floated on the back of the material and are brought to the surface for the design.   (John K. Burch Co.)

Fig. 3-11. Brocatelle is similar to brocade but design stands higher and is more tightly woven. Folded section shows floating of threads forming the design.   (Barrow Fabrics)

CORDUROY. A sturdy, hard-wearing cotton fabric having a cut pile and a rib running in the direction of the warp threads.

CRASH. This heavy, rough-textured fabric is plain woven. It is made up of irregular yarns of jute, flax, hemp and cotton and may be dyed or printed.

DAMASK. Somewhat like brocade but flatter, lighter and reversible, this material can be made of cotton, wool, silk, rayon or a combination of these fibers. Only heavy weights are used for upholstery.

DENIM. Strong twill-woven cotton either plain or figured. Plain denim is usually used under seat cushions. Figured denim is suitable for regular upholstering or for slip covers.

FRIEZE . When used for upholstery, a woven pile fabric with looped and springy fibers of cotton, wool or rayon. Loops may be cut or uncut or a combination forming a pattern. Surface is rough and fibrous. See Fig. 3-12.

MATELASSE. A double or compound fabric with a quilted, puckered or blistered appearance, Fig. 3-13. Heavier weights are used for upholstery.

MOQUETTE. A pile fabric of mohair or wool on a cotton foundation. It may be cut, uncut or a combination of cut and uncut. Usually in solid colors or small jacquard pattern.

REPP (or REP). A ribbed fabric in which the rib is at right angles to the warp threads. Fiber may be wool or cotton. Rib is rounded and prominent.

SATEEN. A variation of the satin weave in which the filling yarns are floated over the warp yarns. Usually made of cotton but sometimes filament fibers are used. Soft and lustrous, the sheen is crosswise of the fabric. Often used as slip covering.

SATIN. Lustrous cloth characterized by long floats of the warp yarns. Silk, cotton or rayon fibers are used. A dressy fabric, it is often used on fine furniture.

TAPESTRY. The pattern of this fabric is woven with colored weft threads. It is used extensively for wall hanging and table covers. In heavier weights, it is also used in upholstery. See Fig. 3-14.

TWEED: A heavy fabric of mixed color in a herringbone or plain twill weave, Fig. 3-15.

VELOUR (or PLUSH). Soft, tightly woven, smooth fabric with a short, thick pile. Often made of cotton, wool or mohair.

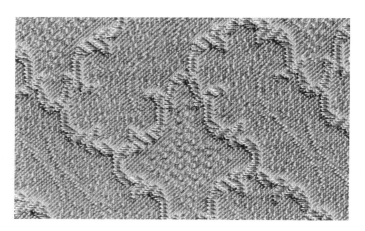

Fig. 3-12. This enlargement shows a frieze fabric. Pile yarns are 100 percent nylon; backing is a cotton-rayon blend.   (John K. Burch Co.)

Fig. 3-14. Tapestry fabrics are made on a loom with a jacquard device. Background fiber is cotton. Pattern threads are rayon. (John K. Burch Co.)

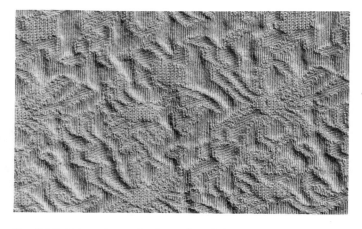

Fig. 3-13. Enlarged sample of matelasse'. Puckered appearance is a distinctive feature of this weave pattern.

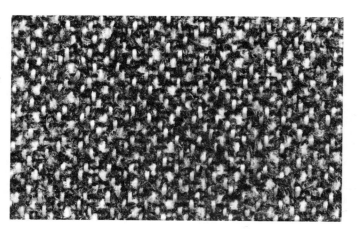

Fig. 3-15. Olefin fabric in tweed pattern. Plain weave is used.

VELVET. Pile woven fabric in which the pile is short and thick. Usually made of silk or synthetic fiber pile with a cotton back. See Figs. 3-16, 3-17 and 3-18.

VELVETEEN. An imitation velvet made with cotton. May be woven in colors and patterns.

NOVELTY WEAVES

Certain weaves which do not fit into the usual classifications are considered novelty weaves. Fig. 3-19 is a heavily textured fabric called "Lattice Texture" by its manufacturer. The warp threads are more widely spaced than the filler threads. The warp threads hold the filler yarns in a knitting stitch. The overlaying pattern of heavy yarns changes directions to form the "box" or lattice design. They are also secured to the fabric by loops of the knitted warp threads.

Another novelty weave, Fig. 3-20, is a needlepoint tapestry called "gros point." In needlecraft terms, "gros point" indicates the fineness of the stitch, in this case, 8 to 15 stitches per inch. The filling yarns are of several colors. They are woven into a base fabric that looks like a rough canvas. It consists of a coarse mesh of stiff threads not unlike metal screening in appearance.

Fig. 3-16. Velvet fabric in a floral patterned jacquard weave. Fiber is rayon. (John K. Burch Co.)

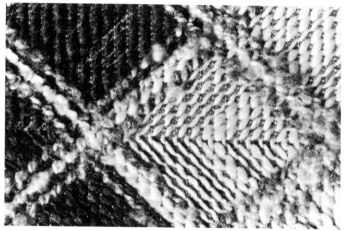

Fig. 3-19. Heavily textured novelty weave. Warp threads are more widely spaced than filler threads. Yarns creating texture are coarse and loosely spun.

Fig. 3-17. Crushed velvet has characteristic pattern of light and shadows caused by variation in lay of the nap or pile.

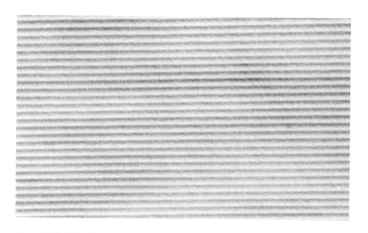

Fig. 3-18. Similar in appearance to corduroy, this velvet has a rib pattern running crosswise. (John K. Burch Co.)

Fig. 3-20. Needlepoint tapestry weave. Filler yarns are woven into base of widely spaced, very stiff, threads. (John K. Burch Co.)

KNITTED FABRICS

Knitted fabrics are made of single filament threads. The knit can be made along the weft or the warp. See Fig. 3-21. The fabric may have raised or unraised loops. Though knitted fabrics are being used at an increasing rate in upholstery they are not as popular as woven fabrics. Most often they are used as a backing for other, nonwoven, materials.

LEATHER AND PLASTIC UPHOLSTERY

Leather and plastic are often classified as nonwoven materials. Leather upholstery, Fig. 3-22, is usually cowhide. It is split into various thicknesses depending on quality. It is sold by the hide or by the square foot. Leather is strong, resists stains, fading and cracking and comes in many different colors.

Coated plastic materials have a spun, knitted or woven backing to which polyvinyl chloride or polyurethane coatings are adhered. The medium and heavyweight materials are intended for upholstery. The plastics are durable, easy to clean and low in cost. They can be made to take on the appearance of leather or woven fabrics. See Fig. 3-23 and Fig. 3-24.

Covering materials are sold by upholstery suppliers, by department stores which maintain yard goods departments, and by fabric stores. Fig. 3-25 will assist you in determining quantity of material needed.

FABRIC CARE

Most modern upholstery fabrics are designed to give long service. But proper care is necessary to preserve the appearance and extend the life of the best fabrics. It is important that this maintenance be performed with the same regularity as vacuuming and dusting the home.

Fig. 3-23. Vinyl plastic upholstery fabrics are sold in many different colors and textures.   (Naugahyde)

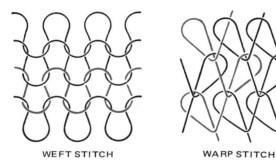
WEFT STITCH   WARP STITCH

Fig. 3-21. Knitted fabric shown in typical weft and warp stitches. Weft stitch allows more stretch than warp stitch.

Fig. 3-22. Sample of top grain cowhide. Leather upholstery is used only on very fine furniture.

Fig. 3-24. Textured plastic upholstering material resembles tooled leather.   (John K. Burch Co.)

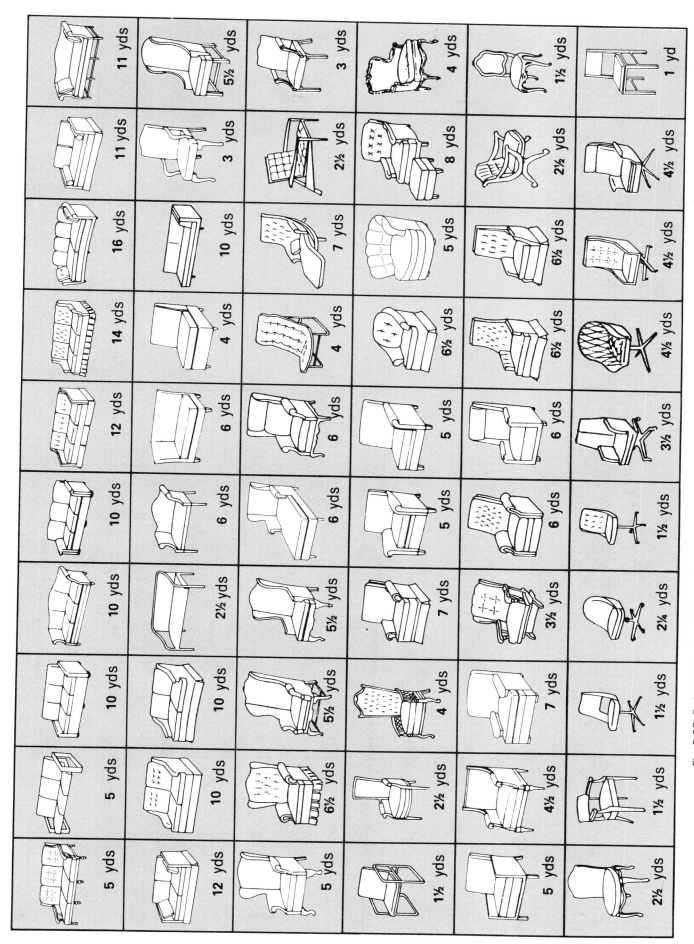

Fig. 3-25. Estimated vinyl or cloth covering yardage needed to reupholster various pieces of furniture. (Uniroyal Corp.)

WEEKLY ROUTINE

Normal care requires a vacuuming of the cushions and backs every week. Nonwoven fabrics should be dusted with a soft cloth or wiped clean occasionally with a mild soap and warm water solution.

Light brushing of woven fabrics with a soft bristled brush will not harm fabrics but hard bristled (metal or stiff fiber) brushes will tear fibers and damage the material. If cushions are reversible, turn them after cleaning. Fluff up loose-filled cushions and pillows to preserve their original softness.

CONTROL SUNLIGHT

Direct sunlight is harmful to fabrics. In time, it will cause fading regardless of quality or type of material. If possible, avoid placing furniture where direct sunlight will fall on it. Pull shades or sheers to block out or reduce solar effects.

CLEANERS AND THEIR USES

WATER. Should be clean. Temperature depends on kind of stain. Use cool or cold water for nongreasy soil. Heat sets most stains. However, for greasy stains, water should be warm or hot. To use: Sparingly used with soft bristled brush, sponge or soft cloth. Shake out or wring out well.

SOAPS. Only mild flakes or liquids should be used. Do not use harsh soaps such as those intended for laundry. To use: Mix with water, agitate and apply sparingly to stain or soil.

DETERGENTS. Same as soaps. Avoid laundry detergents. To use: Mix with water and agitate. Apply with brush, sponge or cloth. Rinse with clean water held in well wrung-out sponge or cloth.

SHAMPOOS. Good for general cleaning. Mix with water and agitate to rich lather. Some are soapless. To use: Apply lather to fabric with soft bristled brush or sponge. Wipe or brush back and forth on stains. Rewipe with clean, dry cloth. Clean one small section at a time. See Fig. 3-26.

HYDROGEN PEROXIDE. Three percent solution makes a strong spot remover. Suitable for washable or dry-cleanable fabrics except white cottons or linens. To use: Dampen stain with cleaner. Expose to direct sunlight until dry. Repeat until stain is gone. Rinse with clean water (wrung-out cloth or sponge) and dry.

CHLORINE BLEACH. Useful for cleaning linen and white cottons. To use: Same as hydrogen peroxide. Dilution may be advisable for some fabrics. Mix with water.

HOUSEHOLD AMMONIA. Used in 10 percent solution (1 part ammonia, 9 parts water) for cleaning. Can also be used for neutralizing acids. To use: Same as hydrogen peroxide. On fabrics containing any wool or silk, dilute 10 percent solution with equal amounts of water.

VINEGAR. Effective as a spot remover when used in a 10 percent solution. To use: Same as for hydrogen peroxide, bleach and household ammonia.

OXALIC ACID. A strong bleach available in crystal form. Dilute at rate of about 1 tablespoon of crystals to a cup of warm water. To use: Dampen stain and keep damp with repeated applications until stain is gone. Rinse thoroughly with clean water (dampened sponge). CAUTION: Use carefully with plenty of ventilation. Oxalic acid can cause damage to eyes and lungs.

COMMERCIAL DRY CLEANING SOLUTIONS. Many of these are nonflammable and safe for most fabrics. Read labels carefully. See Fig. 3-27. To use: Dip a dry, clean, white cloth into the cleaner and apply to the stain. Wipe with clean, dry cloth to pick up dirt, grease and perspiration. For large area cleaning some manufacturers recommend dipping a larger white cloth into a bowl of the cleaner. The dampened cloth is then laid over the area to be cleaned. Smooth the cloth into contact all over area; then remove still dampened cloth and rub the entire area gently. Always read manufacturer's instructions.

FABRICS AND SOILING

Preventive measures against soiling might begin with choice of fabrics. For example, a heavy, rough textured upholstery material in certain darker colors will not show soiling as much as lightweight, light colored fabrics.

Fig. 3-26. Commercial shampoos, such as this one, are used as they come from the container. They will not damage materials not harmed by water. (Albatross Chemical Co. Inc.)

Fig. 3-27. Dry-cleaning fluids are intended to be used as stain removers.

Type of fiber, yarn and fabric construction will also affect the ability of the fabric to shed or mask soil.

FIBERS AND YARNS

Consider some of the fibers. The olefins are the least absorbent. They do not build up static which attracts dirt particles. Water based stains can easily be removed.

Nylon and polyester also have low absorbency rate for watery stains. But they readily absorb oil stains and build up static.

Cotton, flax, rayon and acetate are absorbent. They should be avoided on heavily used furniture unless they are treated with one of the water repellant finishes. Application of the fabric fluoridizer (oil resistant finish) is also desirable.

Wools attract dust more readily than other fabrics. Yet, it is not hard to clean.

Smooth yarns, especially filament yarns, do not attract and hold dust as readily. Certain novelty yarns probably will hide soil better than regular yarns.

CONSTRUCTION

Soil remains on the surface of high-count (thick) pile fabrics. Cleaning is easy if the soil is removed quickly. Allowed to remain, it penetrates to the base of the fabric and becomes harder to remove. Figured fabrics, tweeds and printed fabrics tend to hide soil. Solid colors show soil more readily. Smooth finishes and those less porous (vinyl and smooth leather) can be easily cleaned with a water dampened cloth.

PRETESTING FABRIC

Before using cleaning agents on any fabric, be certain that they will not damage the fabric. Try the cleaning material on a hidden portion of the fabric. Observe the fabric. Is the color running or coming off onto your cloth? Does the fluid cause shrinking?

CLEANING METHODS

General cleaning methods will vary slightly, depending on the type of fiber, finish, soil release treatments and weave. Some synthetic fibers have a natural tendency to release soil. Other fabrics are treated with chemical compounds which cause the treated material to resist stains and soiling. Pile weaves are one type that require different treatment for cleaning.

REPELLANT FIBERS

To clean fabrics such as Herculon or Vectra, which naturally resist staining, brush with a soft bristled brush to loosen soil. Follow brushing with a thorough vacuuming. Water based cleaning agents, such as detergent suds or fabric shampoos, will usually remove stains if they have not been absorbed by a latex backing or a fabric liner.

Facial tissue will absorb fresh spills and reduce danger of staining. Soiled spots can be cleaned by sponging the area with clean water. Blot up moisture immediately. If a stain remains after such treatment use a detergent solution for water soluble stains. For oil or wax based stains, treat the area with a cleaning fluid or solvent. Never dry clean or machine wash the fabric.

Stains which do not respond to the prescribed treatment will usually yield to spraying with household cleaner containing ammonia. Using clean water, rinse with a towel or sponge well wrung-out.

REPELLANT-TREATED FABRICS

Add a small amount of detergent or ammonia to water as a general cleaning agent for fabrics treated with stain and soil repellants. This solution is safe for all except filament rayon fabrics.

To treat staining caused by skin or hair oils, use a dry-cleaning fluid. A foam cleaner (lather) may be required for some stains. Do not allow the cleaner to dry on the fabric where it may ruin the soil repellant properties of the treated material.

PILE FABRICS

Pile fabrics, such as velvets, corduroys and friezes, should be carefully vacuumed before regular cleaning methods are used. If the fabric is stain resistant you can remove soil with a water-dampened sponge or cloth. For rayon piles, substitute a dry-cleaning fluid for water. Commercial shampoos will remove stains which do not respond to the suggested treatment. Always brush in the direction the pile lays.

Cleaning of untreated pile fabrics is the same except that oils will need to be removed with a clean cloth dampened in a commercial cleaning fluid.

On friezes, vacuum against the lay of the pile. Color-fast fabrics can be sponged with a cloth dipped in a detergent solution and wrung out. Rinse with a water-dampened cloth. Wiping strokes should be made against the pile. Brush frequently as the fabric dries to prevent matting.

Suppliers of upholstering materials offer booklets with additional information on fabric cleaning and care.

REVIEW QUESTIONS — CHAPTER 3

1. Fabrics with traditional designs look best on_____ _____ and _____ furniture.
2. If wearability is important, what kind of upholstery fabric should be chosen?
3. List the two basic kinds of fabric.
4. What four things affect the durability, appearance and desirability of a woven cloth?
5. What do the following fibers have in common: cotton, wool, mohair and silk?
6. Synthetic fibers are classified either as_____ based or _____ based.
7. _____ is the surface created by the ends of yarn or loops of yarn fastened to a backing material.
8. Describe a twill weave.
9. What fabric has a pattern of colored threads with the design raised well above its background?
10. Which of the following should be performed as part of weekly care for upholstery?
    a. Brush lightly with a soft bristled brush.
    b. Brush lightly with a hard bristled brush.
    c. Dust nonwoven fabrics with a soft cloth.
    d. Fluff up loose-filled pillows.
    e. Vacuum cushions and backs.
11. How would you test fabric to see if a cleaning agent is suitable for it?
12. Why is it important to immediately blot up spilled materials on upholstery?
13. Should water base detergents be used for cleaning stain repellant fibers?

Section 2
UPHOLSTERING PROCESSES

A well made upholstered piece is comfortable because it skillfully combines many materials and parts. Through understanding the processes, the upholsterer successfully combines them with techniques that bring out the advantages of the materials.

In the next seven chapters you will learn about stripping and repairing old frames; removing old wood finishes and applying new finishes; installing new webbing, springs and padding; installing coverings and making cushions; doing channeling and tufting.

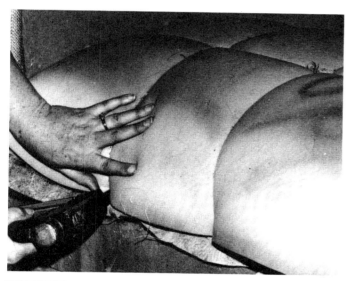

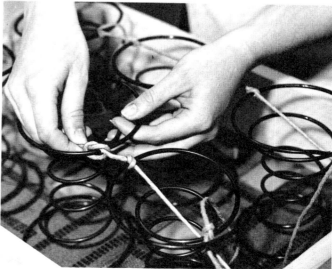

Chapter 4
STRIPPING AND REPAIRING FRAMES

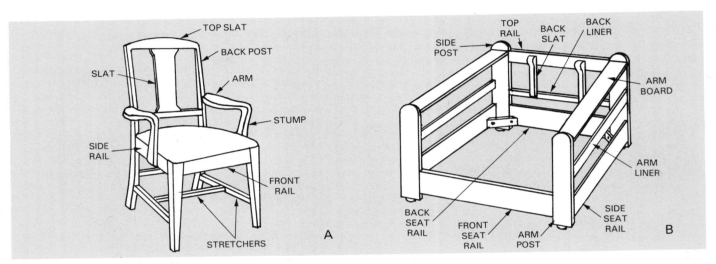

Fig. 4-1. Upholstered furniture has a variety of styles but there are only three basic types. Two are shown here.
A — Padded constuction uses no springs and leaves a great deal of the frame exposed. (Universal Seng)
B — Overstuffed construction uses springs in seat and back for comfort. These frames are usually entirely covered by upholstery.

There are many types and styles of upholstered furniture. Whatever their individual differences, each type has a frame that supports springs and/or padding, Fig. 4-1. Before working on a piece of furniture, the beginning upholsterer should know its basic construction and how the basic types differ.

BASIC FURNITURE TYPES

Upholstered furniture is of three basic types:
1. Padded construction which has no springs. See Fig. 4-2. Padding can be cotton batting, kapok, foam rubber or other material.
2. A combination of padded construction and spring construction, Fig. 4-3. This type is often used in occasional chairs. The seat will be constructed with springs and the back will be padded. Rails for spring seats are at least 3 in. (7.5 cm) wide.
3. Overstuffed construction which uses springs in both seat and back. See Fig. 4-4. Note that most vertical parts of the frame are called POSTS and

most horizontal parts are called RAILS. Refer to Fig. 4-1. These are the main parts of the frame and give the piece of furniture its shape and support.

Some vertical and horizontal pieces have no other function except to provide a place to tack down upholstery fabric. Vertical pieces are called SLATS. Horizontal pieces are called LINERS, Fig. 4-1.

PADDED CONSTRUCTION

In padded construction, the padding is supported by a base or foundation. Sometimes this foundation is made up of jute webbing, steel webbing or a wire mesh. At other times the foundation is a solid platform of plywood or wood slats.

SLIP SEATS

When the seat base is held in place by easily removed screws it is called a SLIP SEAT. Slip seats are commonly used on dining chairs and small side chairs. Padded

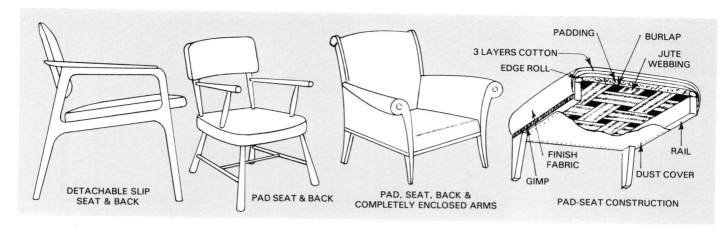

Fig. 4-2. Some upholstered furniture uses only padding applied to a solid or webbed supporting base.
(Craftplans)

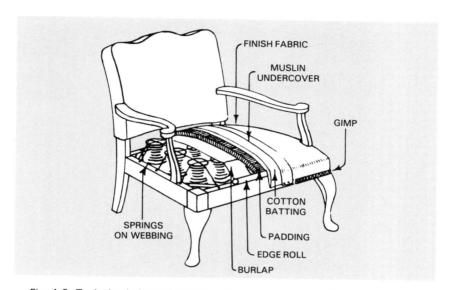

Fig. 4-3. Typical upholstered chair combining spring type and pad type upholstering. This type is sometimes called tightspring construction.

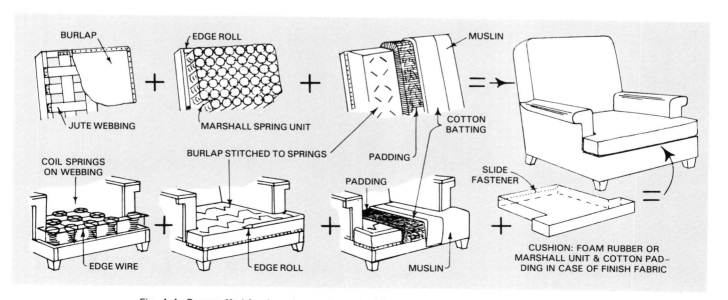

Fig. 4-4. Overstuffed furniture is constructed with generous use of springs and padding.

seats usually have a slight crown or a flat surface. Occasionally the pad may be slightly concave (dished) as with the scoop or sag seats. Slip seats are easily reupholstered since they can be removed from the frame as shown in Fig. 4-5.

COMBINATION - SPRINGS AND PADDING

If coil springs are used in seats of occasional chairs they are supported by jute webbing, metal webbing, wood strips, 3/8 or 1/2 in. plywood, expanded metal lathe or a patented foundation for coil springs. This support material is attached to the underside of the seat frame.

OVERSTUFFED CONSTRUCTION

Overstuffed furniture is often entirely covered with upholstering materials. Only the feet, and sometimes the arms, are left uncovered. Frames for overstuffed furniture are of fairly simple construction.

Basically, the frame is a combination of rectangles which hold the springs and support the padding and final covering. Figs. 4-6, 4-7 and 4-8 are cutaway views of overstuffed furniture.

Fig. 4-5. Slip seat is being removed from old dining room chair. Screws through corner braces hold seat to chair frame.

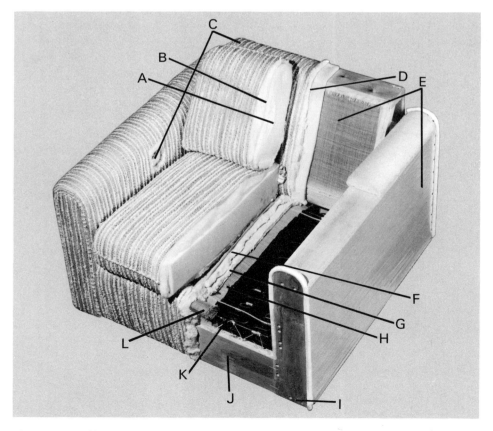

Fig. 4-6. Cutaway shows overstuffed chair construction with sinuous springs. A—Polyurethane core. B—Polyester fiber wrapping. C—Fully padded arms and inside back. D—Cotton layer. E—1/2 in. polyurethane pad. F—Polypropylene sheeting. G—14 ounce cotton. H—Propex deck covering. I—Double-doweled joints. J—Frame lumber. K—7.5 gauge universal wire springs with soft spring edge. L—Anchor edge roll.   (Thomasville Furniture Industries, Inc.)

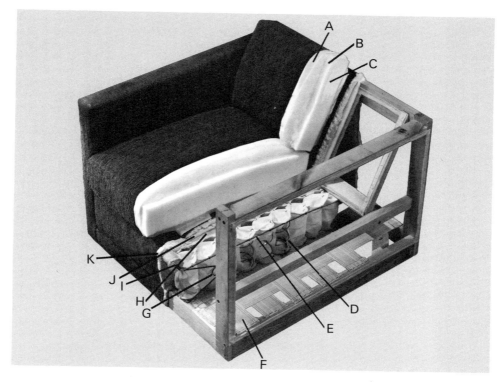

Fig. 4-7. Cutaway view of chair which uses covered coil springs (Marshall units). This is the same construction used in innerspring mattresses. A—Face sewn muslin ticking. B—Polyester fiber wrapping. C—Polyurethane foam core. D— 13.5 gauge muslin enclosed Marshall springs. E—9 gauge spring edge wire. F—Polyethylene webbing. G—Corner support spring. H—Propex deck covering. I—Anchor edge roll. J—Tuftflex cellulose fiber. K—14 ounce cotton.

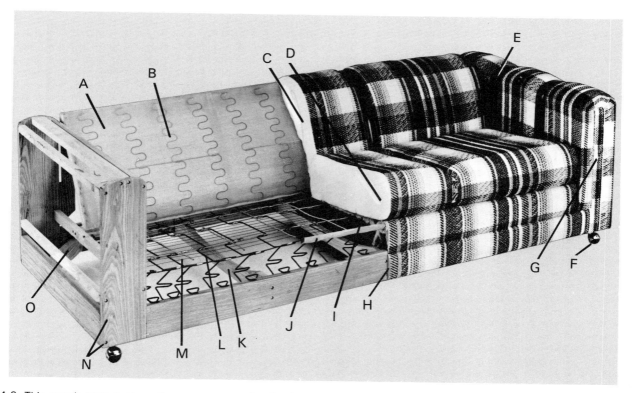

Fig. 4-8. This couch uses a serpentine or no-sag spring in the back. The seat has a wire grid platform with springs. A—Woven polyproplyene. B—Heavy duty back springs. C—Luxuriously foam padded back. D—Solid foam seat cushions. E—Form padded strap. F—Heavy duty rubber ball casters. G—Foam padded panel. H—Foam padded border. I—Cotton seat deck. J—Zip fast for smooth front seat edge. K—Hardwood stretchers for long lasting frame support. L—Heavy gauge body form seat springs. M—Permalator for better support in seat. N—Double doweled joint on all rails. O—Corner blocks and brackets added for long lasting support.   (Basset Upholstery Div.)

STRIPPING THE FRAME

Stripping refers to:
1. Removing used fabric or other upholstery materials from furniture frames.
2. Removing old finishes from wood surfaces and edges.

Details about stripping finishing materials are given in Chapter 5. This chapter will discuss removal of old fabrics, padding and springs.

We strip upholstery materials by pulling or knocking out staples, tacks or furniture nails which hold upholstery to the furniture frame. Upholstery materials are generally removed in reverse order of fabrication. Stripping moves from the bottom up. Usually, the dust cover comes first, then the outside back, the outside arms (or sides), seat, inside back and inside arms. The beginning upholsterer can learn much about the proper upholstering techniques during the stripping process.

STRIPPING TOOLS

The proper tools for stripping are:
1. The ripping tool.
2. The staple lifter.
3. The claw tool.
4. The mallet. This may be made of rawhide, wood or rubber.

These tools are discussed and illustrated in the Tool Chapter. Refer to Figs. 2-9, 2-10, 2-11, and 2-13.

STRIPPING ORDER

It is a good idea to note the order in which your particular piece of furniture was upholstered. Keeping a notebook with detailed sketches during the stripping process should be a valuable aid for refabrication processes. Save final covering pieces for use as patterns.

FASTENER REMOVAL

Remove staples using a wrist-twisting motion on the staple lifter. Tacks and furniture nails are removed with the tack claw or the ripping tool. The tack claw is easier to use and less likely to slip. Beginners will find it easier to use. The ripping tool is faster and more efficient and generally preferred by experienced workers. Tacks cannot clog its smooth edge. It is usually driven with a mallet and the tacks are lifted with a prying wrist action.

POSITIONING FURNITURE FOR STRIPPING

Furniture should be shifted frequently into positions which make stripping easier. The same positions can be used in the reupholstering process.

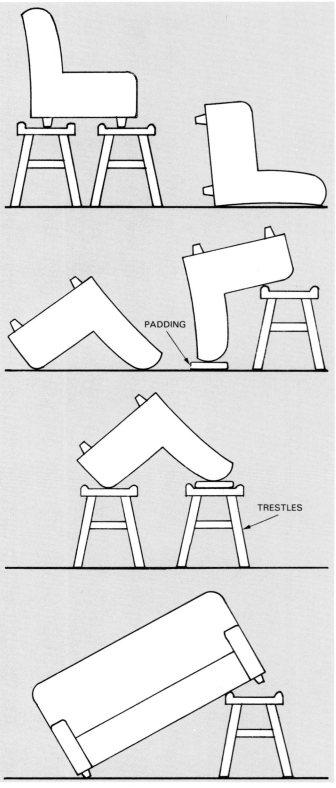

Fig. 4-9. Working on the floor or on trestles upholsterer should turn furniture frame to a position where it will be easiest to work on.

If furniture piece can be placed on trestles, so much the better. If not, working on the floor is satisfactory. Furniture positioned as in Fig. 4-9 should allow you to work in greatest comfort and with most efficiency.

54

REMOVING COVERINGS

Remove bottom covering. Turn furniture frame on its back to expose bottom side. With staple lifter, tack claw or ripping tool, remove cambric from the bottom of frame, Fig. 4-10. This will expose the fasteners holding the side fabric pieces to the frame. Remove these fasteners also. If staples have been used as fasteners, use the staple lifter, Fig. 4-11, to remove them.

Extract upholstered nail panels. With ripping tool or other suitable tool, pry upholstered nail panels from the furniture frame, Fig. 4-12. These panels will be upholstered during refabrication. Remove side panels. With ripping tool remove fasteners at sides. Lift panel up over the arm to reveal fasteners under the arms. Remove these fasteners, Fig. 4-13.

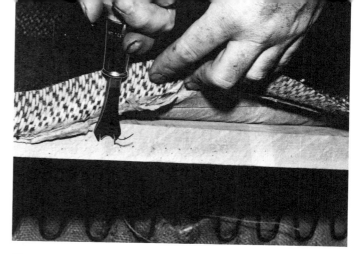

Fig. 4-11. Use staple puller or tack remover to remove fasteners. Be sure no part of the fastener remains on the surface. Remove all broken pieces or drive them into the wood where they cannot cause damage to new coverings.

Fig. 4-10. Removal of cambric dust cover uncovers fasteners holding upholstery covers to bottom of frame. (The Wrenn House)

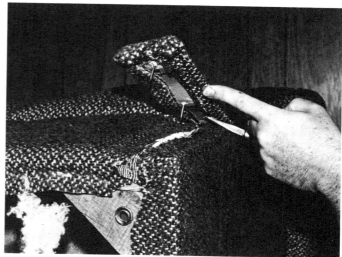

Fig. 4-12. Remove padded furniture panels from front of frame. This will uncover fasteners attaching outer arm panels and seat coverings. (The Wrenn House)

Fig. 4-13. Removal of side panels uncovers fasteners attaching inside arm panels to underside of arm.

Remove back covering. Cut threads, extract fasteners and pull away covering fabric to expose back padding and springs. See Fig. 4-14. This step will also expose fasteners for inside back covering.

Shear covered buttons. With shears, cut the twine holding the covered buttons. Remove them from the seat, back and sides of chair, Fig. 4-15. Remove inside arm coverings. Lift out fasteners from the tack rail on the frame, Fig. 4-16. Then, remove fasteners under the arm on the outside, Fig. 4-17.

Remove seat fabric covering. Using appropriate tools, pull the fasteners holding seat covering ties and seat covering to frame, Fig. 4-18.

Remove all remaining padding from the furniture frame. This will expose the burlap covering the springs. Remove the burlap, Fig. 4-19, so you can inspect the springs and webbing as in Fig. 4-20.

INSPECTING THE FRAME

No reupholstering should be attempted without a thorough inspection of the frame to determine its condition. This inspection should cover the following points:

1. Is the frame straight and solid? Back away and look

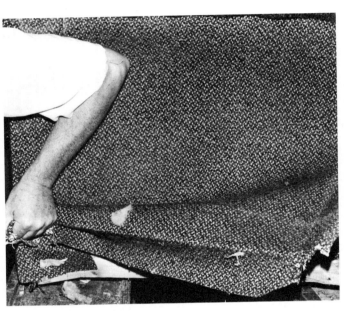

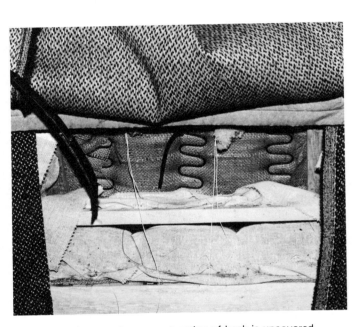

Fig. 4-14. Left. Beginning to remove back cover. Right. Back cover still attached at top. Inner construction of back is uncovered.

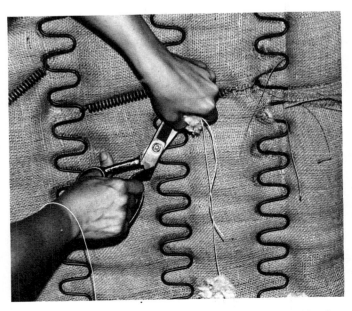

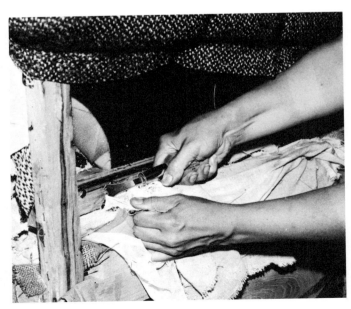

Fig. 4-15. With covers removed, twine holding covered tufting buttons can be removed.   (The Wrenn House)

Fig. 4-16. Removing fasteners holding seat covering to tack rail. White fabric is muslin used as stretcher for seat covering.

at it. Are the legs and arm posts vertical or do they lean? Grasp the frame and try to move it back and forth. Does it wobble and twist (indicating loose joints)? Does it rock, indicating a short leg or twisted, out-of-square parts? Are the arms and back securely fastened to the seat?

2. Inspect joints closely. Are any loose? Dowels broken off? Are glue blocks loose or damaged?

3. Pay close attention to tack rails. Previous reupholstering may have riddled them with holes and splintered surfaces. These will need resurfacing or reinforcement.

4. Check for splits or cracks in rails, posts and liners.

Parts will have to be glued or replaced.

Frames which are not structurally sound should not be reupholstered. Repair of the frame will require some skills in woodworking.

STRIPPING DINING CHAIR SEATS

Stripping padded seats off dining chairs in preparation for refinishing and reupholstering is a simple task. When the seat is part of the frame and cannot be removed, the covering will either be attached to the top of the seat platform or it will be wrapped around the

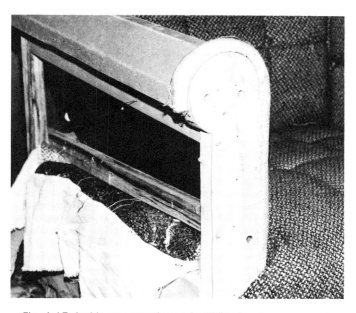

Fig. 4-17. Inside arm covering and padding has been removed.

Fig. 4-19. Chair with seat cover and padding removed. Burlap spring covering is badly worn and must be replaced.

Fig. 4-18. Fasteners holding seat covering to frame are being removed. (The Wrenn House)

Fig. 4-20. Burlap has been pulled away to inspect springs. They appear to be in good condition. (The Wrenn House)

seat rail and tacked to the underside. In the first case, when the covering is tacked to the top, gimp will conceal the tacks. Use a claw or other suitable tool, Fig. 4-21, to remove the metalene nails. Strip away the cover and padding, Fig. 4-22.

Slip seats are frequently used on dining chairs, occasional chairs, vanity benches and stools, Fig. 4-23. Before stripping can begin, the seat must be removed from the frame. This is accomplished by turning the chair upside down and removing the screws which hold the seat to the frame. These screws are located in the corner braces (or glue blocks) which reinforce the seat rails. Refer again to Fig. 4-5.

Using a ripping tool or other suitable tool, lift out

Fig. 4-23. Slip seated dining chair is in need of refinishing and reupholstery.

Fig. 4-21. Use ripping tool or claw tool to remove metalene nails from padded seats.

Fig. 4-24. Slip seat has been removed and fasteners are being removed.

Fig. 4-22. Lifting out old covering and padding from padded seat.

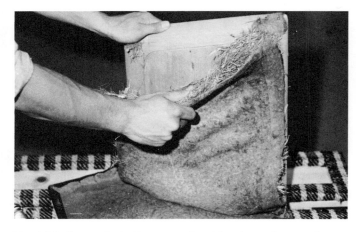

Fig. 4-25. Removal of old cover and padding from slip seat. Cotton batting and fiber filler have become thin and hard from long usage.

fasteners from the underside of the seat. Remove covering and old padding materials. See Fig. 4-24 and Fig. 4-25.

REPAIRING FRAMES

If new frames are being built or old frames must be repaired, a few basic facts about furniture woods (and furniture joints) will be useful. Medium-hard hardwoods are usually recommended for most upholstery frames. It has several desirable characteristics:

1. It is easier to drive fasteners into it than into very hard woods.
2. It holds the fasteners firmly without splitting.
3. Medium-hard hardwoods withstand considerable stress.
4. These woods are economical and readily available.

Straight-grain woods in soft maple, poplar and gum are best for frame parts that will be hidden by upholstery. More expensive and beautiful woods—such as walnut, cherry, birch and mahogany—are usually used only for parts that will be exposed. Hard maple and oak are too hard to use where tacks and nails are to be driven. Basswood and white pine lack strength. Western cedar and redwood split too easily and are also relatively weak.

Lumber should be 1 1/8 to 1 1/2 in. dimension well seasoned and preferably kiln dried to 7 or 8 percent moisture content. It should be reasonably free of large knots to assure adequate strength.

JOINERY

The method of joining the wood at corners where different parts meet is important for strength. See Fig. 4-26 for examples of furniture joints.

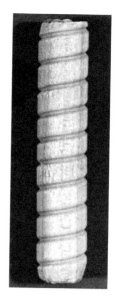

Fig. 4-27. Grooves in dowel release glue trapped in hole during assembly.

REPAIRING LOOSE JOINTS

Usually, the best repair for a loosened joint is to take the joint apart and reglue it. Remove all old glue; apply new glue and reassemble. If the fit is too loose, wrapping the joint with cloth is usually an effective remedy. Saturate the cloth with glue. Trim away excess.

Making/repairing dowel joints

One of the simplest and strongest of joints is the dowel joint. This is how it is made:

1. Select dowels with grooves, Fig. 4-27. They will allow excess glue to escape as the dowel is pressed into the hole. Dowel thickness should be a third that of the furniture part.

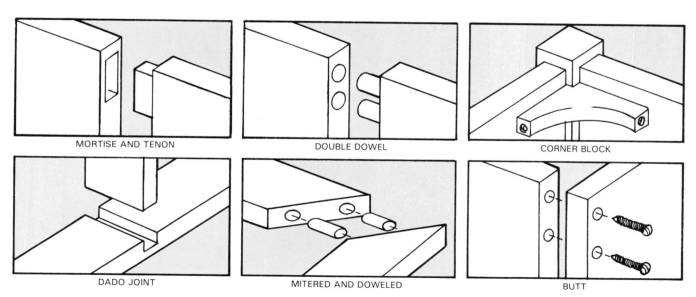

Fig. 4-26. Wood joints used in furniture. Modern quality furniture makes frequent use of double doweling. Butt joint, being weak, is not used in good furniture.

2. Make sure surfaces to be joined are square.
3. Mark the dowel positions on both parts of the joint, Fig. 4-28.
4. Select a drill bit the same size as the dowel. The dowels should be from 2 to 3 in (5 to 7.5 cm) long.
5. Drill the dowel holes. Make the hole half the dowel length plus 1/16 in. (about 1.5 mm).
6. Test fit the dowel before gluing. It should slide in snugly with a light tap or two from a mallet.
7. Apply glue to dowel and push it into the hole.
8. Coat joint and dowel ends with glue. Slip second part over the dowels and force the joint together. Clamp the joint and allow glue to dry.

A loose joint can often be repaired by squeezing glue around the joint. Then, pull the glue into the joint with a string or thread.

Fig. 4-29. Repairing joint with new dowels. Applying glue to both dowel and hole.

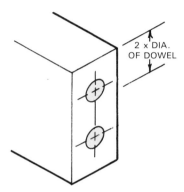

Fig. 4-28. Marking dowel positions on end of furniture rail. Drill holes at points where lines cross. Use of doweling jig would simplify this task.

Fig. 4-30. Use rawhide mallet to drive dowel into hole.

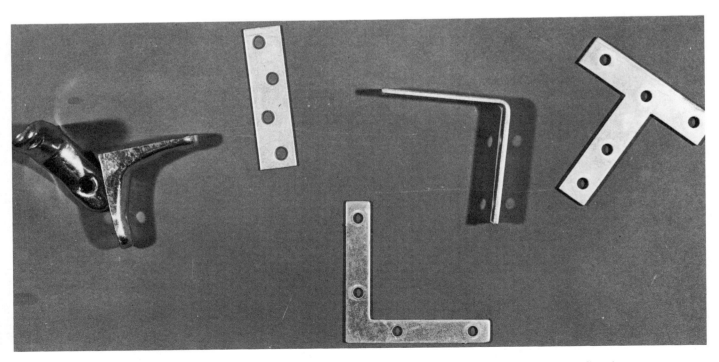

Fig. 4-31. Manufactured metal braces can be used for reinforcing frames. From left, chair brace, flat plate brace, flat corner brace (below), bent corner brace, T plate brace.

Fig. 4-32. Attaching wood corner blocks with glue and screws. Adjustable belt clamp is excellent tool for clamping all four corner joints at one time.

To repair a broken dowel joint, pull the joint apart and scrape away old glue. Using a drill bit of the correct size, clean out the dowel peg holes. This removes old glue and pieces of broken dowel pegs.

Replace the dowel pegs, Fig. 4-29. Dip one end of the dowel peg in a can of glue or squeeze glue onto the peg. Drive the peg into the drilled out hole with a mallet, Fig. 4-30.

JOINT REINFORCEMENT

Sometimes a weak joint must be strengthened by adding reinforcing parts. There are many fasteners on the market which can be added to miter or butt joints for this purpose, Fig. 4-31. Adding wood blocking is another excellent way of strengthening joints. See Fig. 4-32. Blocking is cut from 1 1/8 in. hardwood. Measure length, cut a 45 deg. angle on either end. Drill holes and attach to corners with appropriate size of wood screws. Use a wood clamp until glue dries.

REPAIRING TACK RAILS

After several reupholsterings, tack rails of overstuffed furniture may be in poor condition. If damage is not severe, sanding or planing will remove splinters and provide a new tacking surface. If there are not very many tack holes, they may be filled with plastic wood.

But when damage is severe, additional tacking surface must be provided. Supplementary tack rails (strips of wood) can be added to the old rails. Use gumwood, poplar, or soft maple. The new wood should be straight grained and free of knots. The new rails should be glued and screwed to the old rail. Stagger screws to avoid splitting. New supplementary rails should be at least 3 in. (7.5 cm) wide and at least 3/4 in. (2 cm) thick.

INSTALLING SCREWS

To set screws, two different sizes of holes are needed. One, the clearance hole should be the size of the shank. For flat head screws, the top side of the clearance hole is countersunk to receive the screw head. The pilot (anchor) hole should be a little smaller than the root diameter of the screw thread, Fig. 4-33.

If the screw must be concealed it should be counterbored. You can use a plug cutter to make a wood plug from the same kind of wood. Glue the plug over the screw. When the glue sets, trim the plug flush with the wood surface.

SELECTING SCREWS

Use the smallest screw diameter that will provide the needed holding power. To get maximum holding power, the entire length of the threads should be in the base piece. This is about two-thirds of its length. This is not always possible in thin stock.

Extra length will be needed when the base piece is end grain. End grain does not hold screws well.

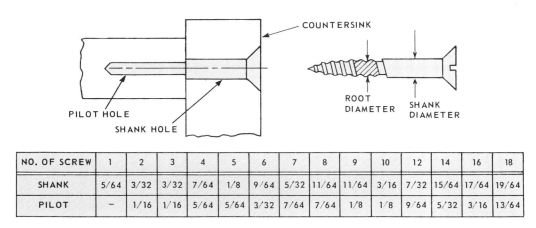

NO. OF SCREW	1	2	3	4	5	6	7	8	9	10	12	14	16	18
SHANK	5/64	3/32	3/32	7/64	1/8	9/64	5/32	11/64	11/64	3/16	7/32	15/64	17/64	19/64
PILOT	–	1/16	1/16	5/64	5/64	3/32	7/64	7/64	1/8	1/8	9/64	5/32	3/16	13/64

Fig. 4-33. Relationship of screws, pilot hole, shank hole and drill sizes for setting common screws. Pilot hole should be a little smaller than root diameter. Shank hole should be same size as shank.

REVIEW QUESTIONS — CHAPTER 4

1. Upholstered furniture which does not have springs is known as _____ construction.
2. Define the following terms:
   a. Posts.
   b. Rails.
   c. Slats.
   d. Liners.
3. What is a slip seat and where is it commonly used?
4. For a beginner, why is it important to keep track of the order in which materials are stripped from an upholstered frame?
5. Describe the method of removing tacks and other fasteners which hold the upholstery materials to the frame.
6. It is best to place furniture on _____ during stripping. It allows you to work more comfortably.
7. How would you determine if a frame is in good condition for reupholstering?
8. Why are medium hardwoods more desirable than hardwoods or softwoods as furniture frames?
9. What is the best repair for a loosened furniture joint?
10. Following is (are) proper repair(s) for a tack rail in poor condition after several reupholsterings (select the best answer or answers):
    a. Cut the rail and install a new one.
    b. If tack damage is not too great, sand or plane to provide a new tacking surface.
    c. If there are not too many of them, fill the holes with plastic wood filler.
    d. With glue and screws, attach wood strips to provide a new tacking surface.

Chapter 5
FINISHING AND REFINISHING

Exposed parts of the upholstered frame (show wood) may need to be finished before any upholstery materials are installed. Old finishes, if any, may have to be removed or covered and new finishes applied. This chapter will discuss the preparation of wood surfaces for finishes. Equally important, it will describe the application of a variety of finishes currently on the market.

REMOVING OLD FINISHES

Often the beauty of fine old furniture is hidden under badly deteriorating finishes or several layers of old paint, varnish or shellac. The process of removing old finishes on wood is called STRIPPING. (The same term is used to mean the removing of old upholstering material from a frame.)

SELECTING A REMOVER

Paint and varnish removers lift or soften old finish for easy removal by wipe-off, scrape-off or wash-off methods. Work area location is an important consideration in the selection of a remover. If you plan to strip furniture in your garage, carport, basement or workshop, make certain the area has adequate ventilation and is not near pilot lights and burner flames. For indoor stripping, use a water base type (nonflammable) remover. It minimizes fire hazard. When stripping in out-of-the-home locations or indoor locations which are well ventilated and free from fire hazards, a flammable type is very effective.

Before removing a finish, cover your workbench with hardboard or sheet metal and old newspapers. Wear protective clothing and rubber or plastic gloves. Pour about a cupful of remover into a tin can.

APPLYING REMOVER

Using a brush, apply the remover to one side of the project, Fig. 5-1. If you are using a thin, liquid remover

turn the piece of furniture so the working side is lying flat. The liquid will be more effective since it will not run as easily.

Continue applying the remover until the finish begins to loosen. Then, using a piece of burlap or coarse cloth, wipe away the loosened finish. See Fig. 5-2. If the finish is thick, scrape it away with a putty knife or spatula. Use an old toothbrush to loosen finish around intricate or irregular shapes.

Remove the finish from one panel at a time. Allow the stripped piece to dry 8 to 10 hours, then sand it with fine sandpaper.

Make certain the furniture frame is sound and joints are tight before it is prepared for a new finish. Use the procedures given under the heading "Preparing Wood Surfaces for Finish," in this chapter. *In addition, read the manufacturer's directions from the label on how to apply the product.*

SAFETY

1. Keep sparks and flames away from the finishing area.
2. Place waste materials and rags in a closed container.

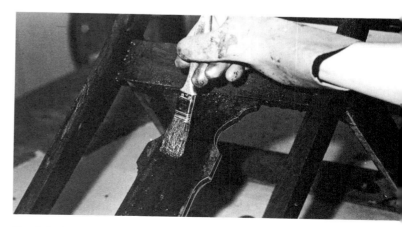

Fig. 5-1. Applying finish remover. Flow on in heavy unbroken film for best results.

Fig. 5-2. Loosened finish can be removed with cloth pad, steel wool or scraper.

3. Work in an area adequately ventilated. Use an exhaust fan, if working in an enclosed area. It is dangerous to inhale fumes while spraying finishes or using removers.
4. Wear goggles and rubber gloves when you handle strong liquids such as bleaches and removers.
5. Clean brushes and store them properly after each use.

6. Seal finish cans tightly. Store them in a metal cabinet.
7. Protect your clothing with an apron.

PREPARING WOOD SURFACES FOR FINISH

Sanding is important in the finishing of wood. It is a required first step on new woods as well as old surfaces from which previous finishes have been removed. Additional sanding will be required at certain stages of the finishing process. Sanding is needed for several reasons:

1. To remove marks left by planers, shapers, saws and other woodworking tools.
2. To smooth and shape the wood.
3. To remove bits of stain, glue or old finish.
4. To remove grain raise caused by applications of bleach or varnish removers.
5. To smooth materials applied during the finishing operations or to make the surface suitable for application of successive coats.

SELECTING AND USING SANDPAPER

Selecting the right abrasive paper for the sanding job is important. If you are not certain of the proper grade and type, refer to Chapter 1, Fig. 1-47. Use open coat on soft materials for less clogging. Close coat abrasives can be used where materials are harder.

A machine sander, Fig. 5-3, may be used for first sanding on large surfaces. Hand sanding is usually

Fig. 5-3. Power sanders can be used for initial sanding. Left. Orbital electric sander. Right. Pneumatic straight-line sander runs on compressed air.

recommended for final sanding. It removes mill marks and smooths the wood in preparation for the final finishing materials. See Fig. 5-4. To use the power sander begin at one side of the surface and move the sander carefully with the grain of the wood. Use only enough pressure to keep the sander cutting. Lap each successive stroke.

For most sanding jobs, grades 60, 100 and 150 can be used. Use the rough or medium grade first followed by the finer grades.

Tear the sandpaper sheets into appropriate size pieces. Power hand sanders usually require a third of a sheet. Fig. 5-5 shows a simple fixture that will make measuring and tearing the paper easier.

The final sanding must provide a smooth surface which will accept stain evenly. If any areas are rough when stained, that portion of wood will become darker. The result is an undesirable, blotchy appearance.

Never sand across the grain. It causes deep scratches barely visible on the unfinished wood but painfully apparent after stain is applied.

When hand sanding large surfaces, use a sanding block, Fig. 5-6. To sand around a curved or irregular-shaped surface, fold a piece of sandpaper into a small pad. Your thumb or fingers will shape it to fit the surface, Fig. 5-7. Steel wool is used to smooth some irregular and curved surfaces where sandpaper is not practical. It may also be used to smooth flat surfaces.

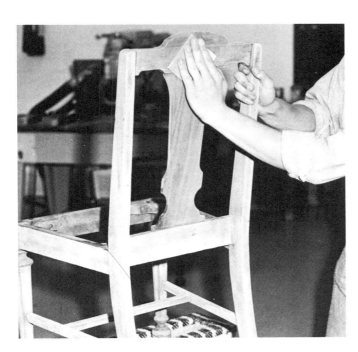

Fig. 5-4. Final sanding should be by hand using fine grit paper.

Fig. 5-6. Always use a sanding block when finish sanding larger flat surfaces.

Fig. 5-5. Fixture for tearing pieces of sandpaper. Old hacksaw blade makes good cutting edge.

Fig. 5-7. Small irregular shaped surfaces are sanded without a block. Use thumb or finger to back up and support sandpaper.

CLEANING UP SANDING DUST

All traces of sanding dust and steel wool must be removed from the wood surface before finishing. This is best done with a tack rag. You can make your own by dampening a pad of soft cotton fabric with thinned varnish. If preferred, ready-made tack rags are sold at paint and hardware stores.

REPAIRING DEFECTS

Surface defects, such as nail holes, small cracks and gouges which cannot be removed by sanding, must be leveled with some type of filler. A number are available including plastic wood, wood putty, water putty and stick shellac. Some are colored to match different wood tones.

The filler should be applied before stain or finish. The surface should be clean and dry. Press the filler into the defect using a putty knife, small spatula or a finger. If the defect is large, apply the filler in shallow layers. Allow each layer to dry before applying the next. The final layer should be higher than the surrounding surface since fillers shrink during drying. Close the container when you are finished with the filler.

Caution: Plastic wood is extremely flammable. Avoid inhaling of fumes. Use only with adequate ventilation.

Some finishers use stick shellac as a filler. It can be used on finished or unfinished surfaces. Fig. 5-8 illustrates the equipment and procedure needed for this product.

Stick shellac is manufactured in various colors. Select a stick slightly darker than the finish you are matching. Use a heated knife or an electrically heated unit to melt the shellac.

Dents in wood where the wood fibers are not broken can usually be raised successfully with the application of heat and moisture. Lightly moisten the dented area, place a wet cloth pad over the dent and apply heat with a soldering iron or a household iron. The water and heat cause the wood fibers to swell and expand returning to its approximate original shape. Allow the wood to dry. Smooth it with fine sandpaper before finishing.

Small defects in finished surfaces can be repaired with putty sticks or blend sticks. Select a stick as close to the color of the finish as possible. Rub it over the hole until the depression is filled. Wipe away the excess with a cloth pad.

BLEACHING WOOD

To lighten wood, remove dark streaks, or to prepare the surface for special finishes, use wood bleach. OXALIC ACID is a mild bleaching solution. A good bleaching solution may be made from 1 part oxalic acid powder and 20 parts of water.

Oxalic acid solutions are usually harmless to skin but should be kept away from the eyes. Apply the bleach with a cloth pad.

COMMERCIAL WOOD BLEACH usually is packaged in two separate containers. One holds sodium hydroxide; the other, hydrogen peroxide. See Fig. 5-9. Mix the two solutions together in small amounts as needed. Follow the manufacturer's instructions.

When working with commercial bleaches, always wear rubber gloves to protect your hands. Wear goggles for eye protection. Use bleach only in a well ventilated area. If the bleach accidentally comes in contact with your skin, wash immediately with soap and water.

APPLYING FINISHES

A wood finish imparts both color and a durable surface which protects and beautifies the wood. Usually, a finish requires several major steps, one to apply the stain and another to apply the transparent finish. The

Fig. 5-8. Stick shellac must be heated and dropped into defects in putty-like state.

Fig. 5-9. Commercial bleach has been used on lighter left hand portion of this wood panel.

finish is applied only after the wood is properly prepared by removal of old finishes, sanding and repairing of defects.

SELECTING AND CARING FOR BRUSHES

In wood finishing, it is important to purchase good brushes. It is equally important that brushes be properly maintained. A brush which is used regularly for the same type of finish may be stored for short periods of time by drilling a hole through the handle, inserting a wire through the hole and suspending the brush in a can or jar of solvent. The brush should be supported so the bristles will not touch the bottom of the container.

If you are using a finish which dries by evaporation (shellac, lacquer, synthetic finish) you can store the brush in a glass jar of the finish. Use a rubber lid as in Fig. 5-10.

To preserve the quality of a brush, clean it after use and store it when dry. Remove excess finish by pulling the brush lightly across the top of a container. Wash the brush in solvent (type used with finish being applied is best) and dry it with a cloth or paper towel. Scrub the brush with soap or detergent and water, and wrap it with paper or aluminum foil to keep the bristles straight.

WOOD STAINS

In wood finishing, stain is used to emphasize wood grain and to impart color to the surface of the wood. Wood stains are classified according to the solvent used in their manufacture. Solvents include oil, alcohol and water.

SELECTING STAINS

There is a bewildering number of good wood finishes on the market. You can select from a great variety of colors and materials. You can also mix colors of the same kind of finish to get new tones to suit your taste.

Although color chips indicate approximately the appearance of the stain on the wood, it is best to experiment on a hidden part of the wood or on a scrap of wood of the same kind. Stains take on an entirely different appearance on different kinds of woods. Remember, softer woods are more absorbent. The same stain will produce darker tones than when used on hardwoods.

OIL STAINS

PIGMENTED OIL STAINS contain finely ground color particles (pigments) which do not dissolve. They are suspended in a vehicle (liquid) such as linseed oil or mineral spirits. Though stains are labeled walnut, mahogany, or some other wood color, the stained wood will not necessarily closely resemble the wood after which it is named. The name implies, rather, a color, such as a brown or reddish tint. Different woods will take the color differently. The pigments remain on the wood surface, providing uniform color and appearance.

Applying oil stains

Stir the stain thoroughly before use. Apply quickly and uniformly, using a soft brush. Flow it on across the grain; then make light finishing strokes with the grain. Check carefully for missed spots (holidays). Allow the stain to set up. When the surface appears to be flat or dull (in 5 to 10 minutes), wipe it with a clean lint free cloth. Excess stain will come away on the cloth. Work only in the direction of the wood grain to bring out the highlights of the wood. See Fig. 5-11.

Fig. 5-10. Frequently-used brushes can sometimes be stored in jars if rubber covers are provided.

Fig. 5-11. Oil stain should be allowed to set up (until finish dulls) before wiping to bring out highlights.

Depth of color may be controlled by the amount of stain left on the wood. Use turpentine or mineral spirits for cleanup. Allow about 24 hours for oil stain to dry before applying paste wood filler or finish coats.

PENETRATING OIL STAINS are made by mixing oil and oil-soluble dyes. One problem experienced in using penetrating stain is that excessive quantities are absorbed by the end grain. A coat of linseed oil applied to the end grain a few minutes before using the penetrating stain will help to equalize the color absorption.

Allow oil stain to dry thoroughly and then coat it with a sealer (shellac or lacquer) to prevent bleeding of the stain into finishing coats.

NGR AND WATER STAINS

Non-grain-raising stains are made by dissolving colored dyes in glycol and alcohol. They will not bleed through finishes and, true to their name, will not raise wood grain.

Water stains are made by dissolving dyes in water. About 4 oz. (113 g) of stain added to a gallon of water makes a gallon (about 3.8 L) of ready-to-use stain.

Water stains penetrate deeply into the wood and tend to raise the wood grain. Before using water stain, the wood grain should be raised by sponging the wood lightly with water. Allow the wood to dry, then sand lightly with fine abrasive paper, working with the grain. Water stained surfaces may be darkened by applying extra coats. These stains do not bleach when exposed to sunlight and are inexpensive. After drying, surfaces should be sealed with shellac or lacquer sealer before applying other finishes.

WOOD FILLERS

Woods consist of countless, interwoven fibers which contain holes or pores. Some woods, like maple, pine and basswood (close-grained woods), have small pores. These small pores need only to be sealed (filled) with such finishing materials as shellac, lacquer, linseed oil or synthetics before applying finishing coats. Other woods, like walnut, oak, ash, and mahogany, have large, visible (open-grain) pores. These large pores should be filled with paste wood filler to produce a smooth surface before applying most other finishes.

Paste wood filler is made from ground silica (silex) mixed with linseed oil, turpentine or paint thinner and drier. It is packed as a heavy paste. It needs to be thinned to a heavy, creamy consistency by adding turpentine or paint thinner. Paste wood filler is available in natural (light buff color) and in colors such as oak, walnut and mahogany. The natural filler tones may be tinted with oil stains. The color of the paste filler should be close to the color of the finished wood.

To fill an open-grain wood, mix paste wood filler to the correct color and consistency. It is a good idea to try the filler on a scrap piece of wood before applying it to your furniture. It can be applied directly to the unfinished wood, or over a thin coat of sealer. Allow the sealer to dry before applying the filler.

Apply the filler along the grain, brushing it into the pores with a stiff brush as shown in Fig. 5-12. If there is a great deal of wood to cover, coat only a small section at a time. Wait a few minutes, until the filler begins to have a dull appearance, then wipe away the excess. Rub across the grain using a lint-free cloth such as cheesecloth, or burlap, Fig. 5-13. Use a softer cloth to remove remaining residue. You can clean out the corners with a piece of cloth wrapped around a pointed stick. Allow the filled wood to dry 4 to 6 hours. Lightly rub the dry surface with 220 sandpaper.

Fig. 5-12. Paste wood filler is applied with brush to fill pores of open-grain wood.

Fig. 5-13. Wipe off paste filler with coarse cloth working across grain.

SEALERS

Sealers are finishes used as a base coat to fill the pores of close-grained wood such as maple, birch, pine and cherry. Shellac, lacquer sealer, sealer stains and synthetics are commonly used for this purpose.

Sealers are available ready-mixed but are often reduced before application. Shellac is reduced with alcohol and usually sold as 4 lb. cut (4 lb. of shellac solids mixed with a gallon of alcohol). The 4 lb. cut is commonly mixed with an equal amount of alcohol to form a 2 lb. cut for brush application.

Lacquer sealer is usually applied by spraying, but it can be brushed on small projects. Lacquer sealer is reduced with lacquer thinner.

Sealer stains are usually reduced with turpentine or paint thinner. Synthetics are reduced with various thinners according to their composition.

WASH-COATING is the application of a thin (six to eight parts of thinner to one part of sealer) coat of sealer. The wash coat is applied over paste wood filler and some stains. It prevents bleeding of the stain into the finish. A wash coat can also be used on wood prior to application of paste wood filler.

You can apply sealers with a brush or spray. See Fig. 5-14. Be sure to follow manufacturer's instructions.

LINSEED OIL and TURPENTINE and DANISH OIL finishes should be allowed to set about 30 minutes after application. Then wipe the excess material off. The remaining finish should dry 10 to 12 hours. Additional coats are applied in the same way. The linseed oil and turpentine finish penetrates the wood better if it is

Fig. 5-14. Using spray finish on small project. Pressurized spray can is practical on small surfaces.

heated to about 140 °F (60 °C) before it is applied. When the final coat is thoroughly dry, apply a coat of wax. Then buff the surface to enhance its beauty and make the finish more durable.

TOP COAT FINISHES

A variety of finishes are used for top coats (over the sealer). Varnish, lacquer, shellac and synthetics are often used to achieve a natural (clear) or transparent finish. Enamel and paint are used to obtain an opaque finish. See Fig. 5-15.

Fig. 5-15. With modern finishes there are many choices for final finishes. All of the above finishes sit on top of the wood without significant penetration. They are called top coat finishes for that reason.

Most of the top coat finishes remain on the surface of the wood to form hard, durable, protective coverings. They can be applied with a brush, roller or by spraying. Usually, when more than one coat of finish is used, the finish should be smoothed between coats with 220 to 280 sandpaper or with 3/0 to 4/0 steel wool.

To smooth the final coat of varnish, lacquer, or shellac to a lustrous finish, sprinkle pumice or rottenstone and rubbing oil over the surface, Fig. 5-16. Using a cloth or felt pad, rub the abrasive and oil over the surface. Wipe off the excess polishing material with a soft cloth. Apply a coat of wax and buff to shine.

PUMICE, derived from lava, is white. Grades FF and FFF are commonly used. ROTTENSTONE is an iron oxide produced from shale. It is red-brown or gray-brown. Rottenstone, being finer than pumice, is generally used after pumice.

ENAMEL

VARNISH and ENAMEL are made from the same basic materials but pigment is added to enamel to give it color and make it opaque. Either is made with both natural and synthetic materials to create a hard, durable, waterproof finish. Drying time varies, but 8 to 10 hours is usually required. Varnish and enamel are reduced (thinned) with turpentine or mineral spirits.

LACQUER

Lacquer dries rapidly by evaporation. Usually applied with spraying equipment, it is well adapted to mass production techniques. But it can also be brushed on small projects if a retarding (slow-drying) thinner is used to reduce it.

Lacquer is reduced with lacquer thinner and should be applied in thin coats. Thick coats dry quickly on the outside but remain soft on the inside. About 30 minutes is usually allowed between coats.

Lacquer produces a clear, hard, durable film which is heat resistant. Pigments can be added to make either transparent or opaque color. Some lacquers are water resistant and some are not.

CAUTION: Lacquer tends to soften and lift varnish, enamel and some synthetics. It should not be used over them.

PLASTIC AND SHELLAC FINISHES

Polyurethane, a clear PLASTIC COATING, is one of the newer finishes. It dries fast and is highly resistant to abrasion and wear. No sealer is needed, and it may be used on all kinds of wood both indoors and outdoors. Polyurethane coatings should be applied with a clean, good quality brush. On new wood, two or three coats are needed. Light sanding between coats will remove the gloss to assure good adhesion.

SHELLAC will produce a fine finish if it is applied in thin coats (2 lb. cut), the same as a sealer coat. It is one of our oldest finishes. It is long-lasting if properly cared for, but it is not water or alcohol resistant. Paste wax should be used after the final coat to enhance its beauty and protect the finish from moisture.

PAINT FINISH

PAINTS are available with oil base or rubber (latex) base in a great variety of colors. Paints are often used to beautify and protect surfaces where an opaque finish is appropriate. Oil-base paint is reduced with turpentine or mineral spirits and usually requires 24 hours or more drying time for each coat. Rubber-base paints are thinned with water and can be recoated within a short time. Brushes used for latex paint should be cleaned in water soon after use.

THINNING MEDIUMS

TURPENTINE is used to reduce oil stains and paints, varnish and enamels. It is obtained from the yellow pine tree. Substitutes for turpentine (paint thinners) are made from petroleum.

SHELLAC SOLVENT is a combination of wood and grain alcohol. Sometimes, it is called "denatured" alcohol.

LACQUER THINNER is a combination of clear liquids. It is used as a solvent for lacquer, lacquer sealer and contact cement.

RETARDING LACQUER THINNER is a special solvent used to slow the drying time of lacquer and to help eliminate "blushing." Blushing is a white or cloudy appearance on a surface caused by small particles of

Fig. 5-16. Final coat may need rubbing down to smooth it. Needed materials are shown. Water is sometimes substituted for oil if additional coats of finish are to be applied.

Fig. 5-17. Materials in antiquing kit. Larger can holds paint-like ground (background) color. Smaller can is a glaze applied over the ground color and wiped.

Fig. 5-18. Sealer can be applied from pressurized spray can.

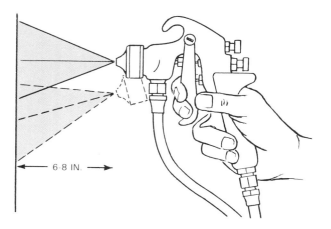

Fig. 5-19. Spray nozzle must be held so it faces area to be finished at right angles.

moisture trapped beneath the finish.

LINSEED OIL, obtained from flax seed, is used in thinning some kinds of paint and as a drying oil in paints, fillers and stains. It is also used with turpentine as a finish. See Fig. 1-51.

ANTIQUING

Antique finishes will make furniture look old and new at the same time. This look is achieved with a color base undercoat and a color glaze. Fig. 5-17 shows a kit containing the items usually needed. Various color combinations are available.

Apply the paint-like latex undercoat to the surface being finished (old paint or varnish). It provides a base color for the glaze.

Allow the undercoat to dry thoroughly, then apply the color glaze. Using a soft, lint-free cloth, wipe or texture the color glaze before it has a chance to dry. If the effect is not satisfactory, wipe off the glaze completely and start over.

SPRAYING FINISHES

Sealers or finishes can be sprayed on with handy pressurized cans, Fig. 5-18, or with refillable spray guns. Air or gas, under pressure, atomizes (mists) the materials so they can be applied in thin, even coats.

However, proper technique must be used. If you are inexperienced, it is best to practice on scrap lumber.

Hold the gun or spray can so the spray strikes at right angles to the surface being coated. See Fig. 5-19.

Begin at one side of the practice piece and move the spray unit toward the other side. Turn on the spray as

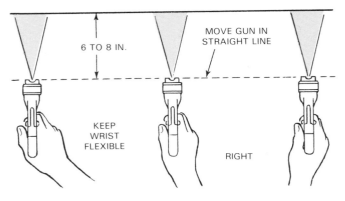

Fig. 5-20. Correct method of moving spray gun across surface being finished. Angle of spray and distance must be maintained for good results.

the unit approaches the first edge. Release the spray as the unit reaches the other edge. Move the gun or spray can in a straight line, not an arc, Fig. 5-20.

When spraying narrow horizontal pieces with a spray gun, turn the air nozzle wings to a horizontal position. This causes the spray pattern to be shortened vertically and lengthened horizontally. Thus, spray is concentrated along the horizontal path of the stroke. See Fig. 5-21.

Similarly, when spraying narrow vertical pieces, turn the air nozzle wings to a vertical position. Fig. 5-22 shows the proper position and technique.

Adjust the mixture of material and air pressure coming out of the nozzle so the material is applied to the surface wet. It if seems to be too dry, add more solvent to the mixture.

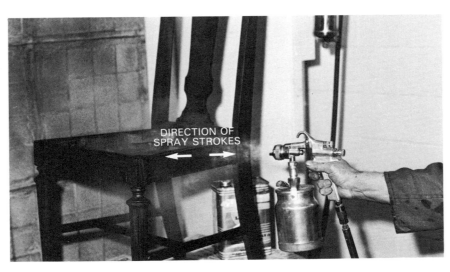

Fig. 5-21. Applying finish to narrow horizontal piece. Air nozzle is adjusted to wide horizontal spread but narrow vertical spread.

Fig. 5-22. Spraying finish on vertical strip. Air nozzle is adjusted for wide vertical spread, narrow horizontal spread.

On a large panel, it is a good idea to spray vertical bands along the ends of the piece first. Then make right and left horizontal strokes, triggering the gun at the beginning and ending of each stroke as in Fig. 5-23.

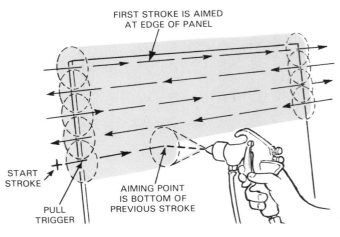

Fig. 5-23. Follow illustrated technique for spraying panels.

Using Minwax wood finishes

Minwax is a penetrating finish which seals and protects wood. It is applied directly to unfinished wood with a sponge, Fig. 5-24, brush or lint-free cloth. Unlike surface stain, wood finish penetrates to become a part of the wood. Thus scratches rarely expose raw wood. See Fig. 5-25.

Since the wood must completely absorb the protective finish, apply liberally without puddling or dripping. After 5 to 15 minutes, wipe off the excess and allow the wood to dry about 12 hours. Then apply a second coat. Sanding between coats is unnecessary because the finish does not raise the grain.

For a soft, flat finish, wait 24 hours and apply finishing wax. For soft lustre in a hard, protective finish, wipe or brush on a generous coat of clear Antique Oil finish. When this is tacky to touch, buff it evenly with a clean, lint-free cloth. If preferred, use buffing attachments on an electric drill or sander. If a semigloss or high gloss finish is desired, apply one or more coats of Deft clear wood finish, lacquer or varnish.

Using Blond-It wood finish

Blond-It is another penetrating finish that gives unfinished wood a deep beauty and charm. Because of its deep penetration, Blond-It also becomes a permanent part of the wood.

Apply the finish with a brush, sponge, cloth pad or spray can. In a few minutes, the tone is absorbed by the wood. No wiping is required. In an hour, the surface is ready for a top coat of clear finish. See Fig. 5-26.

On either light or dark woods, light shades will create bleached effects without the use of strong bleach solutions. Blond-It colors are permanent and can be intermixed to create new tones.

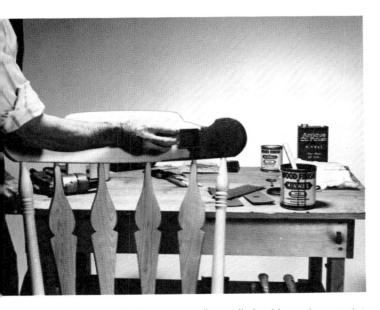

Fig. 5-24. Some finishes are easily applied with an inexpensive sponge. (Minwax Co., Inc.)

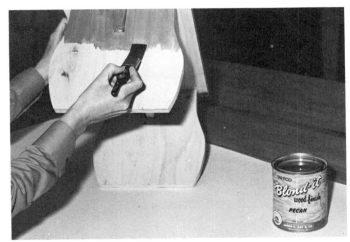

Fig. 5-25. Comparison of wood stain penetration. Left. A surface stain. Right. Minwax wood finish.

Fig. 5-26. Blond-It finishing project. Top. Applying penetrating stain with brush. Bottom. Application of clear alkyd gloss finish.

Finishing with Deft vinyl stain

With a commercial finish such as Deft vinyl stain (water cleanup), a paste wood filler (described earlier in this chapter) is usually not required. The first coat fills open pores and seals the surface of the wood, Fig. 5-27.

Deft vinyl stain is used just as it comes from the container. Apply the material generously with a brush, cloth, felt applicator can, or roller. While the material is still wet, wipe off the excess with a water dampened cloth.

To avoid lap marks, maintain a wet edge. Work back and forth across the surface in narrow bands. Cover one surface before going on to the next. The first coat will be dry enough in about two hours for recoating, if desired. Sand lightly between coats using fine (220 or 280) paper. Finish with Deft clear semigloss wood finish. The latter cannot be cleaned up with water.

Fig. 5-27. Deft stain being applied with a brush. If preferred, a pad may be used as an applicator.

Sealacell finishes

Finishing with Sealacell wood finishes, Fig. 5-28, involves use of three different coatings:

1. Sealacell, a moisture repellent, penetrating wood seal.
2. Varnowax, a penetrating blend of gums and waxes.
3. Royal finish, a blend of gums which also penetrate the wood. Arm-R Seal Heavy Duty, a heavy bodied seal, may be used for a final coat on surfaces which will receive hard use.

Finishing steps

1. Apply Sealacell to the unfinished wood. Use a cloth and liberal quantities of the penetrant seal. Depth of penetration depends on the amount of material applied. Ground-in-oil pigments may be used to add color to the sealer. Allow 10 to 12 hours drying time.
2. Sand lightly with very fine (400-600) wet-or-dry sandpaper before recoating.
3. Apply the Varnowax with a small cloth pad using a circular motion. Use sparingly to lightly cover the surface.
4. Apply Royal Finish or Arm-R Seal Heavy Duty in the same way as the Varnowax.

Fig. 5-28. Cloth pad is being used to apply Sealacell penetrant seal. (General Finishes Sales and Service Corp.)

Using Watco stain and oil finish

Penetrating oil finishes, such as linseed oil, have long been used to preserve gun stocks and other fine woods. Penetrating ''resin-oil'' finishes are a second generation in this family of finishes and preservers. For a deeply penetrating natural (no stain) finish, use Watco Danish oil directly from the can.

For a stain finish, start with Watco 5-Minute Stain, Fig. 5-29. Since it does not seal the wood grain, it allows Danish oil, applied later, to penetrate deeply into the wood. Color test a sample of the wood you are using. Some light woods, like birch, have a tendency to

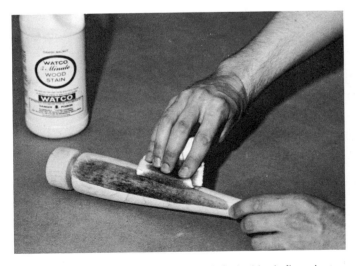

Fig. 5-29. Applying Watco stain with pad. Stain dries in five minutes. (Watco-Dennis Corp.)

take stain unevenly (blotch). Others darken evenly and deeply when stained or finished with penetrating oils.

You can lighten the stain by adding reducer (alcohol) or darken it with additional applications. Stains can be intermixed to obtain new colors and tones.

Before applying stain, sand the surface, using 4/0 or 6/0 garnet sandpaper for the final cut. Wipe on the stain along the grain. Let it dry five minutes. If you want a darker tone, apply a second coat. Let dry 45 minutes before applying Danish oil.

Apply Watco Danish oil with a brush, cloth pad, roller or by dipping, Fig. 5-30. Completely flood the surface. Wait about 30 minutes to allow maximum penetration, adding fresh Danish oil to areas that are drying too fast. Apply a second coat, allowing additional 30 minutes penetration. Then wipe off excess material. (For best results, it is important that oiled surfaces be wiped clean and dry within an hour of the initial application.)

For added lustre, let the finish dry four hours, then wet sand with 600 wet-or-dry sandpaper and small amount of Watco Danish oil finish. Wipe the wood thoroughly dry with a clean cloth. Polish briskly with another clean cloth.

REPAIRING DEFECTS ON FINISHED SURFACES

Water (white) spots. Apply heat and moisture. Place a warm iron over a damp cloth or blotter. Use brief applications and repeat until spot is completely removed. Alternate treatment: try a damp cloth with a few drops of ammonia or camphor on it. Let dry, then rub with 4/0 steel wool and apply wax.

Alcohol spots. Rub area with cloth slightly dampened with ammonia. Then rub with liquid or paste wax, silver polish or boiled linseed oil. Polish with a clean cloth. If deeper treatment is needed, rub with rottenstone and light oil.

Fig. 5-30. Oil finish is applied to stained surface with pad. Surface is made to absorb all the finish it can.

Heat Marks. On varnish or shellac finish, dab with a lint-free cloth dampened with camphor or essence of peppermint. Refrain from wiping, let dry 30 minutes. Then rub with rottenstone and oil.

Milk Stains. Milk has an action similar to a mild application of paint remover. Wipe spills away quickly. Apply cream wax and polish with a soft cloth.

Ink Stains. Ink stains can be removed only if they have not penetrated into the wood. Clean with cream wax or pat with dampened cloth. Refrain from rubbing. If the stain remains, rub with rottenstone and oil.

Candle Wax. Chill wax with a piece of ice to make it easier to remove from the surface. Pare off wax with your fingers. Scrape gently with the dull edge of a table knife. Apply cream wax and polish with lint-free cloth.

Small Blemish. Staining wax will often hide a superficial blemish. If damage extends into the finish, fill with a commercial refinishing compound to match wood. You can use a wax stick or oil stain.

Deep Blemish. For blond finishes, fill with layers of hard wax. For darker finishes, use matching colors of stick shellac. Smooth with fine sandpaper. Rewax surface with several coats of paste wax.

Burns. Remove damaged wood with razor blade or sharp knife. Clean with naphtha. Smooth with 4/0 steel wool and clean again. Fill with layers of stick shellac or wood filler. Stain to match finish, smooth and wax.

Dents. If wood fibers are not broken, use a warm iron over a damp cloth or blotter to raise dent. If wood fibers are broken, use damp cloth and heat, then proceed as if it were a burn.

REVIEW QUESTIONS — CHAPTER 5

1. _____, the removal of old finishes from wooden surfaces, usually requires the use of a _____ and _____ remover.
2. It is important to have _____ _____ in the area where you are using finish removers.
3. Which of the following things should always be done when preparing wood for a finish?
   a. Sand it to shape and smooth the surface.
   b. Wet the surface to raise the grain.
   c. Remove every bit of old stain, sealer and varnish.
   d. Remove dried bits of glue.
   e. Remove dust and other foreign matter.
4. List grades of sandpaper considered suitable for most sanding jobs.
5. Which of the following products are suitable for repairing defects in wood?
   a. Glazing compound.
   b. Plastic wood.
   c. Sealer.
   d. Stick shellac.
   e. Water putty.
   f. Wood filler.
   g. Wood putty.

6. A _____ is used to lighten wood that is to receive a light toned finish.

7. In wood finishing, _____ is used to bring out wood grain and give color to the wood surface.

8. What does NGR stand for and why is it important in wood finishing?

9. Some woods have an open grain, meaning the surface has pits and hollows. How would you treat such wood to fill up the hollows and make the surface level?

10. What is wash coating and why is it used?

11. Which of the following products are top coats?
    a. Enamel.
    b. Lacquer.
    c. Linseed oil.
    d. Pumice.
    e. Shellac.
    f. Stain.
    g. Turpentine.
    h. Varnish.
    i. Wood filler.

12. _____ is a clear, plastic coating for wood.

13. A _____ clear finish is one which, when applied to unfinished wood, is absorbed (soaked up) by the wood and becomes a part of the wood surface.

14. One distinct advantage of penetrating stains or finishes is that accidental scratching of the surface rarely exposes_____.

15. Antiquing is (check which statements are true):
    a. Distressing the wood by denting it with sharp metal objects to make it look old and used.
    b. Use of a colored undercoat and a top coat of glaze so the furniture piece looks both old and new at the same time.
    c. Use of chemicals to "age" the wood before it is finished.

16. Discuss how to remove dents from a wood surface.

Chapter 6
INSTALLING WEBBING AND SPRINGS

Not all reupholstering jobs will require the replacement of springs. Where springs are still in good condition, only minor adjustments or repairs are necessary, Fig. 6-1. In other cases, an inspection will show the need to remove all upholstering materials down to the frame and rebuild the unit. This requires that webbing and springs be replaced with the same or comparable materials, Fig. 6-2.

WEBBING

The purpose of webbing in upholstered furniture is to provide support or backing for springs and padding materials. There are several types of webbing.
1. Corrugated steel webbing.
2. Perforated flat steel webbing.
3. Wire mesh.
4. Jute webbing.

Fig. 6-2. Factory spring unit on this couch is badly damaged. It must be replaced.

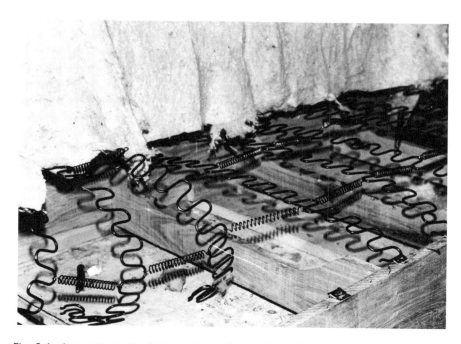

Fig. 6-1. Inspection is the first step in repair of springs. The sinuous spring unit needs replacement of several clips and helical springs.

77

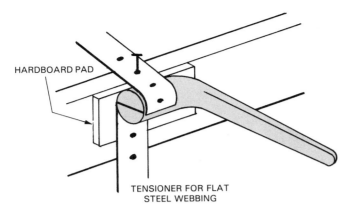

Fig. 6-3. Special tool is needed to tension steel webbing. Hardboard pad protects rail.

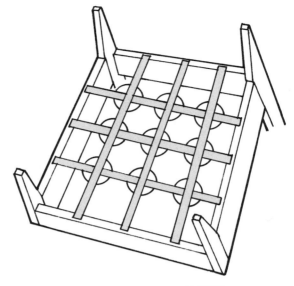

CROSSING JOINTS OVER SPRINGS

Fig. 6-5. Correct layout of flat steel webbing and coil springs.

Though not as popular as jute webbing, steel web materials are sometimes used on the under edges of seat frames to support coil springs. Tensioning some steel webbing requires a special tool, Fig. 6-3.

Corrugated webbing has small loops for holding the coil springs. The open end of the coil is passed through the loop where it will be held securely without need for additional fasteners. When perforated webbing is used, the coil springs must be fastened down with stove pipe wire. See Fig. 6-4. As with perforated webbing, a special tool is needed to tension corrugated webbing.

Fig. 6-5 shows correct use of steel webbing with coil springs. First the webbing is laid down and attached going one direction. Then webbing is laid down in the other direction. Fasten flat steel webbing to the upholstery frame as shown in Fig. 6-6. Nail the webbing to the frame first. Apply tension and nail it at the rear rail. Use ring type nails for greater holding power.

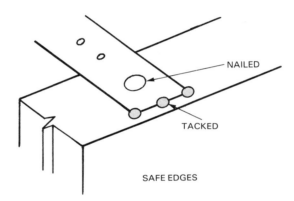

SAFE EDGES

Fig. 6-6. Method of attaching perforated metal webbing. Tacks are used to cover rough edges, protect dustcover.

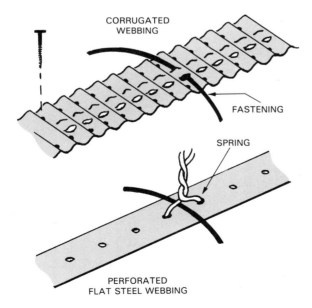

Fig. 6-4. Closeup view of attachment methods used for metal webbing. Bottom coil of spring attaches to built-in slot on corrugated web. On perforated flat steel web, stove pipe wire is used to secure spring.

Cut off the excess webbing with a file, hacksaw or other suitable tool. Tack down rough edges so that a dustcover can be installed neatly when the job is finished.

Perforated flat steel webbing can be ''woven'' over and under crossing strips. Corrugated webbing cannot be woven.

Fasten coil springs at four points to the perforated steel webbing. Coils are located over each point where the webs cross. Refer again to Fig. 6-5.

For most reupholstery purposes, 3 1/2 in. (about 9 cm) jute webbing is most suitable. An average chair will require about 10 yd. (9 m), a sofa about 20 yd. (18 m).

Jute webbing is most often preferred over steel because of its resilience. When used as a foundation for padding only or for Marshall springs units, it should be applied to the tops of seat rails and to the front edges of back rails. When used as support for coil springs, attach webbing to the undersides of seat rails and to the backs of back rails. Fig. 6-7 shows webbing applied to

Installing Webbing and Springs

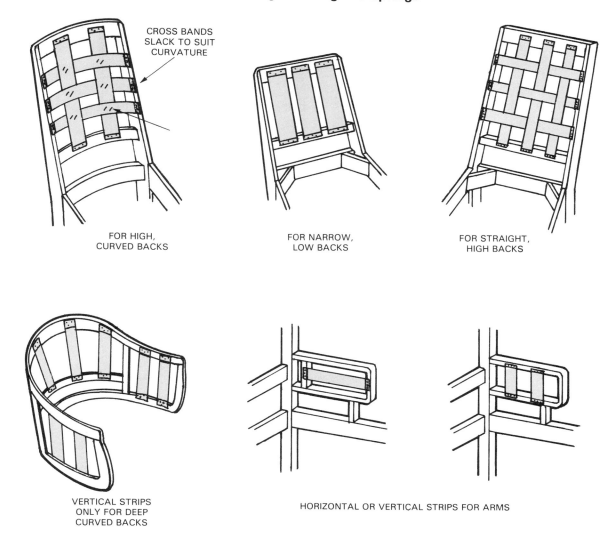

FOR HIGH,
CURVED BACKS

CROSS BANDS
SLACK TO SUIT
CURVATURE

FOR NARROW,
LOW BACKS

FOR STRAIGHT,
HIGH BACKS

VERTICAL STRIPS
ONLY FOR DEEP
CURVED BACKS

HORIZONTAL OR VERTICAL STRIPS FOR ARMS

Fig. 6-7. Correct application of webbing to support padding on backs and arms.

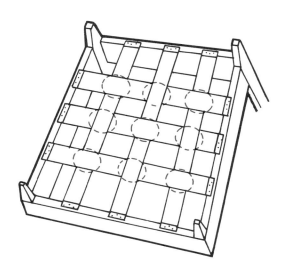

FOR COIL SPRING SEAT

Fig. 6-8. Placement of webbing has been adjusted so coil springs (circles) can be placed where bands cross. This gives springs better support.

backs and arms as a support for padding.

Spacing between bands of webbing should not be closer than 1/2 in. (12 mm). When the webbing is to support springs, spacing should be adjusted so that the springs rest at points where two pieces of webbing cross. See Fig. 6-8.

As with steel webbing, tack the jute webbing to the front seat rail first. Then, using the webbing stretcher as shown in Fig. 6-9, stretch the webbing taut and tack it on the back rail.

Allow an overlap of about an inch at either end of the webbing. Drive in four No. 10 or No. 12 tacks, as shown in Fig. 6-9, fold the extra webbing over the top and drive in three more tacks. Stagger the tacks and space them evenly. Stay at least 3/8 in. (9 mm) away from rail edges. Do not stretch webbing so tight that the cloth tears away from the tacks or that tacks tend to pull out of the wood.

Webbing on backs can be stretched by hand. Not as much pressure is placed upon the back of the chair as on the seat.

If the back is to receive springs, as well, the back

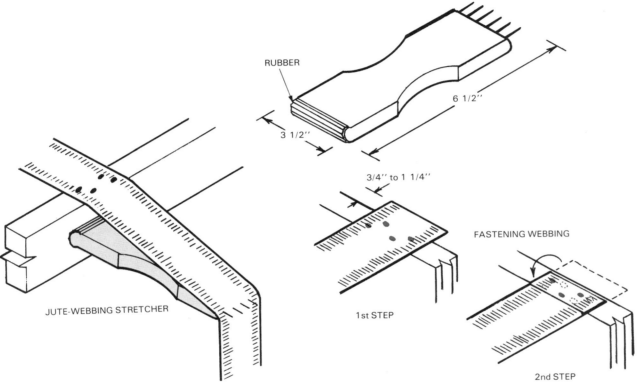

Fig. 6-9. Top. Using the webbing stretcher. Do not stretch fabric too tight. It may tear the material, pull out the tacks or warp rails. Bottom. How to use another type stretcher and how to place webbing tacks.

webbing should be interlaced the same as the seat. But if padding only is used, then vertical webbing alone is enough.

SPRINGS

Springs are one the the best cushioning materials in upholstery. Being resilient and flexible, springs offer the utmost comfort and support when used on upholstery seats, backs, arms and in cushions. Correctly installed, springs can give many years of luxurious and satisfying service. Padding materials are added to springs to:

1. Protect final coverings from rubbing against the wire and wearing out faster.
2. Provide extra comfort for the user.

SPRING CONSTRUCTION

Spring construction is of two general types:
1. Spring supported seats and padded backs.
2. Spring supports in both seat and back, sometimes referred to as OVERSTUFFED furniture.

Overstuffed furniture often has two sets of springs in the seat. The lower set is the BASE and is fastened to the frame. The upper set may be attached to the frame or installed in a removable cushion.

Upholstery springs vary in type, size, style and degree of compression to serve a variety of purposes. They are made with steel wire of several gages. The wire is highly tempered and treated to resist corrosion. Seat springs are heavier, stronger and firmer than those used in arms or backs. Cushion springs are lightest.

Durability, flexibility and resilience of springs are

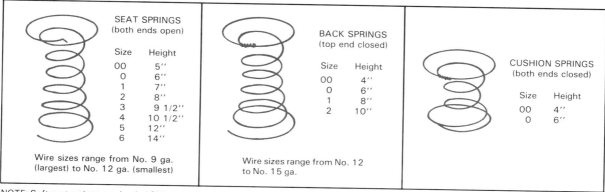

SEAT SPRINGS (both ends open)		BACK SPRINGS (top end closed)		CUSHION SPRINGS (both ends closed)	
Size	Height	Size	Height	Size	Height
00	5''	00	4''	00	4''
0	6''	0	6''	0	6''
1	7''	1	8''		
2	8''	2	10''		
3	9 1/2''				
4	10 1/2''				
5	12''				
6	14''				

Wire sizes range from No. 9 ga. (largest) to No. 12 ga. (smallest)

Wire sizes range from No. 12 to No. 15 ga.

NOTE: Soft seat springs can be tied 2'' below normal height; medium seat springs 1'' below normal height; hard seat springs never below normal height but may be tied 1'' above this. Before tying, seat springs are 1 to 1 1/2'' above normal height.

Fig. 6-10. Coil springs for upholstering are made in several coil shapes and in many, many sizes.

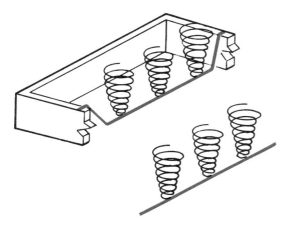

Fig. 6-11. Two styles of spring bars often used on less expensive furniture.

controlled by:
1. Size, gage of wire used and shape of springs.
2. Method of tying springs.
3. Quality of spring supports.
4. Anchorage.

SPRING TYPES

Installation procedures for springs vary according to the type of spring used. Types generally used for upholstering include:
1. COIL COMPRESSION SPRINGS. These are the most common.
2. SINUOUS (sagless or zig-zag) springs which are used where a low profile is desirable or required. They are faster and easier to install and are very durable. However, their major disadvantage is that they are usually not as comfortable.
3. MARSHALL units. These are also called "pocket springs" because each individual coil spring is enclosed in a canvas pocket or bag. They are manufactured in single rows or as complete units ready for installation in a seat, back or cushion.

COIL SPRINGS

The coil spring is used in the backs, seats and cushions of upholstered furniture. Several types are shown in Fig. 6-10. They are manufactured in many heights, shapes, wire thicknesses and degrees of stiffness.

The size number of a spring is related to the number of coils. It will help you remember sizes to know that the size of the spring is five less than the number of coils it has.

The heavier the wire the stiffer the spring. The smaller the center coil the stiffer the spring is in comparison to other springs of the same size.

There are three degrees of firmness:
1. Hard.
2. Medium.
3. Soft.

Seat springs are made with heavier gage wire (9 to 12) because seat springs must stand up to heavier use than back springs or cushion springs. Coil springs used to cushion the backs of chairs and sofas are lighter gage (12 to 15). Top ends are closed so that the springs do not tear padding and covering fabric. Cushion springs are closed at both ends and are softer to provide extra comfort.

For moderate service, seat springs with medium firmness and 4 to 9 in. (100 to 225 mm) in height are often used. Larger springs, 12 to 14 in. (30 to 35 cm) high, are recommended for heavy service.

Coil springs are also available in assembled units called spring bars. Single coils (which are cone shaped) are mounted on a bar. The bars are of various lengths from 16 to 26 in. (40 to 66 cm) and are designed to be mounted to front and back rails. No webbing is needed, Fig. 6-11.

PLACING COIL SPRINGS

The first step in installing coil springs over webbing is to determine where and how close together to locate

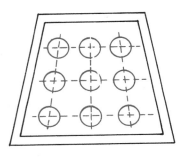
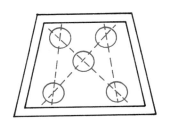
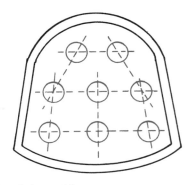

THREE TYPICAL SPRING ARRANGEMENTS
FOR SEATS (SPRINGS ALIGNED IN ROWS)

Fig. 6-12. Layout of springs will vary according to shape and size of the seat frame.

Fig. 6-13. Arranging coil springs on base support. Tops of coils will be tied in a later operation.

them. Springs are usually placed 2 to 4 in. (5 to 10 cm) apart. Fig. 6-12 shows several patterns for arranging springs. Fig. 6-13 shows a double row of coils being arranged and sewn over jute webbing in a small upholstery project.

Placement of the springs is important for comfort and appearance. If placed too closely together, the springing will be stiff and uncomfortable. If too far apart, the springing will be too soft and will "bottom out" (sink down to the spring support) when used. Padding will become lumpy and sag between the springs. The unit will be uncomfortable.

ATTACHING COIL SPRINGS TO BASE

Coil springs need to be firmly anchored to their base support so they cannot shift position or fall over. Each spring should be secured at four points.

Check each spring carefully before attaching. On

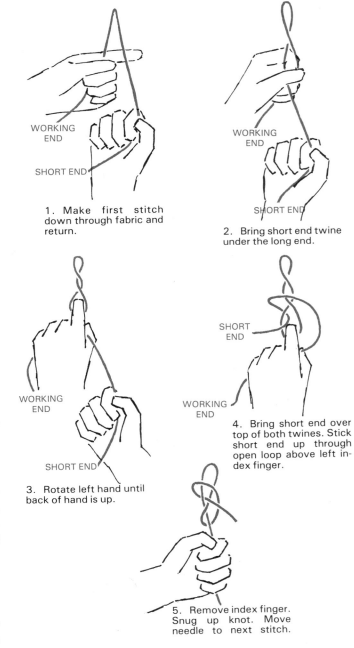

1. Make first stitch down through fabric and return.

2. Bring short end twine under the long end.

3. Rotate left hand until back of hand is up.

4. Bring short end over top of both twines. Stick short end up through open loop above left index finger.

5. Remove index finger. Snug up knot. Move needle to next stitch.

Fig. 6-14. How to tie an upholsterers' slip knot. First stitch has already been taken.

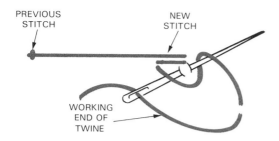

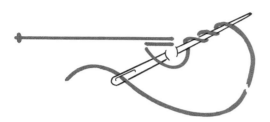

1. AS STITCH IS COMPLETED, SLIDE NEEDLE HALFWAY THROUGH FABRIC AS SHOWN. LOOP TWINE AROUND NEEDLE POINT.

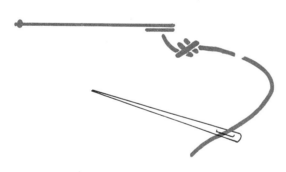

2. MAKE TWO MORE LOOPS AROUND THE POINT OF THE NEEDLE. (KEEP COMPLETED STITCH SNUG.)

3. PULL NEEDLE THROUGH LOOPS. SNUG UP TWINE. LOCK STITCH WITH SHORT JERK ON TWINE. GO ON TO NEXT STITCH.

Fig. 6-15. Tying a twist knot which is used between first and last stitches.

springs which are open on both ends, one end or tip of the spring wire is bent down slightly toward the center. This end of the spring should be up to prevent puncturing padding and covering material placed over it.

On jute webbing material, stitching twine is used for fastening. Measure and cut a piece of twine long enough to fasten down all of the springs. (If the spring unit is large, this is not practical since the twine will twist and ravel. Several shorter pieces will prove easier to handle.)

Tying knots

It is helpful to learn several knots before attempting to sew springs to webbing.

1. The SLIP KNOT, Fig. 6-14, (sometimes called the lock knot) secures the first spring stitch to the webbing. It should be used also on the last stitch of a length of twine. It prevents the last stitch from pulling apart.
2. A TWIST KNOT locks each intermediate stitch before going on to the next stitch. Fig. 6-15 describes how it is made. Loops are made with the hand holding the twine. Keep twine taut.

Use of the knots is considered good practice. Even though it requires extra time on each stitch it can save a reupholstering job later should a twine break between stitches. Without the knots such a twine failure would cause some or all of the stitching to loosen.

STITCHING THE SPRINGS

Before sewing down the coil springs, some upholsterers indicate the position of the springs by marking locating lines on the webbing. These are chalk marks made alongside the bottom spiral of each spring. Loose springs can be moved out of the way during the stitching operation without losing their proper position.

Begin stitching on a corner spring. Using a curved or double-pointed needle, sew the bottom spiral of the coil spring to the webbing at four points. Wrap the twine tightly around the spring at each point.

Secure the twine on the first stitch with a slip knot. As each succeeding stitch is made, secure it with a twist knot. See Fig. 6-16. The last stitch on every length of twine should be secured with a lock stitch.

As stitching proceeds, follow a pattern that will bring the last stitch on each spring nearest the next spring.

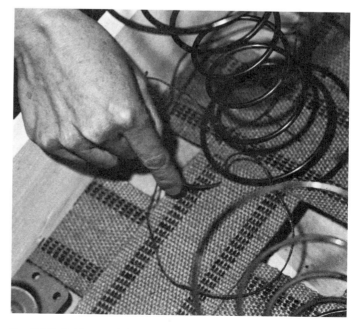

Fig. 6-16. Taking a stitch with a curved needle. Twine loop is made tightly around spring to keep it from shifting.

Fig. 6-17 shows the open square pattern. Another sewing diagram is shown in Fig. 6-18.

TYING COIL SPRINGS

Coil springs are also tied down firmly across their tops to prevent them from slipping sideways out of position. They should be tied to uniform height so that each spring's upward expansion is controlled. Before tying, springs usually stand about 1 1/2 in. (3.5 cm) above ''normal'' height. Firm springs are often tied at freestanding height (1 1/2 in. above normal height). Medium springs are generally tied 1 in. (2.5 cm) below normal height and soft springs 2 in. (5 cm) below normal height.

Springs lose resiliency when compressed by tying. Extra height above the frame increases the resiliency of the springs. In seats, tops of springs, after tying, should be a minimum of 3 in. (7.5 cm) above the frame. This permits them to be depressed without taking up all slack in the spring twine.

Seat springs may be tied to form round or flat tops according to need or preference. Single sets of springs

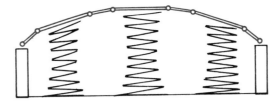
SIMPLE SPRING TIE FOR ROUND SEAT

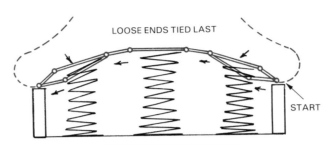
LOOSE ENDS TIED LAST
START
RETURN TYING FOR ROUNDED SEAT

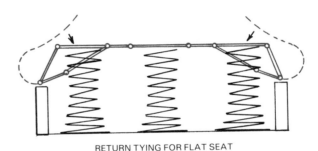
RETURN TYING FOR FLAT SEAT

Fig. 6-19. Tying arrangements for rounded and flat seats. For flat seats, return tie is fastened to the third coil from top.

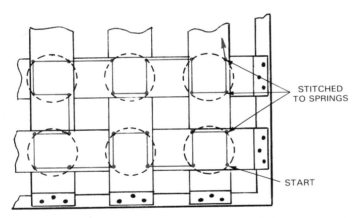
STITCHED TO SPRINGS
START

Fig. 6-17. Arrange stitching pattern so final stitch is nearest next spring to be attached.

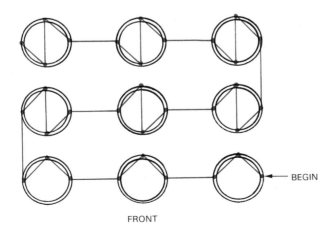
BEGIN
FRONT

Fig. 6-18. Diagram for alternate sewing pattern for attaching springs. Some upholsterers attach front springs at three points only.

used without cushions are usually tied with a round contour for appearance and comfort. See Fig. 6-19. Flat-shaped tops are used particularly when two sets of springs or a removable cushion is used. Fig. 6-20 is a diagram for a two-way (four knot) tie. Fig. 6-21 illustrates a four-way (eight knot) tie.

Tying springs for round seat

The two-way (four knot) tie is often used to fasten round seats. Each row of springs is tied lengthwise and then crosswise. Each row uses a separate piece of spring twine.

To estimate twine length, measure the distance across the frame lengthwise and crosswise. Double each measurement and allow 12 in. (30 cm) extra length for knots. With scissors, cut enough pieces of spring twine for each row of springs.

Fastening springs lengthwise

Using an upholsterers' hammer, drive two No. 12 tacks into the frame opposite the center of each row of

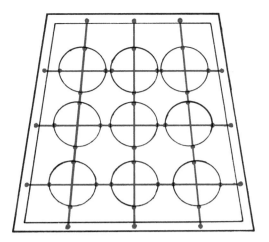

Fig. 6-20. Two-way tie diagram is shown in color.

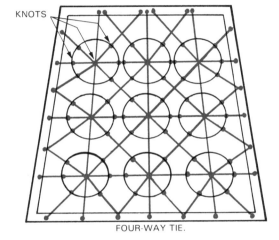

FOUR-WAY TIE.

Fig. 6-21. In four-way tie, ties run in four directions: vertical, horizontal, angled to left, angled to right.

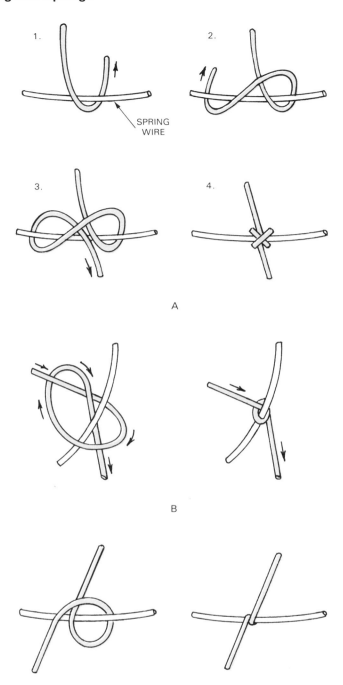

SPRING WIRE

A

B

C

Fig. 6-23. How to make three types of knots used in tying twine to springs. A—Steps for making clove spring knot. B—Procedure for overhand knot. C—Making the simple loop.

Fig. 6-22. One method of forming the knot which hooks over the tacks in rail.

springs at either end. Space the tacks 1/2 in. (12 mm) apart and drive them only halfway into the frame.

Form a clove hitch knot at one end of spring twine piece. Loop the knot around two of the partially driven tacks. Then drive the tacks tightly into the frame against the knot. See Fig. 6-22.

Depress the edge of the first spring (nearest double tack) to the desired height for a round seat. Pull the spring twine tightly around its top coil and make a clove spring knot or an overhand knot. See Fig. 6-23. Then pull the twine taut to the opposite side of the spring and tie another knot. Tie all the springs in the same way. See Fig. 6-24.

Fastening springs crosswise

Drive two No. 12 tacks into the frame opposite the center of each row of springs at each side. Then fasten the twine crosswise in the same way as lengthwise. Shape and tie the springs crosswise by the same method as was used lengthwise, Fig. 6-25.

The four-way (eight knot) tie is sometimes used as extra support to hold coil springs. This method employs diagonal spring twines in the same way that lengthwise and crosswise twine pieces are used in the two-way (four knot) tie method. Clove hitch or overhand knots are tied around each spring and intersecting twine. Fig. 6-26 shows a four-way tie nearly completed.

Tying springs for flat seat with return twine

The two-way (four knot) tie is generally used to fasten flat seats. The procedure is similar to tying round seats. See Figs. 6-21 through 6-26.

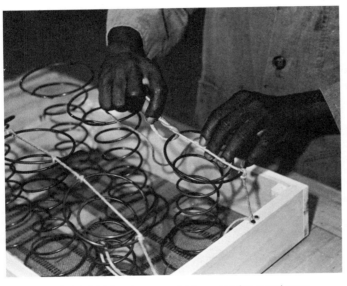

Fig. 6-24. Making ties on outside spring for round seat.

Fig. 6-25. Placing clove knot over rail tacks during cross tying. Pull knot tight and drive tacks rest of way into top of rail.

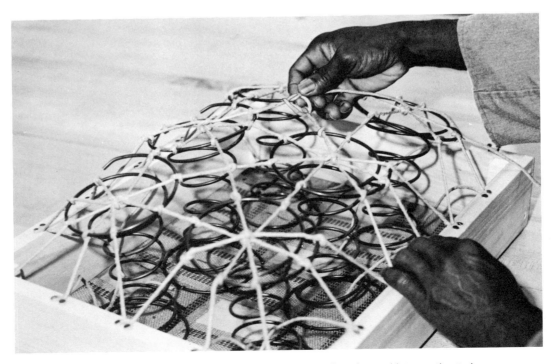

Fig. 6-26. Tie clove hitches or overhand knots at each spring and intersecting twine.

Measure the distance across the frame lengthwise and crosswise. Double each measurement and allow 24 in. (61 cm) extra length for knots and return twines. With scissors, cut the pieces of spring twine needed.

Fasten springs lengthwise. Using an upholsterers' hammer, drive two No. 12 tacks partway into the frame opposite center of each row of springs at both ends. This is the same procedure used with the round seat. Leave about 6 in. (15 cm) of loose end on each piece of twine for tie back. Form a clove hitch knot, loop it around two of the partially driven tacks. Then drive the tacks tightly against the knot.

Wrap long end of the twine around the opposite side of the spring. Then compress the spring to height you want and form a clove hitch or overhand knot, Fig. 6-27.

Fasten the loose (short) end of twine to the first side of the spring (one nearest double tack). Attach it to the second spiral from the top. Use a clove hitch or overhand knot, Fig. 6-28.

Pull the twine taut to the next spring and wrap the twine around its nearest edge. Then compress the spring to the desired height and form a clove hitch or overhand knot. Continue tying the other springs in the same way, Fig. 6-29. Fasten springs crosswise using the same method.

Fig. 6-29. Tying inside spring with overhand knot. Keep spacing between springs even.

APPLYING SPRING EDGE

Spring edge wire, sometimes used in overstuffed furniture, produces a straight, even edge along the top coils of a spring seat or back. It forms a flat, neat platform for a cushion. Since it is manufactured only in straight sections 5-12 ft. (1.5-3.5 m) long, it must be shaped by the upholsterer.

To find the length of wire needed for the spring edge, measure the tops of the springs from front to back and then from side to side. Be sure to measure to the outsides of the top coils. Double the dimensions and add about 8 in. (20 cm) for overlap.

No. 9 or 10 gage wire is used for seats, No. 12 or 14 gage for backs. Special metal clips are manufactured to attach the wire to the springs or twine may be used.

The wire is bent by hand. To cut the wire, file a notch in it; then slip two lengths of 1/4 or 3/8 in. steel pipe over the wire. With one length of pipe on either side of the notch bend the wire back and forth until it breaks. Corners are bent using the pipe method or a vise and hammer.

Attach edge wire with clips as shown in Fig. 6-30. Clips are attached with a spring clip pliers.

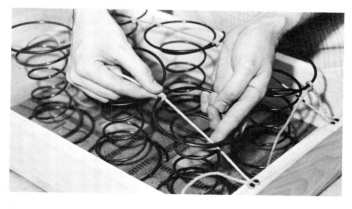

Fig. 6-27. Beginning tie for flat seat with return tie. Spring is depressed on inside of coil and twine is knotted around it in first step.

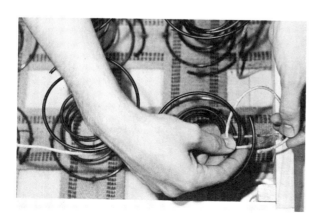

Fig. 6-28. Fasten short (return tie) end of twine to outside of coil on lower spiral of coil spring.

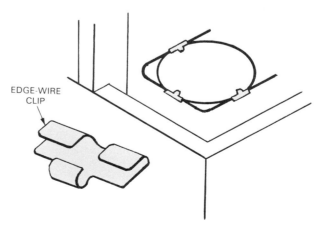

EDGE-WIRE CLIP

Fig. 6-30. Edge wire forms crisp, even edge for flat spring seat or back. Attaching clips are fastened with special pliers.

1. DOUBLE UP LENGTH OF TWINE AND LOOP IT AROUND SPRING AND EDGE WIRE.

2. START WRAP GOING OVER AND UNDER WIRE IN "FIGURE EIGHT" PATTERN.

3. AFTER THREE OR FOUR LOOPS, MOVE TO OTHER SIDE.

4. MAKE SAME NUMBER OF LOOPS USING SAME PATTERN.

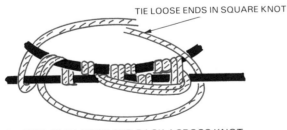

TIE LOOSE ENDS IN SQUARE KNOT

5. PULL ONE LOOSE END BACK ACROSS KNOT AND BRING UP BETWEEN WIRES, BRING OTHER LOOSE END ACROSS AND TIE.

Fig. 6-31. Steps for tying spring to edge wire.

If twine is used for tying the wire to the springs, use the wrapping technique illustrated in Fig. 6-31. Fig. 6-32 shows some special applications of spring edging.

SINUOUS SPRINGS

Sinuous (sagless or zig-zag) springs, Fig. 6-33, are faster and easier to install than coil springs. You can purchase precut lengths or bulk rolls of 100 ft. (30 m) or more in length. Gage ranges from No. 8 to No. 12 in half gage steps. Sinuous springs can be cut with bolt cutters, a fine toothed hacksaw or file. Ends are bent in a vise or bending fixture so that they do not become detached from clips. See Fig. 6-34.

Sinuous spring strips are arched between front and back seat rails and are generally spaced 4 to 5 in. (10 to 12.5 cm) between centers. Bent ends of adjacent strips should alternate right or left and be fastened to frame with spring clips, Fig. 6-35. Small, helical (coil) springs are used to attach spring strips to side rails of frame and between spring strips. (Refer, again to Fig. 6-33.) This provides uniform springing action and helps support padding materials.

Use 3/4 to 1 in. barbed, cement-coated or screw-type nails to fasten spring clips to frame. Ordinary nails tend to loosen or pull out under continuous tension.

Fig. 6-33. Sinuous springs can be used in backs and seats. They make the furniture appear less bulky.

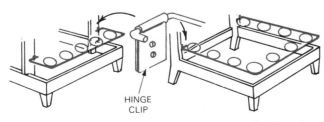

HINGE CLIP

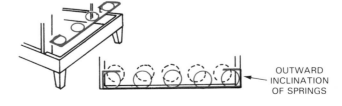

OUTWARD INCLINATION OF SPRINGS

Fig. 6-32. Application of spring edges. Some go only partially around the springs.

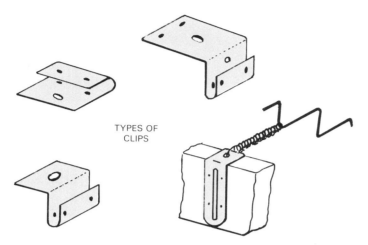

ABOUT 2"   HOW ENDS ARE BENT

Fig. 6-34. Sinuous springs zig zag about 2 in. Ends must be bent so springs do not become detached from clip accidentally.

TYPES OF CLIPS

Fig. 6-35. Fasteners are manufactured in several styles to support sinuous and helical springs.

Fig. 6-36. Sinuous spring clips are quickly attached with ring nails.

Fig. 6-37. Attaching second end of sinuous spring to clips. On longer spans or where more tension is desired, a special stretcher is used.

Fig. 6-38. After attaching sinuous spring to clip secure it by driving additional nails through holes in top of clip.

Fig. 6-39. Helical springs connected between loops of sinuous springs keep springs aligned.

INSTALLING SINUOUS SPRINGS

With a rule, measure the distance lengthwise and crosswise between top edges of the frame. Allow 4 to 5 in. (10 to 12.5 cm) between centers for springs and 1 1/2 to 3 in. (4 to 7.5 cm) of space between outer springs and end rails of frame.

Using bolt cutters or hacksaw, cut the required number of spring strips. Should the measured length fall where the spring loop is going the opposite direction of the starting end, make the cut at the next longer bend.

With rule and chalk, lay out locations for spring clips. Position each spring clip and, with a hammer, drive two 1 in. barbed nails through the clip, into the edge of the back rail, Fig. 6-36.

Insert end of spring strip into clip and drive two more nails through the top of the clip to lock in the spring and reinforce the clip.

To attach spring to front rail, locate front spring clip over layout mark made earlier. With hammer, drive 1 in. barbed nail through hole in clip, into top edge of front rail as in Fig. 6-36. Insert the end of the spring strip into the clip, Fig. 6-37, and drive two more nails through the clip into the frame, Fig. 6-38.

INSTALLING HELICAL SPRINGS

As was explained earlier in this chapter, helical springs are used to interconnect sinuous springs. This causes the sinuous springs to act as one unit in counteracting weight placed upon them. Similarly, helical springs are used to connect sinuous springs to furniture frames.

To connect center spring strips, select helical springs of appropriate length. Fasten the end hooks of helical springs around loops of sinuous springs. Fig. 6-39 shows a typical arrangement between springs. Install one or more helical springs between adjacent sinuous springs.

With hammer, drive two staples partway into the top edge of the rail at both sides of the frame. Select helical springs of appropriate length. Fasten one end of each helical spring around a loop of the nearest sinuous spring. Then insert the other end through the staple and set the staple with a hammer. See Fig. 6-40.

An edge wire can be used with sinuous spring by using a special ''U'' shaped connector. This is shown in Fig. 6-41.

MARSHALL UNITS

Marshall or innerspring units, Fig. 6-42, are springs sewn inside individual pockets of muslin or burlap. They are joined together into banks of springs large enough to cover an entire seat, back or cushion. Marshall units can be purchased in ready-made strips or entire units.

APPLICATIONS

Marshall units are used in cushions for greater resilience. The coil units are 3 in. (7.5 cm) in diameter and 3 1/2 in. (about 9 cm) high. Larger coils—up to 6 in. (15 cm) high—are used for chair backs.

ATTACHING MARSHALL UNITS

When Marshall units are used in a chair or couch back, the supporting webbing should be attached to the front edge of the frame. Webbing should be arranged so that a web supports each row of springs. Attach springs by stitching outside coils to the webbing. On these units, no burlap covering is needed between padding and springs.

Marshall units can also be mounted on sinuous springs. Place the sinuous springs vertically and tie

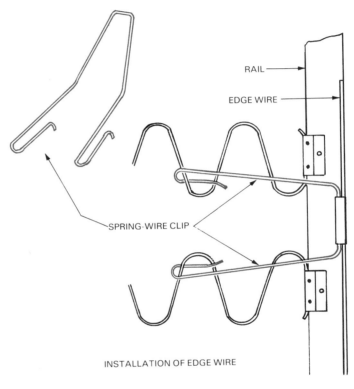

RAIL

EDGE WIRE

SPRING-WIRE CLIP

INSTALLATION OF EDGE WIRE

Fig. 6-41. Special U shaped clips are used to attach spring wire edging to sinuous springs.

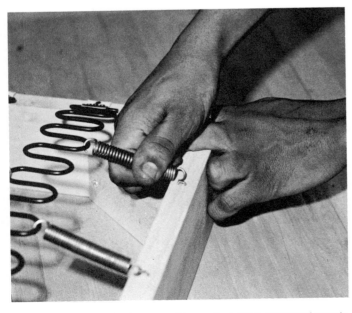

Fig. 6-40. Drive staples into top of frame for helical spring and attach helical spring between sinuous spring and frame.

Fig. 6-42. Marshall spring unit is ready to be used as purchased.

them horizontally with twine. Stitch the bottoms of the coils to the loops and bars of the sinuous springs. Hog rings may be used instead of stitching twine.

REPAIRING MARSHALL UNITS

It is not usually advisable to repair Marshall units. The coils tend to lose their resilience. However, if they are less than six months old and appear to be in good condition, new pockets can be sewn for them.

Cut strips of muslin or burlap 15 in. (38 cm) wide. Fold them to 7 1/2 in. (19 cm) wide. Sew across the narrow width at 9 1/2 in. (24 cm) intervals to form open pockets. Insert springs and sew pockets shut. The pocket should be snug enough so spring does not shift but loose enough so it can fully expand.

Springs can be added to or removed from innerspring units. For example, T shaped backs will need additional springs above the arms. These additional springs are attached to the unit with twine or hog rings.

ATTACHING BURLAP OVER SPRINGS

With a tape rule or string, measure the distance lengthwise and crosswise over the contour of the springs between the frame's top edges. Add 2 in. (5 cm) extra length each way to allow for folds. Then, with scissors, cut a piece of burlap to size.

Fold under about an inch (25 mm) of the burlap along one side. Lay the folded edge over the frame's edge. With an upholsterers' hammer, drive three No. 3 tacks near the center of the frame through the fold. Fold under about an inch of the opposite edge of burlap. Pull the burlap firmly over the springs and fasten it with three tacks near the center of the frame. Space the tacks about 1 to 1 1/2 in. (2.5 to 3 cm) apart. Fasten the other edges of burlap in the same way. Start each tack with the magnetic (small end) of the hammer and finish driving with the other end, Fig. 6-43.

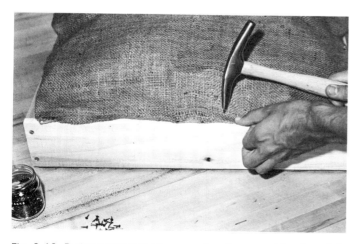

Fig. 6-43. Burlap cover tacked over springs keeps padding from falling through.

Fig. 6-44. Stitching over top of burlap attaches burlap to springs. Upholsterer is adding edge roll.

Continue fastening each edge from the center toward each end. This helps prevent wrinkles in the material. Then stitch the burlap to the tops of springs with a curved or double-pointed straight needle and sewing twine, Fig. 6-44.

REVIEW QUESTIONS — CHAPTER 6

1. What is the purpose of webbing?
2. _____ is the most popular webbing material because of its resilience.
3. List the two types of spring construction used in upholstered furniture.
4. Coil springs are made of _____ _____ in several gages.
5. _____ springs are used where a low profile is desired or required.
6. Describe the proper location of coil springs over jute webbing.
7. The _____ knot and the _____ knot are useful in securing coil springs to webbing.
8. What treatment is given the tops of coil springs to keep them in place when used in a seat or back?
9. The following tie is generally used to fasten flat seats with coil springs (select the correct answer):
    a. Two-way tie.
    b. Four-way tie.
    c. Four knot tie.
    d. Eight knot tie.
10. Name the knots used for tying down coil springs.
11. The part used to form a straight, even edge along the top coils of a seat or spring back is called a _____.
12. What is a sinuous spring and what are its advantages?
13. What additional parts should you have for installing sinuous springs?
14. Which of the following form a suitable base (support) for Marshall unit springs:
    a. Webbing.
    b. Sinuous springs.
    c. Burlap.
    d. Muslin.

Chapter 7
INSTALLING PADDING

Upholstered furniture, with or without springs, requires padding materials. The purpose of padding is to provide softness for comfort. Not only should the padding material be soft, it should remain soft after years of use. Materials which will provide softness when compressed and then expand to original shape and size are the best for padding. The ability of a material to spring back into its original shape is called resilience.

SELECTING PADDING

There are a number of padding materials to choose from. Some are obtained from plants and animals. Some are produced by manufacturing processes. Among the commonly used materials are:
1. SISAL. This inexpensive material comes from the large leaves of the hemp plant. The fibers are long, white and coarse. Sisal is manufactured as padded material or as loose fibers. It is sometimes rubberized for greater durability. Since it has a tendency to pack (lose its springiness) it is best used as a base for better grades of padding.
2. RUBBERIZED CURLED HAIR. Hogs, cattle and horses are the source of hair padding. The hair is soaked in hot water to make it curl. Then the strands are coated with rubber and made into pads. Curled hair which has not been rubberized is sold loose.
3. FOAM RUBBER and FOAM PLASTIC. These two products are, today, the most popular of all the padding materials. Both are made in sheets with foam plastic being made in thicker dimensions than foam rubber.
4. COTTON MAT and DACRON POLYESTER FIBER-FILL. These materials are intended as a topping over other padding to provide additional softness.
5. WHITE WADDING. This is a thin cotton padding sold in narrow widths. It is intended as a light padding over structural surfaces of the furniture such as fronts of arms and around seat rails.
6. MOSS. This air plant is harvested from trees in southern states. It is alternately soaked and dried to

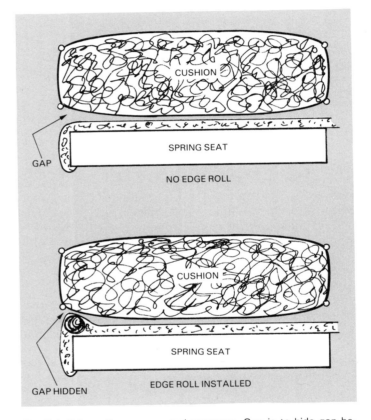

Fig. 7-1. Edge roll serves several purposes. One is to hide gap between seat and crowned cushion.

remove the outer covering. This treatment exposes a tough fibrous material that was once popular as bulk padding. It is no longer popular.
7. KAPOK. A soft, silky, resilient material. Kapok is highly resistant to moisture. It is sometimes used in pillows and cushions.

These materials are illustrated in Chapter 1. See Figs. 1-29 through 1-37.

EDGE ROLLS

Loose or formed resilient materials are sewed inside fabric to form a long, narrow, rounded pad called an

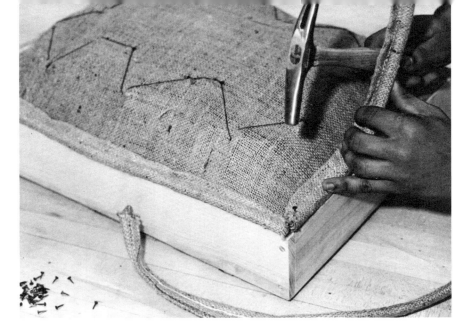

Fig. 7-2. Manufactured edge roll is being tacked to furniture rail.

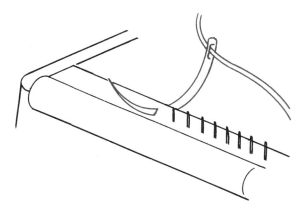

Fig. 7-3. Edge roll must be sewed to burlap when it is being attached to spring edges. Curved needle works best.

edge roll. The roll can be handmade or purchased already formed. It is used on wood or spring edges. It cushions hard, sharp edges and its soft, spongy surface prevents regular padding from shifting or coming in contact with the hard edge and wearing thin. In the same way, it reduces wear on the final cover and makes the padding more comfortable.

A third advantage of the edge roll is that it fills the gap between a crowned cushion and the upholstered seat of furniture, Fig. 7-1.

Edge rolls are attached to wood surfaces with tacks, Fig. 7-2. On spring edges there are no wood parts for support. The edge roll, therefore, must be sewed to the burlap which covers the springs, Fig. 7-3.

MAKING AND INSTALLING EDGE ROLL

Edge roll can be purchased ready-made to suit most applications. Diameters range from 1/2 to 1 1/2 in. (12 to 37 mm) and there are a variety of shapes. Some are shown in Fig. 7-4.

The upholsterer can make edge roll from strips of muslin or burlap, filling it with any resilient stuffing material. This is not difficult.
1. Estimate the width of muslin or burlap covering from the diameter of the edge roll wanted. Be sure to allow an extra inch at each edge for attaching the roll to the furniture, Fig. 7-5.
2. Measure and cut material into strips required.

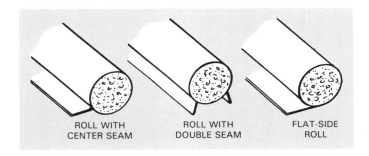

ROLL WITH CENTER SEAM

ROLL WITH DOUBLE SEAM

FLAT-SIDE ROLL

Fig. 7-4. Manufactured edge roll is made in several styles. Not all have round contour shown here.

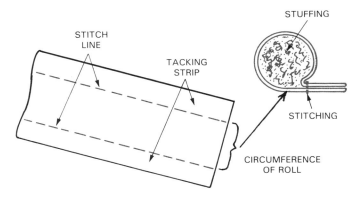

STITCH LINE

TACKING STRIP

STUFFING

STITCHING

CIRCUMFERENCE OF ROLL

Fig. 7-5. Measuring and cutting burlap or muslin for making edge roll. Allow extra width for tacking or sewing the roll to furniture.

93

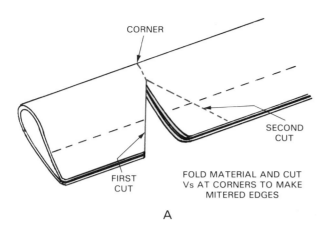

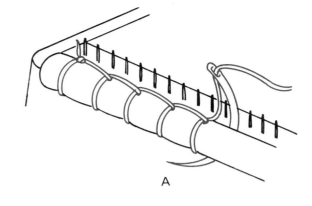

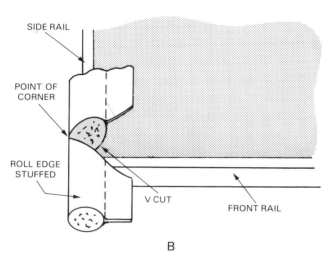

Fig. 7-6. Cut miters in burlap or muslin for corners of edge roll. A—Cut V before stuffing. B—Stuffed edge roll mitered and ready for turning corner.

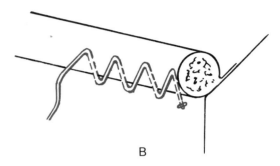

Fig. 7-8. Securing padded portion of edge roll to spring edge. A—With series of half hitches. First and last hitch are knotted. B—With series of loop stitches.

3. Measure and mark where corners will be on the covering. Cut a notch at these points with the material folded double. Make the notch no deeper than three-quarters of the width of the folded material, Fig. 7-6. Angle of the notch should be about 45 deg. (After the roll is stuffed, the notch

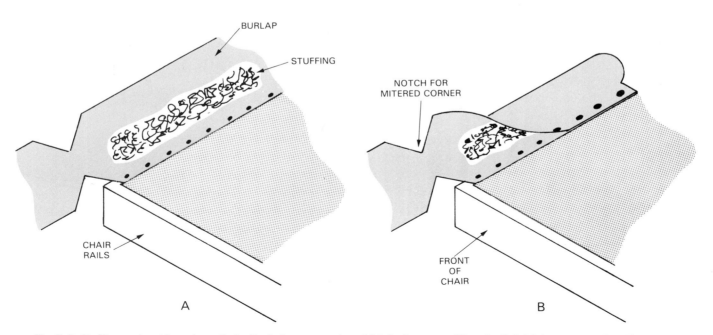

Fig. 7-7. Stuffing and tacking edge roll. A—Tack down one edge of fabric. Lay on stuffing. B—Roll fabric over top of stuffing and tack down.

can be cut deeper, if need be.)

4. Attach one edge of the material to the frame or spring edge. Use No. 6 tacks on wood. Stitching twine will be needed on spring edges.

5. Add stuffing and fold the material over it. Pack the stuffing firmly.

6. Tack or sew the second edge over the first edge, Fig. 7-7.

7. If rolls are very large, it may be advisable to stitch back and forth through the stuffing materials to keep them from shifting.

8. When very large edge rolls are attached to spring edges the roll must be lashed down to the springs with a second set of stitches, Fig. 7-8, view A. This set is a series of half hitches made around the entire roll with a curved needle. Push the curved needle down through the top of the edge roll at the point where the padding starts. The twine must be carried in back of the edge spring and out the front through the burlap covering. Exit point should be as near the front edge of the edge roll as possible. Knot the first and last stitches with several half hitches. Fig. 7-8, view B, shows another stitching method.

Ready-made edge roll can be shaped to turn corners and follow curves smoothly. Mark the corner, cut a V shaped section out of the inside of the corner at that point. To make a smooth curve, pleat the edge or make a series of small V cuts on the inside of the curve. See Fig. 7-9.

PADDING FURNITURE WITH SPRINGS

Padding materials, of whatever type used, should cover the surface smoothly and completely. There should be no gaps in the padding for the final cover to bridge. See Fig. 7-10.

In most cases, the padding must be anchored to keep it from shifting on the springs. Stitch it to the burlap which covers the springs. Start the stitching in the center, Fig. 7-11. Sew in a pattern of expanding squares or circles.

Foam paddings are easy to fasten with spray adhesives. This method is described later in this chapter.

INSTALLING RUBBERIZED HAIR PADDING

The following procedure is typical for attaching rubberized hair pads to upholstery frames having springs:

1. Using a tape rule, measure both dimensions of the frame. Pad should extend from edge to edge, fitting up against the previously installed edge roll.

2. Transfer measurements to the hair pad and mark the pad with chalk.

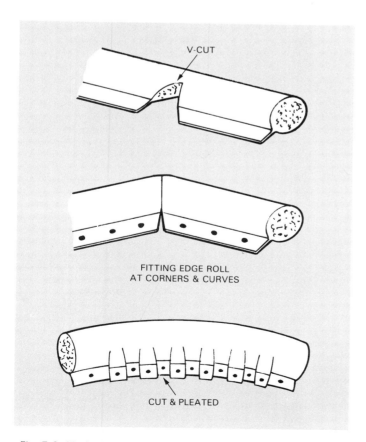

Fig. 7-9. Methods of cutting and shaping manufactured edge roll.

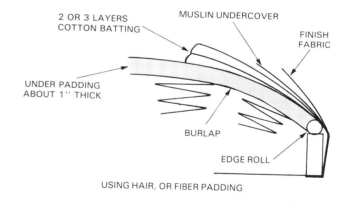

USING HAIR, OR FIBER PADDING

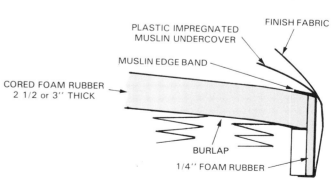

USING FOAM RUBBER PADDING

Fig. 7-10. Two different types of padding in cross section as used over springs. Padding fills all gaps so final cover goes over a smooth surface.

Fig. 7-19. Padding can be installed over wood bases. Use No. 3 or No. 4 tacks. Mat is fairly rigid and makes very staple padding where firmness is needed.

Fig. 7-20. Foam adhesive is applied to top of slip seat which is being repadded.

Fig. 7-21. Position foam pad carefully along one edge of slip seat. Then lay it across entire seat.

PADDING WITHOUT SPRINGS

Many upholstering jobs require the use of padding directly over a solid wood platform, such as is found on a stool, Fig. 7-19, or a dining chair slip seat.

To apply a new foam pad to a slip seat:

1. Lay the slip seat on a piece of rubber or plastic foam 1/2 to 1 in. (12 to 25 mm) thick. Trace around it with chalk.
2. With an upholsterers' shears or tin snips, cut along the chalk lines.
3. Using a spray can or brush, apply foam rubber cement or contact cement at several locations on the surface of the slip seat, Fig. 7-20.
4. Beginning at one edge, carefully position the foam pad over the slip seat, Fig. 7-21.
5. Using the fingers, tear a layer of cotton felt 1/2 in. (12 mm) thick to fit the slip seat and apply it over the foam, Fig. 7-22. The seat is ready for the final cover.

Some of the old padded seat chairs do not use a slip seat. A smaller padded area may be surrounded by exposed wood, for example. The reupholstering process then requires a slightly different approach. The following steps are a typical solution:

1. Cut a piece of 1/8 in. hardboard to fit beneath the chair seat.
2. Drill five or more 1/4 in. diameter holes through the hardboard so the foam rubber padding can "breathe."
3. Turn the chair upside down.
4. Attach the hardboard to the chair frame using ring nails or screws, Fig. 7-23.
5. Cut a piece of foam rubber or plastic, medium density and about an inch thick. Trim it to fit the chair seat recess, Fig. 7-24.
6. Cut a second piece of foam 1/4 to 1/2 in. thick. Make it an inch (25 mm) wider and longer than the chair seat recess.

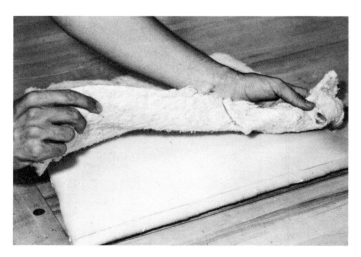

Fig. 7-22. Cotton felt, 1/2 in. thick, is laid over foam for extra comfort and to soften contour of edges.

Fig. 7-23. Hardboard base is attached to seat frame with ring nails. Note venting holes in hardboard so foam padding can "breathe."

Fig. 7-24. Inch thick, medium density foam pad fills cavity in old seat frame.

Fig. 7-25. Second foam pad is cut to provide a smooth top over first, thicker pad. This must be held in place with an adhesive. Foam rubber cement is being applied with a brush.

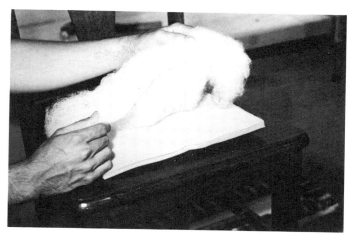

Fig. 7-26. Polyester fiberfill is arranged over foam padding.

7. Apply foam rubber or contact cement to the bottom of the second piece, Fig. 7-25. Position it over the chair seat recess. Press it firmly onto the first piece of foam.

8. Use your fingers to tear a thin layer of Dacron polyester fiberfill to fit over the second piece of foam. Spread the fiberfill over the second piece of foam. See Fig. 7-26.

PADDING OVER WEBBING

Jute webbing also provides a suitable base for padding. Either rubberized hair or foamed slabs can be used for padding. Cut the padding material with shears or knife. Attach it to the frame with staples or upholstery tacks. Tear cotton felt to size and lay it over the padding and the side of the frame.

REVIEW QUESTIONS — CHAPTER 7

1. List at least five materials used as padding in furniture.
2. Where is edge roll used and what is its use?
3. To keep padding from shifting on a seat or back, it must be _____ to springs or other supporting materials.
4. Foam padding is attached by the following method(s):
   a. Adhesives.
   b. Sewing back and forth through the padding.
   c. Sewing on tufting buttons.
   d. Stapling.
5. Cotton felt padding is added to other padding for _____.
6. Explain how to build up foam padding to thickness wanted.
7. What padding materials might you use in reupholstering a slip seat for a dining room chair?
8. Is it advisable to use jute webbing as a base for padding?

Chapter 8
INSTALLING FINAL COVERINGS

The upholstery fabric is the last material to be installed on the piece of furniture. It is called the FINAL COVERING. In most cases, this fabric goes on over the top of the padding. However on tufted furniture or where the final covering is lightweight, a muslin covering is first placed over the padding. Then the final cover goes on.

Muslin is a light-to-medium weight, unbleached fabric in a plain weave. It usually comes in 36 and 39 in. widths. It is installed for several reasons:

1. It smooths the surface and rounds the corners, improving the appearance of the final cover.
2. It separates the padding material from the final cover. This can be important if the final covering is a loose-woven fabric. Padding materials, unless contained by the muslin, could work up through the fabric and spoil the appearance.

MEASURING AND CUTTING

As a rule, final coverings should not be ordered until you are quite sure how much material is needed. You can roughly estimate the amount by referring to the chart in Chapter 3, Fig. 3-25. However, for greater accuracy and economy, there are other methods which are worth learning.

OLD COVERS AS PATTERNS

Old coverings, if available, make the job of measuring easy. They can be laid out so you can see how much material is needed. Later, the old pieces can be used as a pattern for cutting new ones.

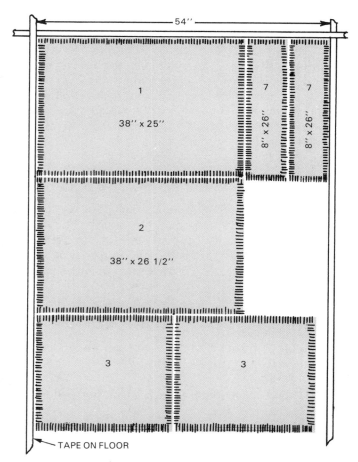

Fig. 8-1. One method of figuring quantity of new material needed for final covering. Tape has been layed out to mark standard width for upholstery fabric. Old coverings are carefully layed out inside the tape boundaries. Part numbers refer to Fig. 8-2 and Fig. 8-3

PART NO.	PART NAME	PIECES NEEDED	WIDTH	LENGTH
1	SEAT (S)	1		
2	INSIDE BACK (IB)	1		
3	INSIDE ARM (IA)	2		
4	OUTSIDE ARM	2		
5	BOTTOM BAND (OR SEAT BOXING)	1		
6	OUTSIDE BACK (OB)	1		
7	FRONT PANEL (FP)	2		
8	WELTING (W)	6		
	(ABBREVIATIONS)			

Fig. 8-2. Prepare chart to record measurements of upholstery panels.

To find out the amount of material needed, lay the pieces out on the floor as though you were placing them on the new fabric. Make the layout no wider than the width of the material, usually 54 in. wide. It may help to lay down masking tape to mark the width, as shown in Fig. 8-1.

Remove all stitching including that on welting. Lay out the pieces. Iron them, if necessary, to get turned edges to lay flat.

When all parts are in position, measure the length and convert it to yards. This is the amount of material you will need. Order to the nearest half yard over the measured amount.

TAKING MEASUREMENTS FROM THE FURNITURE

Taking of measurements when there are no old coverings to use as a pattern must be done on the piece of furniture. Accuracy at this point will save time and prevent waste of material. The beginner is advised to set up a procedure such as the following:

1. Make up a chart of the final cover pieces to be measured. This chart should have several columns. See Fig. 8-2.
2. Select a flexible tape for measuring. Carefully measure each surface of the piece of furniture which will require a separate piece of material, Fig. 8-3.
   a. Always take the measurement at the widest point. Extra material can be trimmed away during fitting.
   b. Refer once again to Fig. 8-3. See how some measurement lines curve around edges? This indicates that the measurement must be taken in the same way so that the material will go around corners and overlap with other parts.
   c. Also be sure the tape measure is tucked into corners and crevices as far as it will go.
   d. Allow extra material as necessary. You will need:
      For seams and tacking, from 1/2 to 3/4 in. (13 to 19 mm).
      For attaching stretchers (to be discussed later), 2 in. (75 mm).
      For pulling fabric around a frame edge for tacking, 4 in. (100 mm).
   e. Always take the width measurement first and then the length. It is important always to know that the first dimension is width. It helps you lay out the pieces properly on the new fabric.
3. Write down the dimensions immediately on the chart, Fig. 8-4. Make sure they are opposite the right piece on the chart. You will work from this chart:
   a. While determining amount of material you will need.
   b. While laying out the pieces to be cut from the material.

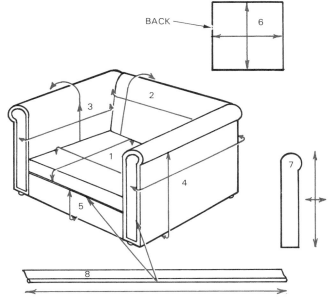

Fig. 8-3. When there are no old covers, take measurements from the piece of furniture. Top. Old chair needing recovering. Bottom. Lines and arrows show where to take measurements should they be needed.   (The Wrenn House)

PART NO.	PART NAME	PIECES NEEDED	WIDTH	LENGTH
1	SEAT (S)	1	38"	25"
2	INSIDE BACK (IB)	1	38"	26½"
3	INSIDE ARM (IA)	2	26½"	26½"
4	OUTSIDE ARM	2	26½"	23"
5	BOTTOM BAND (OR SEAT BOXING)	1	37"	8"
6	OUTSIDE BACK (OB)	1	36"	25"
7	FRONT PANEL (FP)	2	8"	26"
8	WELTING (W)	6	54"	1½"
	(ABBREVIATIONS)			

Fig. 8-4. Chart with sizes of panels recorded. Width measurement should always be in first column.

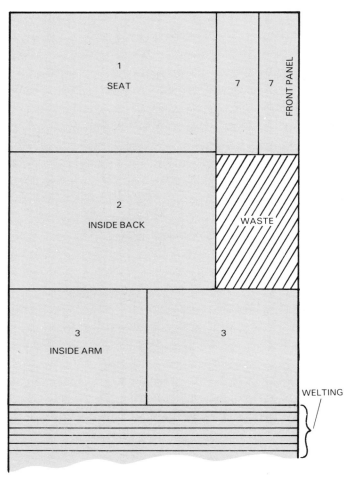

Fig. 8-5. Some upholsterers prefer to work with small scaled drawings rather than full size layouts.

4. Prepare full size paper patterns taking the dimensions off the chart.

5. To determine the amount of material to purchase, lay out the pattern pieces on the floor. (Follow the same procedure described for using old coverings for patterns.)

6. Some upholsterers prefer to make a small-scale drawing or sketch instead of a full-size layout. It will work very well in helping to determine amount of material and how the pieces can be laid out on the new fabric. For example, you can let 1/16 in. equal 1 in. as in Fig. 8-5.

7. If the material has a pattern or a nap, layout of pieces will require more care and there probably will be more waste. Be careful to center the pattern on the seat and back pieces. Parts must also be arranged so the pattern matches after the parts are installed on the furniture.

With napped material, sections must be arranged so the nap runs from back to front on the seat and from top to bottom on other sections. Welting should be laid out on the bias.

STRETCHERS

To save on expensive upholstery materials, it is common practice to attach stretchers (also called pull strips) to sections of covering materials which will be hidden by cushions, pillows or overlapping of covering materials. Stretchers are made from strong, inexpensive material—denim, for example. In addition to saving on expensive fabrics, the denim or other stretcher

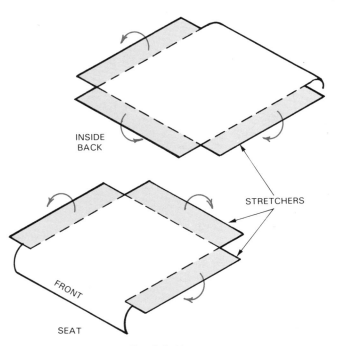

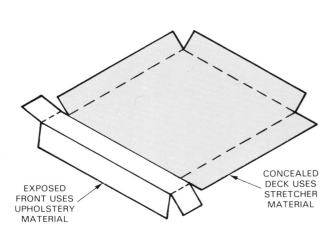

Fig. 8-6. How stretchers might be used on chair covering. Left. Stretchers shown in color will be used to tack coverings to furniture rails. Right. Hidden part of seat covering is made of stretcher material.

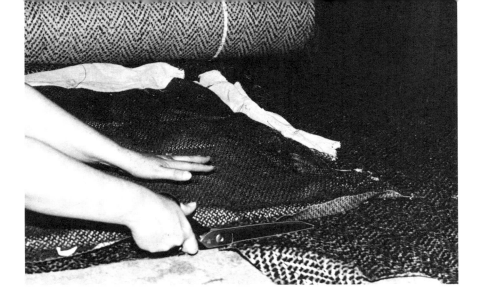

Fig. 8-7. Using an old covering as a pattern. Chalking is not needed. The old cover is the cutting guide.

material is often stronger.

Stretchers are also used to pull the final coverings taut in areas that would otherwise be inaccessible or hard to reach. In recording dimensions, allowances must be made when stretchers are used. Fig. 8-6 shows a situation where stretchers are used.

MARKING AND CUTTING

Using one of the methods described, arrange and mark off the pieces of upholstery for cutting. If chalk is used to mark cutting lines, lay the new material face down so you will not be soiling the face side with chalk marks. If old covering pieces are used, you can work face up as no chalking is needed. See Fig. 8-7.

Label each piece immediately with the number given on your chart so you will be able to identify it later. Use a shears to cut out all the pieces. Stack pieces face to face so chalk markings will not soil the face sides. Keep paired parts together.

SEWING FINAL COVERINGS

Usually, there is some sewing to be done before coverings can be installed. Sewing might include:
1. Attaching stretchers to sides and backs of sections.
2. Sewing welting strips together end-to-end.
3. Sewing cordage inside of strips to form welting.
4. Sewing welting to upholstery panels.
5. Sewing various cover sections together.

Fig. 8-8 shows various sections that should be sewed before they are installed. Not all upholstered furniture will require as much sewing as is illustrated.

MAKING MACHINE SEWN SEAMS

Machine sewn seams are made with right sides of the material facing. If pieces are heavy or large it is advisable to baste the sections together using straight

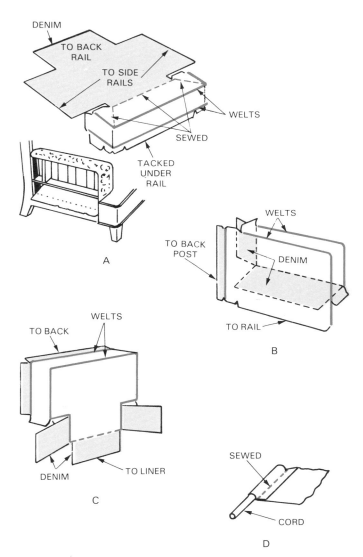

Fig. 8-8. Many parts of a cover can be sewed on a machine before they are attached to the furniture. A—Sewing mitered corners, attaching stretchers and welting to seat deck. B—Attaching stretchers and welting to arm sections. C—Attaching stretchers and welting to back sections. D—Sewing cordage inside welting. Tinted portions are stretcher material.

103

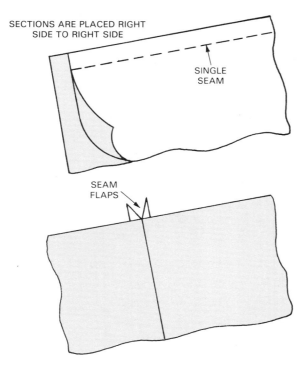

Fig. 8-9. Plain seam. Single row of stitching is used to combine two panels of fabric.

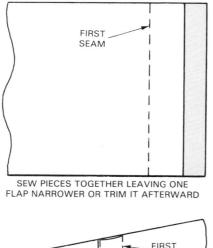

SEW PIECES TOGETHER LEAVING ONE FLAP NARROWER OR TRIM IT AFTERWARD

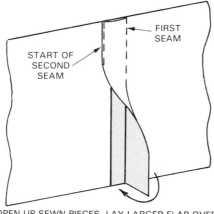

OPEN UP SEWN PIECES, LAY LARGER FLAP OVER NARROWER FLAP AND SEW SECOND SEAM

Fig. 8-10. Welt seam. Double line of stitching is used. Seam is stronger and lies flat.

pins or long, loose, hand-sewn stitches. These should be made parallel to the permanent stitch.

Common upholstery stitches are:
1. The plain seam, illustrated in Fig. 8-9.
2. The welt seam shown in Fig. 8-10.

FABRICATING WELTING

Welting can be purchased already made up. However, most welting is made of the same material as the final cover. It must be sewn up from strips of the upholstery fabric. Layout and cutting of the strips was explained earlier in this chapter.

To make welting:
1. Sew welting strips together until you have the lengths needed. Use the method shown in Fig. 8-11. It avoids bulkiness at the seams when folded over. See Fig. 8-12.

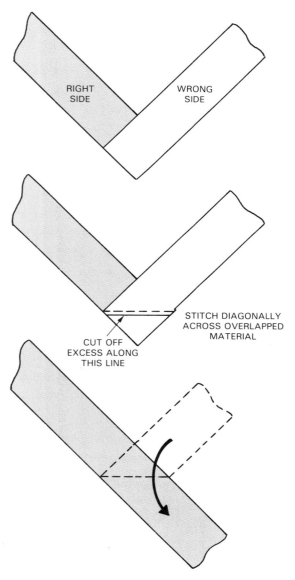

Fig. 8-11. Welting strips are sewn together with a diagonal seam.

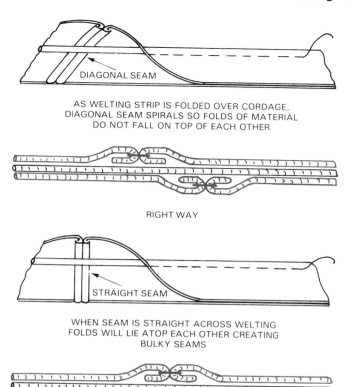

AS WELTING STRIP IS FOLDED OVER CORDAGE,
DIAGONAL SEAM SPIRALS SO FOLDS OF MATERIAL
DO NOT FALL ON TOP OF EACH OTHER

RIGHT WAY

WHEN SEAM IS STRAIGHT ACROSS WELTING
FOLDS WILL LIE ATOP EACH OTHER CREATING
BULKY SEAMS

WRONG WAY

Fig. 8-12. Why diagonal stitching makes welting seam less bulky.

2. Lay lengths of cord in the centers of the strips.
3. Fold the fabric, top side out, over the cord.
4. Sew the cord inside keeping the seam as close to the cord as possible. The fabric must be stretched smoothly around the cord.

This task is made easier if the sewing machine used has a welting or cording foot.

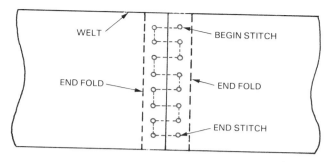

Fig. 8-13. Blind stitch. Circles mark points where thread is visible. This stitch is used to sew sections of covering together after they have been attached to furniture.

BLIND STITCHING

Blind stitching is so called because the threads are nearly concealed under the folded edges of the fabric. It is a technique of hand sewing used in joining top cover sections at points where a sewing machine cannot be used and where tacking would show. The outside back cover, for example, is blind tacked at the top and blind stitched at the sides.

To blind stitch, use a thread about twice as long as the length to be stitched. Knot one end and thread the other end onto a curved needle.

Fold under the edges of the panels being joined if they are not already folded. About 1/2 in. (12 mm) will be enough.

Begin stitching on the underside. Pass the needle through the folded edge and pull it out of the top. Pass the curved needle back down through the material and across the seam. Bring it up through the other panel. Keep the stitch very short. It should loop across only two or three threads of the fabric. Make each stitch at right angles to the one preceding, following the pattern shown in Fig. 8-13. Method of making the stitches with a curved needle is shown in Fig. 8-14.

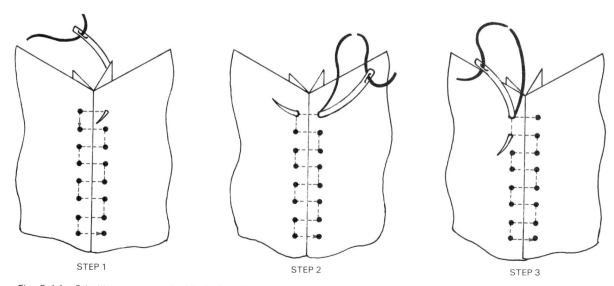

STEP 1   STEP 2   STEP 3

Fig. 8-14. Stitching sequence for blind stitch. Needle emerges from and reenters material at points marked by black dot.

TACKING FINAL COVERS

While tacking of final covers is not much different than tacking of other material in upholstery, there are some variations which the upholsterer must master. The ones you will need to learn are:

1. Pin tacking.
2. Blind tacking.

PIN TACKING

Pin tacking is simply driving tacks partway into the upholstery material to hold it in place temporarily. It is used in two situations:

1. When the material is to be tacked in place but may need to be adjusted or shifted to improve appearance.
2. When the material is going to be sewn in place and needs to be held until after the sewing is completed.

In the first situation, start pin tacking at the middle of one edge. Then move to the opposite edge. Repeat this operation with the other two sides.

Stretch the fabric as you tack. Work all sides alter-

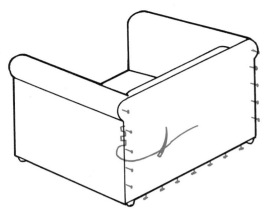

Fig. 8-15. Pin tacking is used to hold covering in place during blind sewing.

nately. Tacking should proceed from centers to corners. Space tacks about an inch apart.

Examine the pin tacked panel. Adjust as necessary. When satisfied with the appearance, drive in the tacks.

Pin tacking in preparation for blind stitching follows essentially the same procedure except that:

1. All edges must be folded under and nearly butt against other finished edges.

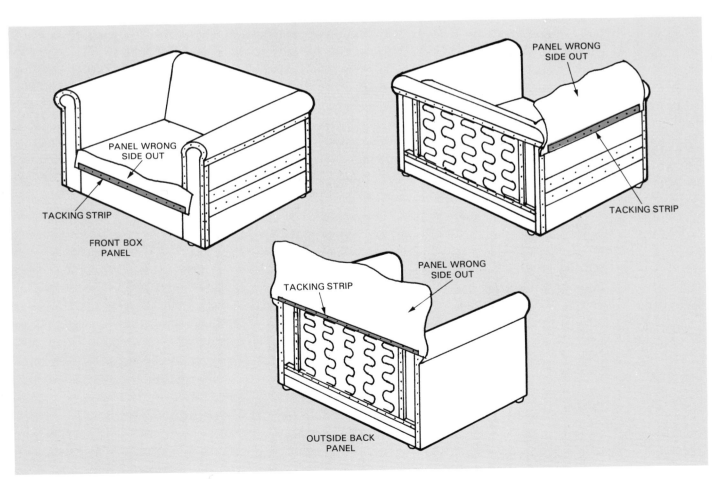

Fig. 8-16. Blind tacking allows material to be folded over the tacks to conceal them. Colored sections shows blind tacking in place before fold is made.

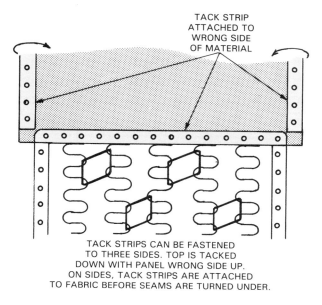

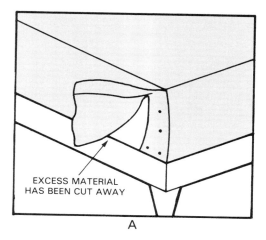

TACK STRIP ATTACHED TO WRONG SIDE OF MATERIAL

TACK STRIPS CAN BE FASTENED TO THREE SIDES. TOP IS TACKED DOWN WITH PANEL WRONG SIDE UP. ON SIDES, TACK STRIPS ARE ATTACHED TO FABRIC BEFORE SEAMS ARE TURNED UNDER.

EXCESS MATERIAL HAS BEEN CUT AWAY

A

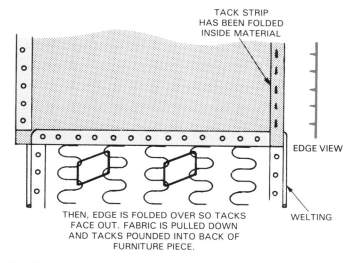

TACK STRIP HAS BEEN FOLDED INSIDE MATERIAL

EDGE VIEW

THEN, EDGE IS FOLDED OVER SO TACKS FACE OUT. FABRIC IS PULLED DOWN AND TACKS POUNDED INTO BACK OF FURNITURE PIECE.

WELTING

Fig. 8-17. Making a blind tack where material cannot be folded back over tacking afterward.

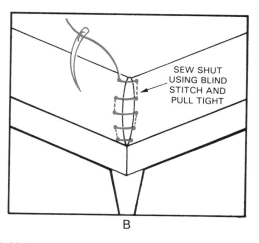

SEW SHUT USING BLIND STITCH AND PULL TIGHT

B

Fig. 8-18. Method of producing a square corner. Blind stitch is used to close the gap.

2. The tacks are removed after the blind stitching is completed.

Carefully examine the pin tacked panel. Adjust to remove wrinkles and pulls. Adjust edges so there are no large gaps or overlapping. Begin blind stitching at one end. Do not remove any tacks until all seams have been sewed. Fig. 8-15 shows beginning of blind stitch used to attach the last panel on a chair.

BLIND TACKING

Blind tacking is a method of fastening top covers with concealed tacks. It is used often to attach the first edge of a final cover, Fig. 8-16. In some instances it may be used on several edges of a panel, such as the outside back. In such cases the tacking strip is attached to the wrong side of the panel before the edges are turned under, Fig. 8-17.

MAKING CORNERS

One of the operations often required to get a seat covering to fit properly is the fitting of corners. There are several types of corners.
1. The pleated square corner.
2. The round corner pleat.

MAKING PLEATED SQUARE CORNERS

1. Draw the seat material down firmly on both sides and tack all the edges up to about 2 in. (51 mm) from each corner.
2. Pull the material on the side to the front and wrap it around the corner. Tack it at the front.
3. Cut out a large V-shaped piece to do away with the surplus material, view A, Fig. 8-18. Leave enough material to fold under.
4. Fold the extra material in front and pull it toward the corner.
5. Temporarily pin or tack the pleat at the corner.
6. Sew the pleat shut using a blind stitch, Fig. 8-18, view B.
7. Repeat operation at each corner.

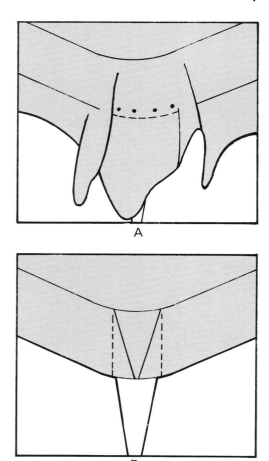

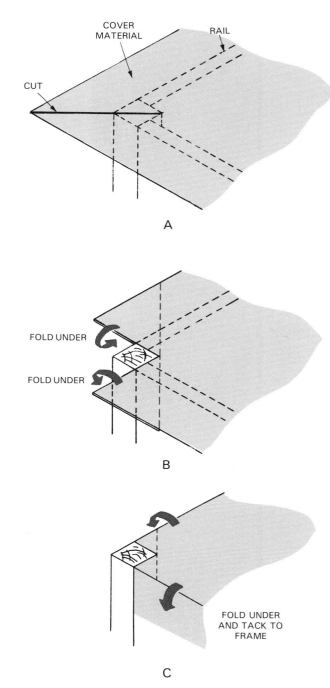

Fig. 8-19. Pleating a round corner. A—Pull material down and tack it leaving large folds to either side. B—Fold extra material back to center and tack it down underneath frame.

PLEATING ROUNDED CORNERS

1. Carefully pull the material down over the corner, stretching it to the firmness you want.
2. Tack it at several points directly on the corner leaving equal folds on either side, view A, Fig. 8-19.
3. Pull folds toward each other forming a V.

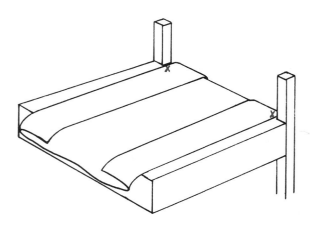

Fig. 8-20. Position material and mark point where it must be cut and folded to fit around corner post.

Fig. 8-21. Cutting and folding to fit covering around corner posts.

4. Tack the material on the underside of the rail or blind stitch each side of the V, view B, Fig. 8-19.

FITTING AROUND POSTS

Some measuring, cutting and folding will be necessary to fit the final cover around chair legs and posts.

When the post is on a corner:

1. Mark the material at the point where it will touch the corner of the post, Fig. 8-20.
2. Cut the material diagonally from the outside corner

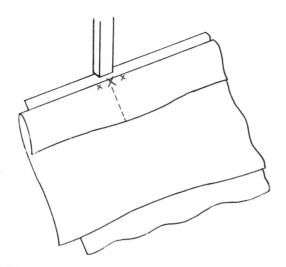

Fig. 8-22. Fold and mark underside of fabric covering so it can be cut and folded around side post.

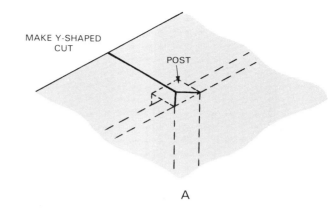

A

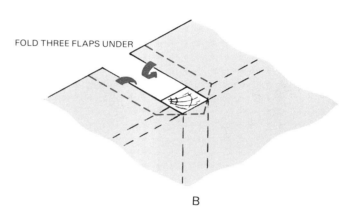

B

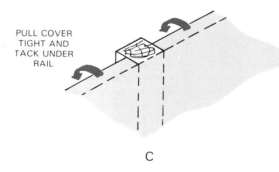

C

Fig. 8-23. Make cuts and folds to fit covering around post which is not in corner position.

to the point marked, view A, Fig. 8-21.

3. Fold each cut edge under adjusting until each edge fits smoothly around the post, view B, Fig. 8-21.

4. Tack the cover to the frame. See view C, Fig. 8-21.

When the post is not in the corner:

1. As shown in Fig. 8-22, find the point where the material will touch the inside edge of the post. Mark in three spots, the center, then the right and left corners.

2. Cut from the outside edge of the material toward the center mark. Do not cut all the way to the center mark. Stay half the width of the post away. Then make two angled cuts toward each of the outer marks. The cuts will be in the shape of the letter ''Y,'' as shown in view A, Fig. 8-23.

3. Fold under the three flaps created by the cutting. Fit them snugly around the post. View B, Fig. 8-23 shows the procedure.

4. Tack the covering to the rail as in view C, Fig. 8-23.

PLEATING CURVES

Coverings must be pleated to fit around and over a convex (curved) surface or edge such as an arm. See view A, Fig. 8-24. It is easier to make even, attractive pleats using a drawstring.

Prepare the drawstring by making basting stitches along the edge of the material as in view B, Fig. 8-24. Pull the string tight to bunch up the material and form the pleats. Flatten the pleats neatly and secure them with tacks, Fig. 8-24, view C.

ORDER FOR INSTALLING COVERS

Usually, new coverings are installed in this order:
1. Seat.
2. Inside arms (or inside back).
3. Inside back (or inside arms).
4. Outside arms.
5. Boxings (if any), front and sides.
6. Outside back.
7. Skirt, if needed.
8. Dust cover.

It is a good practice for beginners to keep a record of the order in which old coverings are removed during a reupholstery job. When working with a frame that is new or one that has already been stripped by someone else, the order above should be followed.

The reason for the order will be apparent to the upholsterer once the work of recovering begins. An arm or back recovered first, for example, might make it impossible to install the seat covering. Often, the same tack rail is used for securing several panels.

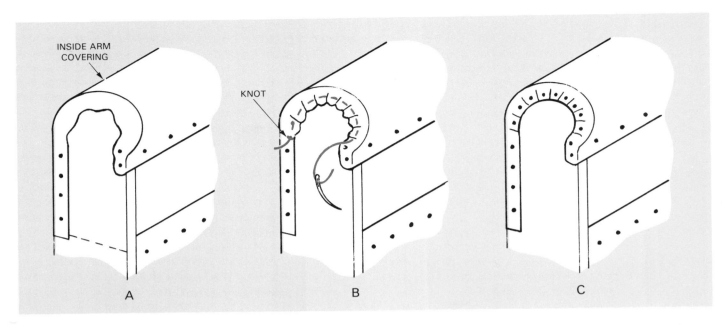

Fig. 8-24. Method of making smooth, even pleats where fabric is fitted around curved surfaces. A—Tack down panel along straight edges. B—Make evenly spaced basting stitches along edge of fabric with strong stitching twine. Fasten one end securely to fabric; pull on other end to gather it. C—Neatly fold and tack fabric.

INSTALLING WELTING STRIPS

Welting strips may be needed between sections of the top cover. In some cases the welting is sewed to the covering. In other instances it will be tacked to the frame. Fig. 8-11 and Fig. 8-12 will show how welting, if not purchased, should be made.

When tacking welting always begin at one end. To go around curves pleat the flat tacking edge of the welting. Cut narrow notches nearly up to the stitching

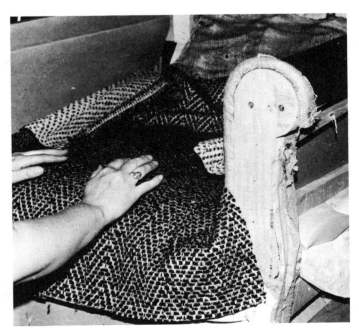

Fig. 8-25. Position fabric on seat in readiness for tacking. Pull material through sides and back.   (The Wrenn House)

and overlap the material as it is being tacked. Wider notches are used when welting must turn corners.

Pull firmly on the loose end of the welting as it is tacked. This will prevent an uneven wavering line.

INSTALLING THE SEAT COVER

The seat covering may be one single piece of material or it may be made up of several pieces with the addition of boxings or stretchers.

If the covering has a pattern, center it carefully. Lines or figures should not run at an angle. If the material is napped, the nap should lay forward. On all other pieces the direction of nap should be downward. Fig. 8-25 shows a tweed covering being installed on the chair pictured in Fig. 8-3.

If the chair has posts, Fig. 8-26, mark and cut the material to fit around them. Use the method explained in this chapter. Refer to the section on ''Fitting around posts.''

Pull the material carefully through the sides and back. Let the material lie over the rails where it will be tacked. Begin tacking, Fig. 8-27, using No. 4 to No. 6 tacks.

TACKING

Using a tack hammer or stapler, drive one tack or staple through the cover into the center of the front rail. If using a tack hammer rather than staples, pin tack the cover first. In pin tacking, the tacks are driven in only about half way. They can easily be removed if covering needs to be adjusted.

The second pin tack is driven at one of the front corners. Pull the material tightly to the corner. Drive in a

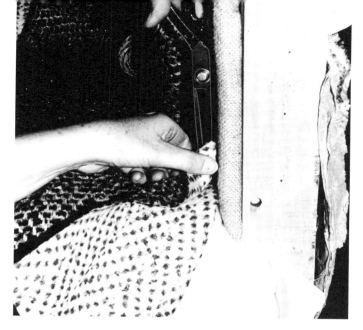

Fig. 8-26. Cut fabric to fit around posts. See Figs. 8-20 through 8-23 for proper technique.

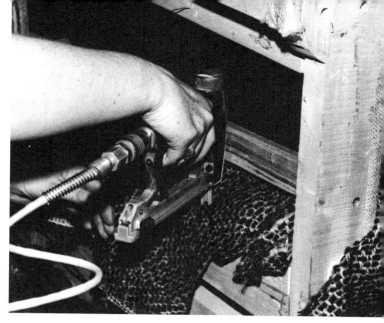

Fig. 8-28. Tacking sides of seat. Use care in pulling the material. Too much tension will distort the pattern or cause depressions.

Fig. 8-27. Use stapler or No. 4 to No. 6 tacks for fastening fabric to front and back of seat frame.   (The Wrenn House)

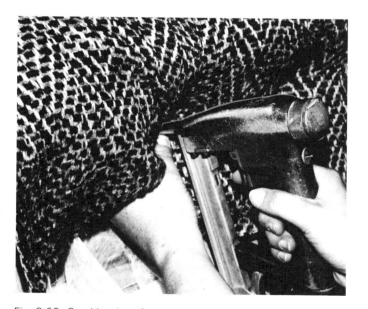

Fig. 8-29. Outside edge of arm covering is attached first. Start tacking at center, then work to right and left.   (The Wrenn House)

pin tack at the corner and then pin tack toward the center.

Pull the cover tightly to the opposite corner. Pin tack it in the same way and pin tack back to the center.

Moving to the back rail, repeat the pin tacking procedure used on the front rail. Pull the material firmly toward the back so it is stretched lightly over the seat from front to back. Pull the fabric before each tack is put in place. The properly stretched covering will be tight without compressing springs and padding.

After the front and back are pin tacked, move to one of the sides. Pull the cover in the same way and pin tack the center. Pull the cover to the front corner and tack. Pull and tack the rear corner. Pin tack the entire edge, Fig. 8-28.

Move to the other side. Pull the cover and pin tack it at the center of the rail. Repeat previous steps until the side is entirely pin tacked.

Inspect the pin tacked cover carefully. It should be smooth and even. Pattern must be centered and straight. If the appearance is not satisfactory, remove tacks where necessary, adjust the cover and retack. When the cover is satisfactory, drive tacks all the way into the frame.

COVERING INSIDE ARMS

Position fabric for the inside arm. Napped material must be directed downward. Tack the outside edge as shown in Fig. 8-29. Pull the fabric through the opening

111

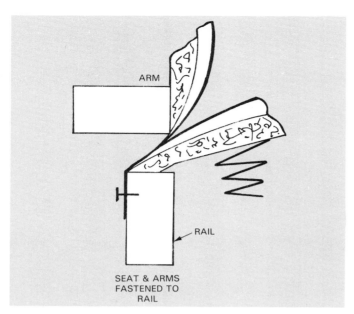

Fig. 8-30. Seat cover and inside arm cover can be tacked to side of seat rail. Seat cover must be attached first.

between the side of the chair and the seat rail. Cut the fabric to fit around the posts (Fig. 8-21 and Fig. 8-23). Pull fabric tightly and tack it to the seat rail, Fig. 8-30.

INSTALLING INSIDE BACK COVER

Lay the inside back cover on the chair and position it carefully. Allow enough material to fall over the back for tacking. If the material is patterned, align it with the seat covering. Make sure that the nap on napped material is directed downward.

When the material is in the right position, pin tack the upper edge to the back of the top rail. Tack the center

first, then the corners. Pull firmly to the corner before tacking. Install pin tacks back to the center. Repeat the same tacking procedure at the opposite side. Fig. 8-31 shows the inside back cover being attached with a stapling gun.

When the top is pin tacked, you are ready to tack the bottom. Pull the material between the opening formed by the back liner (bottom cross rail for the back) and the seat rail. The material must be tacked either to the back liner or to the seat rail.

Pull the material until it stretches across the padded back firmly without distorting the contour of the padding. Pin tack the bottom following the same procedure described for the seat and inside arm coverings.

Inspect the covering for proper alignment and positioning of tacks. Remove tacks, adjust and retack as needed. When satisfied with the appearance, drive the tacks all the way into the rails.

BUTTONS

Buttons are often installed in the backs and sides of upholstered furniture for the sake of appearance and to keep padding from shifting. Heavy twine attached to the buttons passes through the padding, springs and webbing where it is tied. The buttons are usually covered with the same upholstery fabric used on the furniture.

Covering the buttons

Using a button covering machine, Fig. 8-32, cover enough buttons for the seat, sides and back of the chair. Local upholstery shops often will supply this service for a small charge.

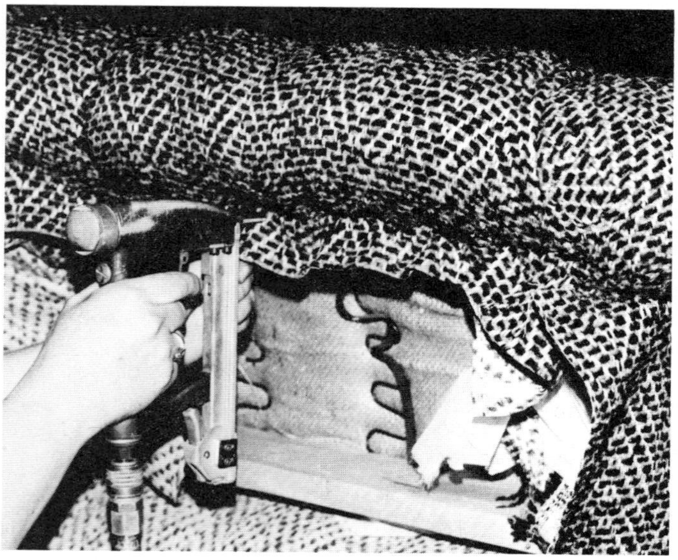

Fig. 8-31. Inside back panel is attached. Top is being attached first, then bottom will be tacked to frame member showing. (The Wrenn House)

Fig. 8-32. Button covering machine is needed to cover buttons.

Installing buttons

Thread nylon tufting twine through the eyelet of the covered button. Then thread it through the eye of a double-pointed straight needle. See Fig. 8-33.

Locate and mark the button positions. Attach the buttons one by one. Push the needle through the upholstering, Fig. 8-34. Pull the twine to the proper tension. Check the depression made by the button in the surface and adjust the tension. Tie off the twine as shown in Fig. 8-35. Knots are made around a tuft of cotton. This will prevent the knot from pulling through the material and causing the button to fall off.

INSTALLING OUTSIDE ARM COVERS

Outside arm coverings, sometimes called side panels, are installed next. Lay the covering over the top of the arm with the wrong side up. Position the edge for blind tacking. Blind tacking is done on the wrong side of the material. When the material is folded back over it the tacking is concealed. Use several tacks to hold the material in place. Then attach a cardboard tacking strip along the tacking edge. Tack it at evenly spaced intervals to the frame. See Fig. 8-36. Fold the covering down. Pull it tight and tack the bottom.

INSTALLING BOXING

Install welting (if it is to be used) between the seat covering and the bottom band or boxing. (Boxings are the narrow panels which cover the part of the frame below the front of the seat covering. Sometimes they are also placed between the arm panels and the bottom.) Tack the welting to the frame with tacks or staples with the piping up.

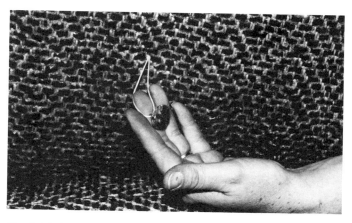

Fig. 8-34. Locate buttons and push double-pointed needle through from front to back. (The Wrenn House)

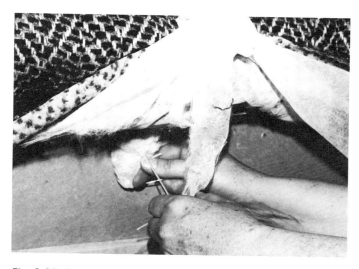

Fig. 8-35. Tying off twine holding button. Cotton tied into knot prevents cord from pulling through back and loosening button.

Fig. 8-33. Nylon tufting twine threaded through button and eye of double-pointed needle.

Fig. 8-36. Installing outside arm panels. Start with panel wrong side up. Tack on blind tacking strip. (The Wrenn House)

Blind tack the boxing over the top of the tacked edge of the welting, Fig. 8-37. Add padding over the still exposed frame.

Pull the boxing over the padding. Turn the chair upside down to make the next step easier. Pull the boxing taut and tack it to the underside of the chair frame.

Turn the chair to a convenient work position. Install outside back panel using blind tacking or blind tacking and blind sewing. See Figs. 8-17 and 8-38.

NAILING PANELS

Nailing panels are the upholstered pieces often used to face the front posts of a piece of furniture. They are usually padded with a thin layer of cotton or fiberfill and upholstered before being attached with a tacking strip or headless nails, Fig. 8-39. If welting is to be used, it should be attached to the back of the panel after the

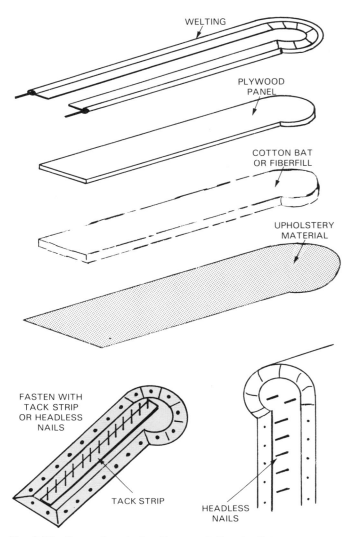

Fig. 8-39. Parts of typical nailing panel. Panel will be attached to furniture post with tacking strip or headless nails.

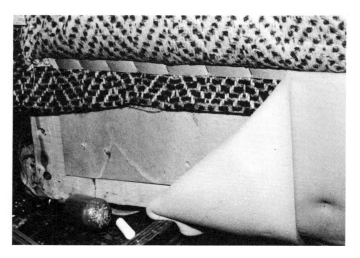

Fig. 8-37. Attaching box panel to front of chair. Blind tack strip has been tacked in place. Foam padding will add extra softness to boxing.

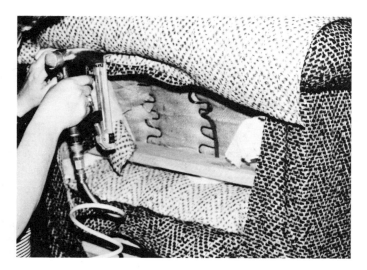

Fig. 8-38. Attaching outside back panel. Blind tack top first. Sides can be blind tacked or blind sewed.   (The Wrenn House)

Fig. 8-40. Attaching nailing panel conceals tacks used to attach other panels to front posts.

Fig. 8-41. Kick pleat skirt has folds at each corner only.

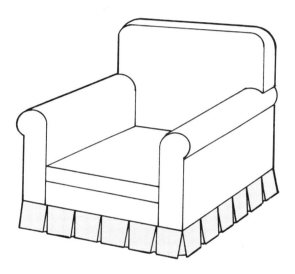

Fig. 8-42. Box pleat skirt has folds at regular intervals.

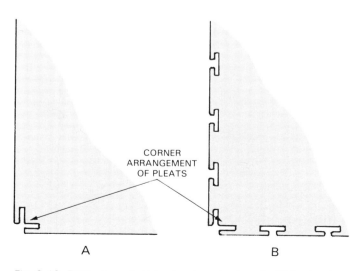

Fig. 8-43. Edge view of skirts showing pleating. A—Kick pleat has folds at corners only. B—Box pleat skirt has folds at regular intervals on all sides.

covering has been attached. Fig. 8-40 shows an upholstered nailing panel being installed.

MAKING AND INSTALLING SKIRTS

The last section of the final cover to be installed is the skirt. This is a narrow band of upholstery material which conceals the legs and add a decorative touch to the bottom of the piece of furniture.

Skirts are usually one of two types:
1. Kick pleat skirt, Fig. 8-41.
2. Box pleat skirt, Fig. 8-42.

The kick pleat, being the most popular, is found on all standard pieces of furniture. It is sometimes called the inverted V pleat. Kick pleats are almost always lined with muslin. The box pleat skirt is popular on colonial furniture.

When estimating amount of material needed for skirts, measure the distance around the piece of furniture and the height from the floor to the frame where the skirt is attached. Allow about 12 in. additional material at each corner for a kick pleat. See Fig. 8-43. A box pleat will require much more material—about double the distance around the base. Skirts are blind tacked to the frame, Fig. 8-44.

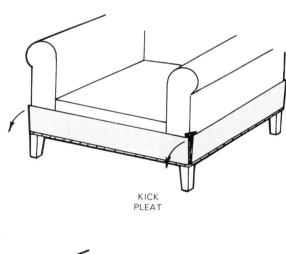

KICK PLEAT

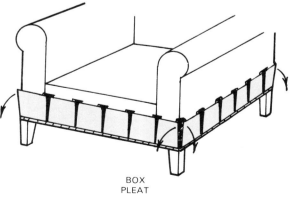

BOX PLEAT

Fig. 8-44. Skirts are blind tacked to bottoms of furniture frames. Allow about 1 1/4 in. extra width to take care of hemming and blind tacking.

REVIEW QUESTIONS — CHAPTER 8

1. _____is an unbleached, plain-woven fabric. One of its uses is to_____ padding material from the final cover.
2. Give two methods of finding the quantity of material needed to recover a chair.
3. Why should old coverings (if available) be saved?
4. Napped fabrics and patterned fabrics require more skill in layout and installation than plain fabrics. Why?
5. _____are pieces of strong but inexpensive fabric attached to final cover fabric to save expensive material for where it will show.
6. List at least three instances when final coverings are machine sewn.
7. _____is a temporary tacking down of an upholstery panel so it can be adjusted before final tacking.
8. What is blind stitching?
9. Blind stitching is most easily done with a_____ needle.
10. How are the tacks concealed in blind tacking?
11. A tacking strip is used in blind tacking to provide a _____edge.
12. What is pin tacking and why is it done?
13. What tool is used when you want to attach upholstery buttons?
14. A_____is a narrow decorative band of final covering attached to the bottom of a piece of upholstered furniture. One of its purposes is to_____the legs.

Chapter 9
CUSHIONS

Many pieces of upholstered furniture have loose cushions. They may be used on the backs of chairs or sofas as well as on the seats.

Basically, a cushion is made of some type of stuffing covered with upholstering materials. The stuffing can be loose materials such as down, feathers, shredded plastic foam or foam rubber. It can be a spring unit surrounded by padding or a solid block of foamed plastic or foam rubber.

Cushions come in all different shapes. Some have straight, flat sides and edges. Others are more like pillows with high crown and hardly any sides at all. Some are carefully shaped to fit uneven contours of backs or seats. Some are simple rectangles, squares or more complicated circles. Many are in the shape of a T or a half T. A few of the shapes are shown in Fig. 9-1. This chapter will show you how to cover many of these types of cushions.

MEASURING AND CONSTRUCTING CUSHIONS

An old cushion and its coverings may be used as a pattern for constructing a new one. The old coverings are carefully removed. Seams are ripped out and pieces pinned to the new fabric so new cover parts can be made. Even the old padding—if it is in one piece like foam or innersprings—can be used as a guide in fashioning a new cushion.

If there is no old cushion to work from, new patterns must be made. The chair or sofa must be carefully measured for exact dimensions.

TAKING MEASUREMENTS

Measurement must take place over the point of greatest width and depth or length of the space the

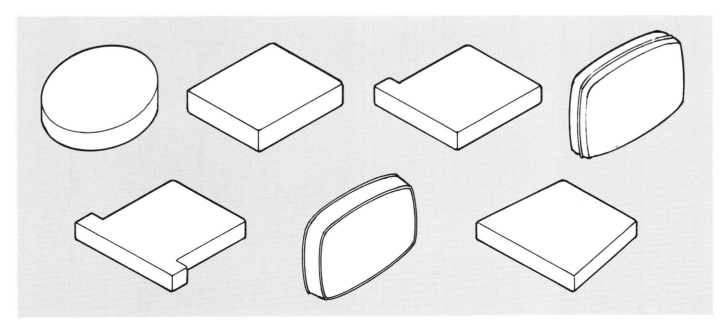

Fig. 9-1. Furniture cushions are made in all kinds of shapes: round, square or rectangular, T-shaped, half T or irregular like pillows.

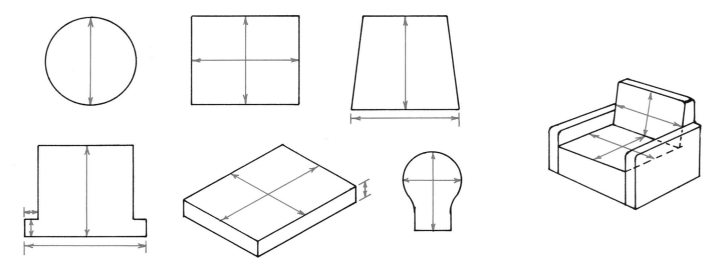

Fig. 9-2. Cushion dimensions must be taken differently for different shapes of cushions. If old cushions are not available for measuring, take measurements on the chair or piece of furniture itself.

cushion is to fill, Fig. 9-2. Additional measurements must be taken if the cushion has an irregular shape such as a full or half T. Dimensions taken can be used in making patterns.

MAKING A PATTERN

Cushion patterns are useful for several parts of the cushion:
1. They can be used for cutting and shaping foam rubber or foam plastic to be used as the cushion filler.
2. They can be used for making casings and final coverings for the cushion.

To make the pattern, transfer the dimensions to a large piece of paper. Rough cut the pattern, allowing a little extra material. (The casing material or even the final covering material may be used in place of the paper, if preferred.)

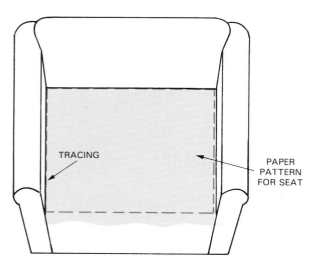

Fig. 9-3. Getting pattern of seat cushion by laying pattern on seat and tracing edges with marking pencil. Dotted line represents completed tracing.

Lay the pattern material over the seat or back for which a cushion is being made. Adjust the pattern to the contour of the seat or back. Using a marking pencil, trace the outline, Fig. 9-3.

Remove the pattern and trim it to the new shape. Allow 1/4 to 1/2 in. (6 to 12 mm) extra on each side for seams.

MARKING AND CUTTING COVERINGS

Lay the pattern on the covering material. If the material has a pattern, make sure that figures are centered and that lines run straight. If the material has a nap, it should lay forward on a seat cushion, downward on a back cushion.

Cut the material following the shape of the pattern. If a seam allowance has not been made on the pattern, cut the material 1/4 to 1/2 in. (6 to 12 mm) larger.

Patternless cutting

Cushion covers can be measured and cut without a pattern, if desired. First, cut the material roughly to size allowing a little extra material. Lay it on the seat or back wrong side up. Push the material tightly to the edges. Use a piece of tailors' chalk to mark the shape of the cushion.

Start cutting the material along the chalk line. But only cut along one side. Follow the chalk mark, allowing for the seam. Cut out only half of the cover. Fold the cut portion over the uncut portion. Finish the cutting using the cut part as a guide. The finished piece will be the same on both sides. See Figs. 9-4 through 9-7.

Cutting bottom cushion cover

You can use the covering just cut to fashion an identical covering for the underside of the cushion. Lay the cut piece on top of the cover material wrong side to

Cushions

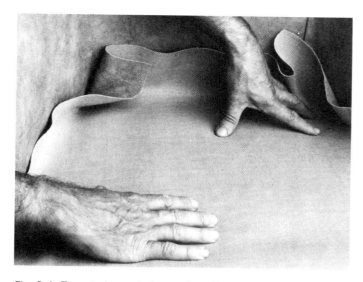

Fig. 9-4. To get size and shape of cushion covering, cut piece of covering material slightly larger than widest dimension of cushion. Lay it on the piece of furniture wrong side up.

Fig. 9-7. With covering half cut out, fold it in half lengthwise and complete the cutting using the cut half as a pattern. Sides will then be identical. (Uniroyal Coated Fabrics Dept.)

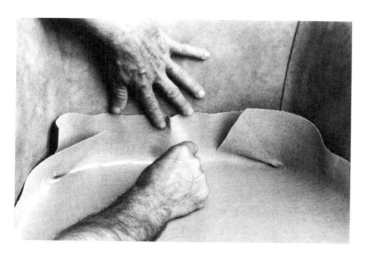

Fig. 9-5. Press upholstery material smoothly against all sides. Use chalk to mark exact dimensions of cushion area. (Uniroyal Coated Fabrics Dept.)

Fig. 9-6. Remove the marked material to work area. Cut out one side of the covering.

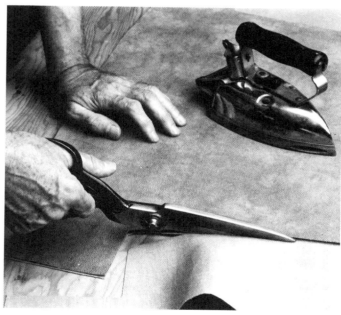

Fig. 9-8. Use top covering as pattern for cutting identical covering for bottom of cushion.

wrong side. Mark the new piece with chalk or weight the pieces down and cut it out following the shape of the pattern piece. See Fig. 9-8.

If you are upholstering with one of the vinyl plastics on the market, consider making the underside covering of denim or some other durable cloth so the cushion will "breathe." (Some vinyl materials are "breathable" making this precaution unnecessary.)

An alternative, when using nonbreathing vinyl plastic on reversible cushions, is to use vents. These are installed in the boxing panels of the cushion.

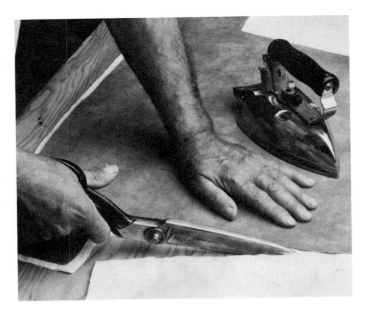

Fig. 9-9. When muslin coverings are used under the final cover make them the same size as the final cover. Use the final cover as a pattern in cutting them out. (Uniroyal Coated Fabrics Dept.)

Casings

Some upholsterers use a muslin casing over foam padding to keep vinyl plastic covers from slipping during use. Make the muslin pieces the same size as the final cover. The final cover can be used as a pattern, Fig. 9-9.

Square or rectangular cushions

Square or rectangular cushions, as well as T or half T cushions, must be cut in a special way if they are crowned. To compensate for the crown, a wedge of material must be cut away from the corners as shown in Fig. 9-10. *This is important. Square cut corners will appear to be pointed and the sides will be dished instead of straight after the cushion has been stuffed.*

Measuring boxing

Boxings must be carefully measured as they must be just the right width for the best appearance. To determine the width of the boxing strips measure the height of the padding. Allow 1/2 in. (13 mm) for each seam. Then deduct about 1/2 in. so the finished cushion cover will stretch tightly over the padding.

At least four sections of boxing will be needed. One will go across the front of the cushion and partway down each side. A second piece will go across the back and partway up the sides. Two pieces will fill in the gaps at either side. These pieces will not be cut until the front and rear box strips have been fitted to the top cushion cover. This procedure will be explained later.

LAYING OUT AND CUTTING FOAM FOR CUSHIONS

Foam padding; because it compresses, must be cut slightly larger than the size of the cushion so it will fit

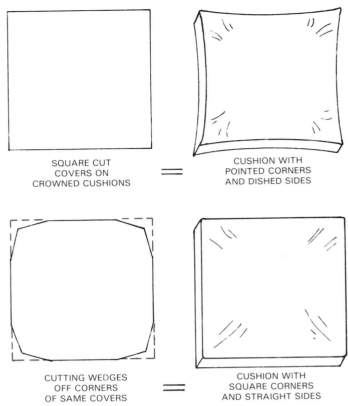

Fig. 9-10. To get finished cushions that are square, wedges must be cut away from corners of coverings used on crowned cushions.

DIMENSION	ALLOWANCE
under 6 inch	1/4 in.
6-12 in.	1/2 in.
12-23 in.	1 in.
24-35 in.	1 1/4 in.
36-47 in.	1 1/2 in.
48-59 in.	1 3/4 in.
60-71 in.	2 in.
72-83 in.	2 1/4 in.

Fig. 9-11. Cushion padding must be slightly larger than its covering for snug fitting covers and plump looking cushions. Follow allowances in chart above.

snugly in its coverings. For oversize allowances, refer to the chart in Fig. 9-11.

Position the top covering or the pattern on the slab of foam and mark the foam with a marking pen as shown in Fig. 9-12. Using shears or utility knife, cut the foam, Fig. 9-13. A power cutter, if available, will make the job easier. See Fig. 9-14.

ALTERING PADDING SHAPE

Foamed plastic is made in slabs up to 5 in. (127 mm) thick. Special thicknesses can be constructed by putting two or more thicknesses together. A crowned cushion can be fabricated by "sandwiching" a series of

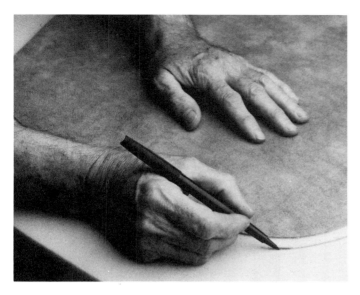

Fig. 9-12. Using top covering as a pattern trace the outline on foam cushioning material. Use a felt tip marker. (Uniroyal Coated Fabrics Dept.)

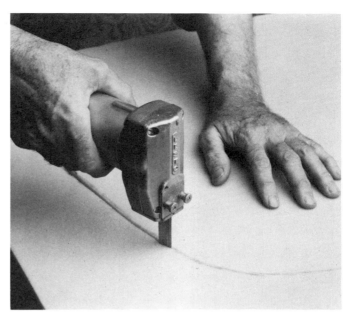

Fig. 9-14. Using a power cutter on slab of foam padding. (Uniroyal Coated Fabrics Dept.)

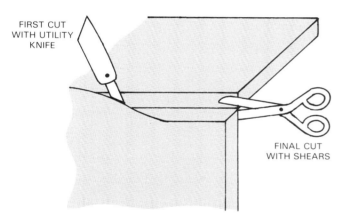

Fig. 9-13. Cutting thick slab of foam plastic. Mark out shape on top with pattern. Cut on trim lines. Make first cut with utility knife. Finish with shears. If preferred, knife and straightedge can be used to make second cut. Then make second cut from other side.

thinner foam sheets between two thicker slabs. Bonding cement or foam cement is used as an adhesive. Edges can be trimmed to round them, Fig. 9-15.

FITTING BOXING PIECES

All parts of the cushion have been cut except the filler boxings. These are the strips needed to fill in the sides of the cushion. Their length is determined after fitting the front and rear box strips to the top cover. This procedure follows:

1. Fit front boxing piece to the top cover.
   a. Fold front boxing strip in half and notch center at both edges.
   b. Fold top and bottom panels from front to back and mark centers with notches also.
   c. Place the front boxing on the top cover right side

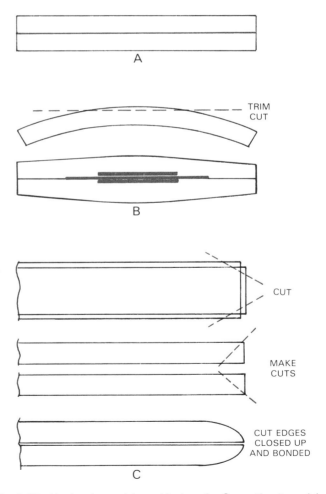

Fig. 9-15. Altering foam slab cushioning. A—Cementing two slabs together to make thicker pad. B—Adding "sandwich" of thinner slab foam to create crown in middle. C—Methods of reshaping edges of foam cushioning.

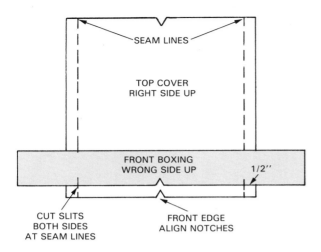

Fig. 9-16. Lining up front boxing before sewing it to top cover. Slits at edges are key to sewing square corners on cushion covers.

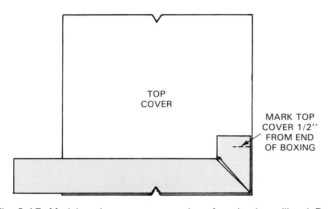

Fig. 9-17. Mark location on top cover where front boxing will end. Do not make mark at actual end. Half inch allowance is for seam.

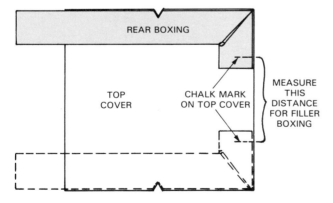

Fig. 9-18. Finding length of filler boxing needed. Rear boxing has been fitted like the front (dotted outline). Distance between end of front boxing and end of rear boxing is amount of filler boxing needed. Allow 1/2 in. extra at ends of each piece for seams!

to right side with notches aligned. Then make shallow cuts on the boxing 1/2 in. in from the corner of the top, Fig. 9-16. This is where the seam will be when the boxing is sewed to the top cover.

d. Turn the corner with one end of the boxing and

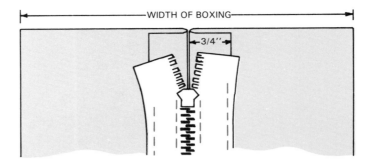

Fig. 9-19. Fold seam edge under and attach boxing strips to zipper. Folded edge must be brought to center of zipper so the zipper is concealed when closed.

put a chalk mark on the top cover 1/2 in. before the end of the boxing strip, Fig. 9-17. (This is where the seam of the front boxing strip will be.)

e. Repeat Step d at the other corner. Markings made in Steps d and e are important in measuring how much filler boxing is needed between the front and rear boxing.

2. Fit rear boxing piece by repeating the procedures in Steps 1a through 1e.

3. Measure and cut filler boxing. Be sure to allow for 1/2 in. seams. See Fig. 9-18.

MAKING ZIPPERED REAR BOXING

Some cushion covers are constructed so that padding can be inserted or removed when the cover is completely assembled. This is accomplished with a zipper closure sewed between two boxing strips. To make a zipper boxing:

1. Cut two boxing strips the length of the zipper opening plus 1/2 in. at each end for a seam. For square or rectangular cushions, the zipper will be the entire width of the back of the cushion. On a T cushion, the zipper opening should span the entire back and continue 4 in. (102 mm) up either side. To determine width of boxing pieces, divide front boxing width by two and then add 1 1/4 in. to each piece. This allowance is for seams.

2. Sew zipper to boxing strips, Fig. 9-19.
   a. Turn under 3/4 in. (19 mm) of one of the strips. Align the fold with the center of the closed zipper. Baste together and sew.
   b. Fold under 3/4 in. of the second strip. Place the fold against the fold of the first strip. Baste and sew. Fit and notch as described under "Fitting Boxing Pieces." Zippered boxing is now ready to be attached to other boxing pieces.

ASSEMBLING BOXINGS AND COVERS

When all boxing strips are fitted and marked, proceed as follows:

1. Sew boxing strips together, Fig. 9-20, forming a circle. Use 1/2 in. seams. (Some upholsterers prefer

to leave the last seam unstitched, finding it easier to sew the boxing to the top and bottom. The last seam is then machine stitched just before the last few inches are sewed to top and bottom.)

2. Assemble enough welting for the top and bottom edges of the cushion. If you do not have any made up, fabricate it following instructions in Chapter 8. (This step can be omitted if the cushion is to be made without welting.)

3. Attach boxing to top panel.
   a. Spread out the top panel in front of you right side up. Lay boxing on top of the panel, right side down.
   b. Orient boxing to the top panel. Find the seam connecting the left side filler panel to the front boxing. Align the boxing seam with the corresponding mark on the left side of the top panel. Slip welting between panel and boxing. See Fig. 9-21. Allow about 2 in. (51 mm) of welting to extend beyond the mark. Begin sewing toward the first corner.

c. Make sure the slit on the boxing is 1/2 in. from the corner of the top panel. Stitch up to the slit, make a 90 degree turn and continue sewing, Fig. 9-22. You will need to cut a slit in the welting so it will turn the corner smoothly.

d. Make certain the next slit is 1/2 in. from the next corner of the panel. Pin all three pieces of material in place to keep the slits aligned at each corner.

e. Continue sewing. Turn the next corner.

f. Match up the seam on the box panel with the mark on the top panel.

g. Continue sewing, matching up corners as described, until near the starting point.

h. Trim the welt, join it and complete the sewing. The boxing is now completely stitched to the top panel, Fig. 9-23.

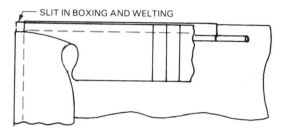

Fig. 9-22. Slit sewing edge of welting and boxing to within 1/16 in. of stitching at point where 90 degree turn is made.

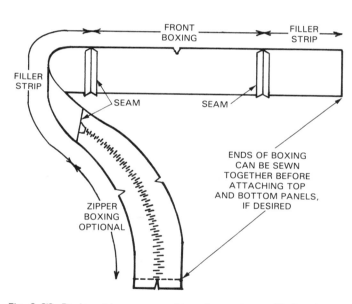

Fig. 9-20. Boxing strips are sewed together end-to-end before being attached to top and bottom cushion panels.

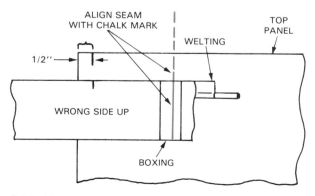

Fig. 9-21. Aligning panels. With seam of boxing at mark on edge of panel, slit in boxing should be 1/2 in. from corner.

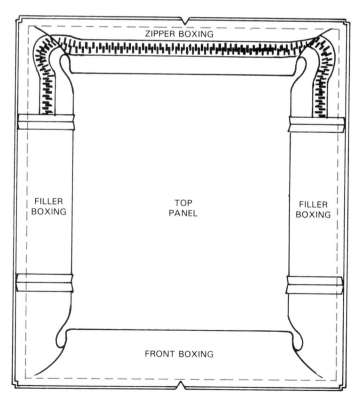

Fig. 9-23. Boxing attached to top panel. On square or rectangular cushions it is not necessary to make the zipper longer than the width of the cushion.

ATTACHING BOTTOM CUSHION COVER

If the cushion cover is zippered, the bottom cover can be sewed to the assembly before the padding material is installed. The procedure follows:

1. Open up the zipper partway. This will allow you to turn the cushion cover right side out when you are finished sewing it.
2. Since there are no markings or slits on the bottom boxing or the bottom cover, mark the corners on the boxing.
   a. Fold the boxing exactly at each corner.
   b. Cut a short slit on the fold, Fig. 9-24.
3. Sew the bottom cover to the boxing matching slits to corners of the cover. Be sure to include welting as before.
4. Open zipper wide and turn cushion right side out, Fig. 9-25.

If the cushion is not zippered, only a portion of the bottom cover is attached as follows:

1. Mark the corners of the boxing with small slits as described in Step 3 above.
2. Match up slits on the front boxing with the front corners of the bottom cover.
3. Slip in the welting as previously described.
4. Sew the front edge of the bottom cover to the box-

ing. The partially assembled cover is now ready to receive the cushion materials.

MAKING INNERSPRING CUSHIONS

The foundation of the innerspring cushion is the inner spring or Marshall unit which provides most of the

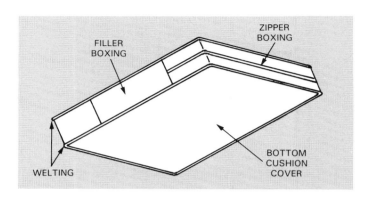

Fig. 9-25. Completed cushion cover. Zipper allows complete machine fabrication before padding is inserted.

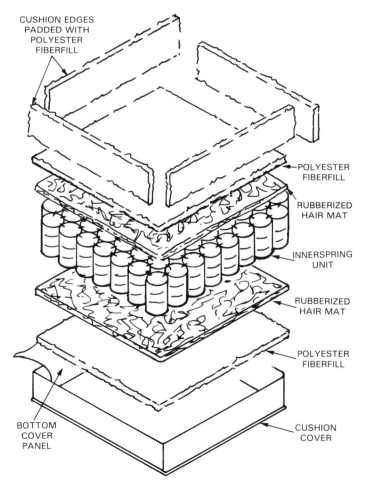

Fig. 9-26. Constructing innerspring cushion. Several layers of padding are placed around the Marshall unit. Bottom cover panel is blind stitched in final step.

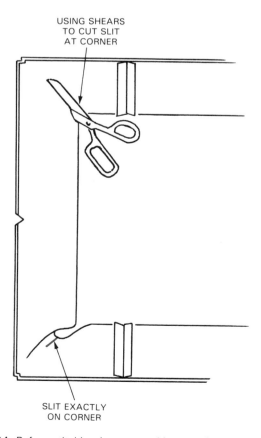

Fig. 9-24. Before stitching bottom cushion panel to partially completed cushion cover, cut slits exactly at the corners of the boxing. These slits must line up with corners of bottom panel so the completed cover will be straight.

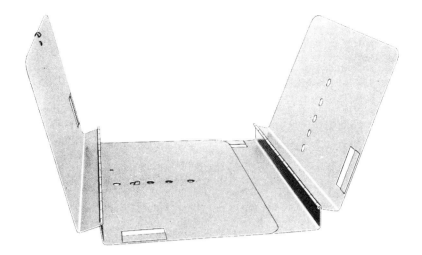

Fig. 9-27. Hand operated cushion filler. Padding is placed inside the metal case to compress it. Cushion cover is slipped over cushion filler, then filler is removed, leaving padding inside. Foot operated cushion filler is shown in Chapter 2, Fig. 2-45. (Lochner Mfg. Co.)

resilience of this type of cushion. These are individual springs enclosed in cloth pockets. They are made in various heights and degrees of stiffness. Cushion springs are usually no more than 4 in. (102 mm) high and are quite soft. The springs are sold in single rows already installed in the cloth pockets.

To construct an innerspring cushion:

1. Sew together as many rows of Marshall springs as needed for the size and shape of the cushion.
2. Construct the casing or final cover. This procedure is described earlier in this chapter.
3. Lay the casing or cover on a table open side up.
4. Cover the bottom with a layer of cotton felt. (Some upholsterers precede this with a thin layer of dacron polyester fiberfill for extra softness.)
5. Add a layer of coarser padding such as rubberized hair 1 1/2 to 2 in. (38 to 51 mm) thick.
6. Place the innerspring unit on top of this layer.
7. Add 1 1/2 to 2 in. of padding followed by cotton felt and fiberfill, if the latter is being used.
8. Cut sections of cotton felt for all four edges of the cushion and install. Cut and install fiberfill, if being used. See Fig. 9-26 for order of construction.
9. Sew the cushion shut using blind stitching. Follow blind stitching instructions given in Chapter 8.

If the innerspring unit is first encased in muslin, the final cover can be completely fabricated and zippered. The cushion is inserted in the covering with the aid of a cushion filler, Fig. 9-27. The filler compresses the cushion materials so they can more easily be slid into the cushion cover.

REVERSIBLE CUSHIONS

Whether or not a cushion is reversible will have some bearing on what covering materials are used for the bottom cover. A reversible cushion is one which can be used with either side up. The bottom side must be made of the same upholstery material as is used on the top or it will not look right. The design must be centered with the same care.

If the cushions are not designed to be reversed, the bottom cover could be made of less expensive material. The plain fabric is hidden from view and will be just as durable.

LOOSE-FILLED CUSHIONS

At one time, expensive furniture had cushions filled with loose stuffing such as down, feathers or kapok. These materials have, for the most part, been replaced by foam stuffing. When such loose materials are used, arrangements must be made to keep the materials from shifting too much inside the casings. Several methods are used to prevent shifting:

1. Use of casings with compartments, Fig. 9-28.

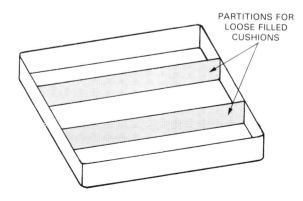

PARTITIONS FOR LOOSE FILLED CUSHIONS

Fig. 9-28. Loose-filled cushions may need compartments inside to keep stuffing in place.

2. Use of buttons on either side. This method is shown in Fig. 9-29.

MAKING COMPARTMENTED CASINGS

Construct the casing in the same manner as those intended for innerspring or solid foam cushions. Then:
1. Divide the bottom cover into three separate compartments across its width and mark them.
2. Cut panels from muslin to be used as dividers.
3. Sew the panels into the casing at the points marked. Attach them to the bottom, sides and, finally, to the top.
4. Leave openings at one side so stuffing can be added to each compartment, Fig. 9-30.

ATTACHING BUTTONS TO REVERSIBLE CUSHIONS

When reversible cushions are to be buttoned on both sides, follow these steps:
1. Mark the location of the buttons carefully on both sides.
2. Thread a long needle with nylon tufting twine.
3. Put the thread through the loop of an upholstery button.

4. Push the needle carefully down through two corresponding marked positions on the cushion. Thread the twine through the loop of another button and pass the needle back through the cushion at the same locations, Fig. 9-31, view A.
5. With the long end of the twine, make a slip knot around the short end of the twine as in view B, Fig. 9-31.
6. Pull the slip knot tight, view C, Fig. 9-31. When buttons are depressed to the desired depth, tie a square knot around the button and cut the twine. If any twine shows, tuck it neatly under the button.

MAKING T-SHAPED CUSHIONS

T cushions are found both in seats and backs. Construction is the same as for rectangular or square cushions. Of course, extra lengths of filler boxing will be needed to cover the additional corners.

The marking of the boxing and the top cover is the

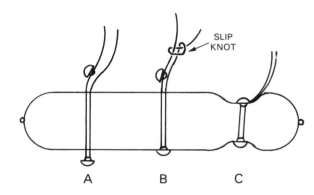

Fig. 9-31. How to attach buttons to loose-filled cushions.

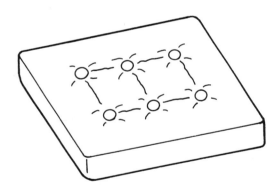

Fig. 9-29. Buttons are also used to keep loose fill from shifting and causing a lumpy cushion.

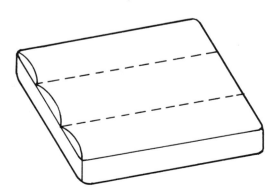

Fig. 9-30. Casings or coverings for compartmented cushions are left open along one side to allow stuffing of the compartments. In the final step, they are sewed shut with blind stitching.

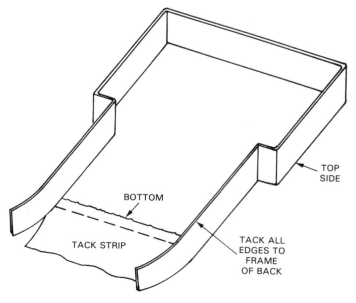

Fig. 9-32. T cushion covering constructed for inside back. Since it will be nailed to frame, no back panel is needed. However, tack strip must be added to bottom.

same except that here are two additional corners to mark. Inside corners do not need to be marked since material does not tend to stretch when changing direction on an inside corner.

Zipper boxings must be wider since the front of the cushion is wider. It will not easily fit through a zipper opening no wider than the narrower back edge of the cushion. The zipper should extend partway up each side of the cushion cover. Refer to Fig. 9-23. Half T cushions are made the same way as the T cushion, the only difference being one less corner to turn.

BACK CUSHIONS

Some back cushions are not reversible. In such cases, no bottom cover is required. The boxings are tacked to the frame. Before the boxings are stitched to the top cover, attach a tack strip along the bottom, Fig. 9-32. Be sure to allow additional material when determining the width of the boxing strips. It will be needed for backing.

REVIEW QUESTIONS — CHAPTER 9

1. Stuffing for cushions can be made of (select correct answer or anwers):
   a. Down.
   b. Feathers.
   c. Springs surrounded by padding.
   d. Shredded foam.
   e. Solid slabs of foam plastic or foam rubber.
   f. All of the above.
2. Describe how to make a pattern for a cushion.
3. If upholstery material has a nap, the nap should lay _____ on a seat cushion and _____ on a back cushion.
4. Describe how to cut the corners of upholstery coverings when the cushion is crowned.
5. What are boxings?
6. Foam padding for a cushion should be cut slightly _____ than the cushion covering.
7. In a zippered cushion, where in the covering is the zipper placed?
8. Some cushions use springs to make them resilient. These springs vary in height but are usually no more than _____ in. or _____ mm high.
9. Explain what knot or knots might be used in attaching buttons to both sides of a reversible cushion.
10. Explain how a loose-filled cushion is constructed to prevent padding from shifting too much.
11. Zippers on T cushions must be (longer, shorter) than zippers used on square cushions. The zippers extend partway up each _____.

Chapter 10
CHANNELING AND TUFTING

Of all the upholstering techniques, the two demanding the most skill are channeling and tufting. Channeling, sometimes called fluting or piping, is a series of padded, usually parallel ridges generally seen as a part of the design of a chair back, Fig. 10-1. It is normally done only on the backs of chairs and sofas.

Tufting is a series of raised and depressed sections created with alternating use of padding and buttons. The effect of the alternating pattern is a repetition of diamond shaped or square tufts (hence the name). See Fig. 10-2. Tufting is done both on the backs and seats of upholstered furniture.

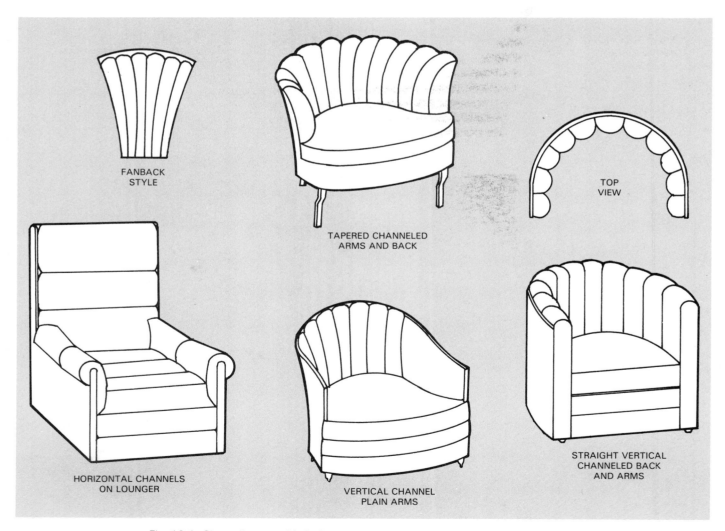

FANBACK
STYLE

TAPERED CHANNELED
ARMS AND BACK

TOP
VIEW

HORIZONTAL CHANNELS
ON LOUNGER

VERTICAL CHANNEL
PLAIN ARMS

STRAIGHT VERTICAL
CHANNELED BACK
AND ARMS

Fig. 10-1. Channeling, a padded tube, is often found on the backs of furniture especially where the back is curved. Horizontal channeling is rarely done.

Fig. 10-2. Examples of tufted furniture. A—Diamond tufted barrel chair with three rows of buttons. B—Chair back and ottoman with square tufts. C—Couch with combination tufts and channels.

MAKING CHANNELS

The channel is seen as a series of straight, parallel ribs running up and down the back of a chair or up and down the arms. Or it is seen as fan shaped with tops of the ribs being wider than the bottoms (tapered).

Some upholsterers prefer to work directly on the piece of furniture when making channels. Others prefer the ease of constructing the channels before attaching them to the furniture piece.

LAYING OUT THE CHANNEL AS A SEPARATE UNIT

The following procedures are for channeling the back of a chair:

1. Measure the surface to be covered by channeling.

2. Decide on the width, and number of channels. (If you can use the old tufted cover as a pattern, you will not need to make these decisions. Go on to Step 3.) Divide the area being covered by the number of channels you plan to have. If the channels are to be fan shaped, be sure to measure both the top and the bottom of the area. Divide each measurement by the number of channels. Set the figures aside. You will use them in Step 5.

3. Find the center of the chair back. Mark it with a soft lead marker top and bottom. These marks will help you center the channels as they are later attached to the chair.

4. Cut a piece of muslin slightly larger than the inside back. This will become the under side of the channels. Mark the center top and bottom so you will have a means of centering the finished channeling on the chair. Draw a line connecting the marks.

5. Mark off the width of the channels which you determined in Step 2. See Fig. 10-3. (If you are using an even number of channels, lay out an even number on each side of the centerline. If an odd number, measure off half the width of a channel on either side of the centerline.)
6. Using a straightedge as a guide, draw lines as in Fig. 10-4. These will be the stitching lines between the individual channels.
7. Cut away excess material around the edges of the pattern just drawn.
8. Determine the depth of the channel (thickness of its padding). This is your choice to make and is important to know at this point. It determines the width of each channel section of the top cover (and, of course, the total width of the top cover).
   a. Experiment with a wide strip of cardboard, bending it until you have the shape and size of channel you wish. See Fig. 10-5. Trim off the

edge of the cardboard when you have found a shape the right height and width.
   b. Lay the cardboard pattern flat and measure its width. This dimension represents the amount of final covering it takes to stretch over the bulge of the padding to form one channel.
9. Measure and mark the final cover.
   a. Find the width of material needed for all of the channels. (Multiply the cardboard's width by the number of channels.)
   b. Working from the center of a piece of final covering large enough to cover the chair back, lay out the channels as you did on the muslin underside. Use chalk and work on the underside of the upholstery material. *Note: the channels will be several inches wider than the corresponding channels on the muslin underside. This is to cover the "bulge" of the padding.*
   c. Allow enough extra material at top and sides so the upholstery material can be wrapped over edges and tacked to the chair. A tack strip or stretcher will be attached to the bottom for tacking.
   d. Draw in lines following the same technique shown in Fig. 10-3 and Fig. 10-4.

ASSEMBLING CHANNELS

1. Place the final cover on top of the muslin underside previously marked and cut. Right side of the cover should face up.

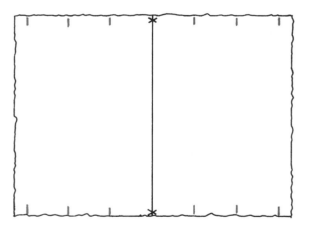

Fig. 10-3. Mark top and bottom of muslin for divisions between channels. If there are an even number of channels, arrange them on either side of centerline. If an odd number, center one channel on centerline.

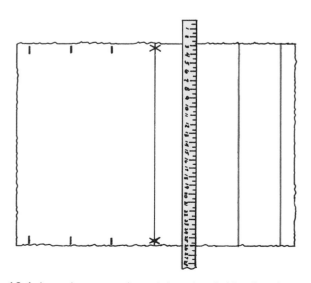

Fig. 10-4. Lay rule over marks and draw in stitching lines between channels.

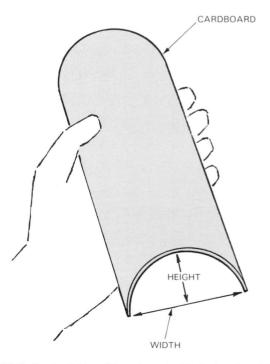

Fig. 10-5. Bend a fairly stiff cardboard with the hand until it has the height and width of the channel you want. Trim cardboard to width and use it as guide for width of channels on top muslin or final cover.

2. In preparation for sewing, match up the lines chalked on the wrong side of the cover with the lines on the muslin underside. It is very important to have exact alignment. If matching is done carelessly, channels will be uneven.

3. Sew in the channel seams, Fig. 10-6. Use pins or a basting stitch to hold the pieces in alignment and to guide the machine stitching along the lines.

4. Most upholsterers do not sew in the last seam on each side. This is sewn in by hand or tacked to the frame after the end channels are stuffed.

STUFFING THE CHANNELS

Stuffing the channels may give the beginner some difficulty depending on the stuffing materials used. Foam padding, cotton padding, kapok or other loose stuffing can be used. However, loose stuffings should be avoided by the beginner. They are difficult to handle.

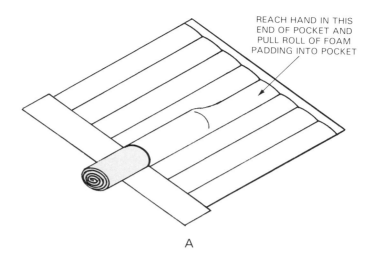

REACH HAND IN THIS END OF POCKET AND PULL ROLL OF FOAM PADDING INTO POCKET

A

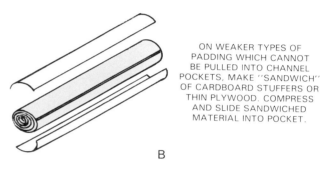

ON WEAKER TYPES OF PADDING WHICH CANNOT BE PULLED INTO CHANNEL POCKETS, MAKE "SANDWICH" OF CARDBOARD STUFFERS OR THIN PLYWOOD. COMPRESS AND SLIDE SANDWICHED MATERIAL INTO POCKET.

B

Fig. 10-7. Stuffing padding into channel pockets. A—Roll of foam rubber or plastic can be pulled into pocket. B—Cotton batting or polyester fiberfill should have cardboard or plywood stuffers laid on either side of roll as stiffener as it is being forced into pocket. Allow stuffing to extend beyond each end. It can be adjusted later.

White wadding, cotton mat, foam rubber or foam plastic are best for stuffing channels. Especially with foamed products, thin slabs are best; they are easier to shape into rolls.

Make the rolls slightly longer than the length of the channels. Padding can be trimmed off later as the cover is being tacked to the chair back.

If you have difficulty sliding the rolled padding into the channel pickets, cut two pieces of cardboard or thin plywood as long and wide as the roll. "Sandwich" the roll between the cardboards or plywood, compress the roll and slide it into the channel, Fig. 10-7. Stuff all but the two end channels which are not sewn. These will be stuffed as the cover is installed on the chair back.

Before installation, sew a tack strip to the bottom of the cover. This can be done any time after the final cover is cut out.

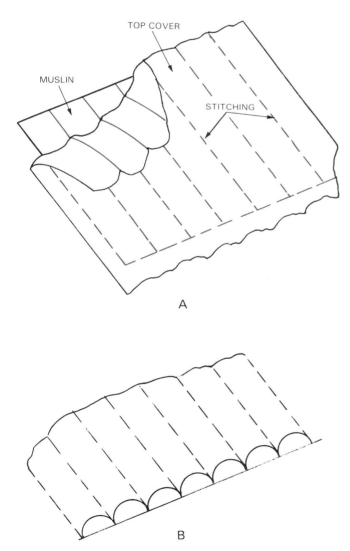

Fig. 10-6. Forming channel pockets with top cover and muslin underside. A—Final cover atop muslin and sewing in progress. B—Pockets formed after sewing finished.

INSTALLING CHANNELED COVER

1. Lay the completed cover on the chair seat wrong side up and push the tacking strip down between the

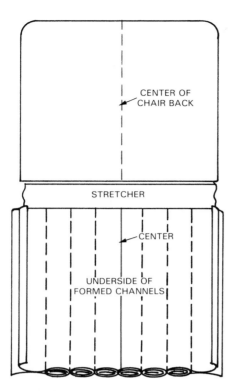

Fig. 10-8. Installing formed channel back covering. Shove stretcher between seat and back. Center channeled covering on back.

seat and the bottom of the chair back, Fig. 10-8.

2. Align the center of the cover with the center mark on the chair back.
3. Tack it down temporarily to the rear seat rail. Make sure that the channels are not too low.
   a. Lay the cover over the top of the back. Adjust position if necessary.
   b. Recheck for center alignment. If satisfactory, tack the bottom permanently.
4. Center the top of the cover with the center mark on the chair back and tack it too. Stretch the material taut before tacking. Fig. 10-9 shows several styles which call for varied methods of attaching the top.
5. Pin tack the top, starting with the center of the channeled unit. Stretch the cover tight before tacking.
6. Move from the center to either side, smoothing and pulling the cover tight as tacking progresses.
7. Examine the work done. If it is properly centered and straight, permanently tack it.

The outside channels require a different method for stuffing. Padding materials must be laid in before the channel is closed.

1. Lay the rolled padding into place. Use the same padding material as with the other channels.
2. Wrap the final cover over the top of the padding and around the chair back. Stretch it taut and tack the edges to the tack rails.

ALTERNATE CHANNEL CONSTRUCTION

Sometimes it is necessary to construct the channeled covering by cutting out and sewing on each channel covering separately. An example is the tapered channel backed chair shown in Fig. 10-10.

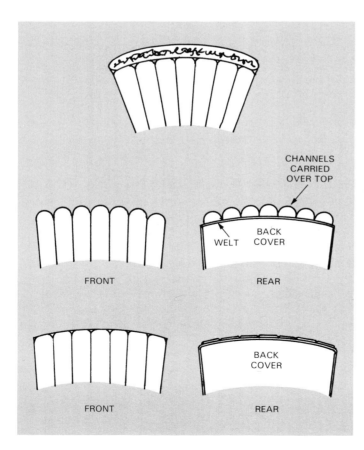

Fig. 10-9. Several styles of channeling on chair backs. Each requires varying the stuffing and tacking procedure. Cut back padding as required.

Fig. 10-10. Upholstered chair with tapered channeling. Pockets are narrower at bottom. Top cover must be made from individual pieces.

LAYING OUT TAPERED CHANNELS

The procedure for measuring and laying out a tapered channel is similar to that used for straight channels.

1. Measure top and bottom of the chair back and divide each measurement by the number of pockets desired.

2. Lay out the pockets on a piece of muslin and use a marking pencil to mark the edges of each pocket. This will be used as a stitching guide and as the underside.
   a. Locate the centerline at top and bottom.
   b. Working outward from the center in each direction, mark the widths of each pocket across the top.
   c. Do the same on the bottom, again working outward from the center in each direction. (Remember: The width of the pockets is narrower at the bottom.) Your layout will look similar to Fig. 10-11.

3. Determine the dimensions of the top channel cover which will complete the pocket. It must be larger than the pattern just layed out on the muslin since it must bulge outward to hold the padding.
   a. If there is an old covering, take it apart and use it as a pattern.
   b. If there is no pattern, use the curved cardboard technique shown in Fig. 10-5. As a rule, adding 2 in. (51 mm) to each channel should be sufficient.

4. Lay out the pieces on the final covering. Do not attempt to save material by laying out some of the channels upside down. Both pattern and nap will be running in opposite directions and the appearance of the back will be spoiled, Fig. 10-12.

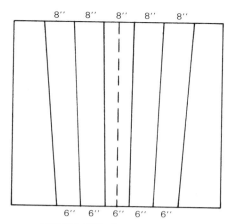

NOT LIKE THIS: WEAVE, NAP AND PATTERN WILL LAY ON A BIAS, RUINING JOB'S APPEARANCE

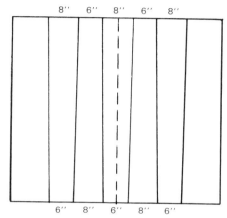

NOR LIKE THIS: REVERSING TAPER ON EVERY OTHER CHANNEL WILL REVERSE PATTERN AND NAP, SPOILING APPEARANCE

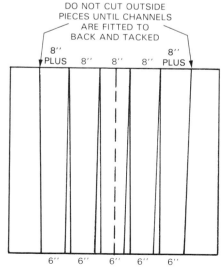

DO NOT CUT OUTSIDE PIECES UNTIL CHANNELS ARE FITTED TO BACK AND TACKED

BUT LIKE THIS: TAPERED PANELS CUT STRAIGHT WITH PATTERN AND WEAVE

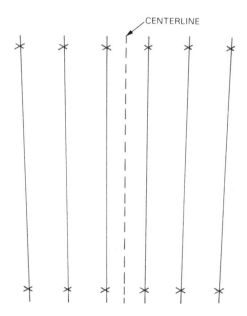

Fig. 10-11. Muslin marked up for tapered channels. This will be the underside. Final cover or other pieces of muslin will be sewed to it to form pockets.

Fig. 10-12. Proper cutting pattern for tapered channels when preparing the final cover. Individual pieces must be marked off and cut along the "straight" on the fabric. Be sure to include seam allowance on both sides.

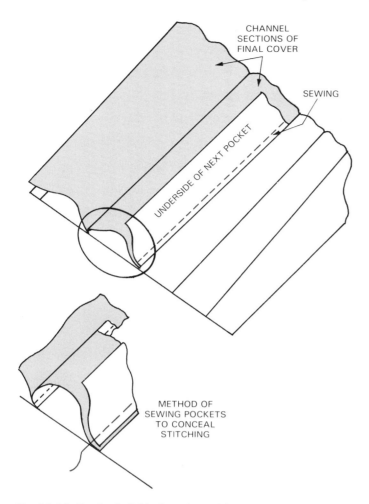

Fig. 10-13. Sewing individual sections of final cover to muslin base marked for tapered channels. Lay edges of sections over stitch lines and sew each edge except first and last. These will be tacked down on the chair back.

5. Stitch each channel separately to the muslin, Fig. 10-13. Leave the outside seam on both outside channels open. These will be stuffed and outside edges will be tacked to the chair after the covering is installed.

Channeling may be constructed directly on the back of the piece of furniture. In this method, the base is layed out on muslin or burlap. It is usually attached to the chair back after marking, Fig. 10-14. The channel covers are cut out and sewed individually to the back. They can be stuffed either before or after they are sewed in, as you prefer. If loose or weak stuffing materials are used, it is better to stuff the channels before sewing.

TUFTING

Tufts are added to furniture as a decoration. Because of the buttons used, they must be constructed right on the piece of furniture. Tufts are used on seats as well as on backs. Fig. 10-15 shows common tufting patterns.

LAYING OUT A TUFTING PATTERN

Tufting forms a pattern of diamonds or squares with buttons forming depressions in the padding. If reupholstering an old piece of furniture that has been tufted you can use the old underside and the old cover as patterns. Press them and lay them over the new pieces of material. Mark the button positions with a marking device.

If there is no old pattern to follow, you must make one. It is best to work right on the piece of furniture. But you can also make a pattern and then transfer it to the furniture. Just be careful that the pattern is the right size and proportion for the back or seat on which you are working.

DIAMOND TUFTING

To place a diamond tuft pattern on a chair back:
1. Find and mark the centerlines of the back for both height and width.
2. Draw up a pattern on a grid of squares or rectangles.
   a. Determine width and height of the diamond. The size should be such that it is in proportion to the size of the chair back.
   b. Divide the height and width in half and make a grid large enough to contain the entire pattern. Vertical lines of the grid must be spaced to half the width of the diamond; horizontal lines to half the height, Fig. 10-16.
   c. Mark position of buttons, Fig. 10-17. Begin to draw in the diagonal lines. Start from the centerline and work outward.

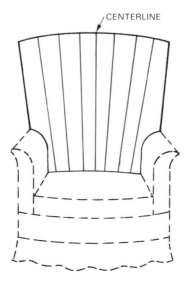

Fig. 10-14. Marked up chair back ready for sewing channel pockets directly onto the back. Stitching must be done by hand with large curved needle.

BARREL BACK CHAIR WITH
5-6-5-4 BUTTON PATTERN
FORMING DIAMOND TUFTS

DEEP TUFTED ANTIQUE
CHAIR WITH SAG SEAT

BEDROOM CHAIR WITH
4-3-4-5 TUFT PATTERN

MODERN THREE-PILLOW COUCH
WITH SQUARE 3-3 TUFTING
PATTERN ON BACK CUSHIONS

DINING CHAIR WITH
SINGLE ROW OF TUFTS
IN 3-4-3 BUTTON PATTERN

Fig. 10-15. Tufting patterns on various types of furniture. To get diamond pattern, alternate rows of odd-even numbers of buttons must be used. Square or rectangular tufts are formed by aligning buttons vertically.

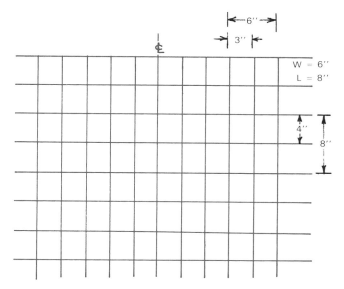

Fig. 10-16. Design of diamond tufting pattern begins with layout of full size grid.

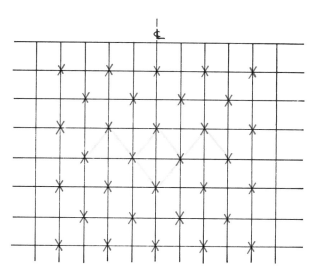

Fig. 10-17. Working from centerline of grid, mark button positions at intersection of grid lines. Begin to connect button positions with diagonal lines. Lines are not necessary to the pattern but to show if pattern is straight or lopsided.

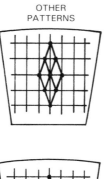

OTHER
PATTERNS

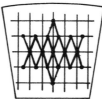

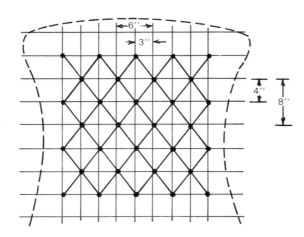

Fig. 10-18. Completed tuft pattern with suggestion of contour of chair. Other patterns are possible for either horizontal or vertical treatment.

MUSLIN OR
FINAL COVER
WRONG SIDE UP

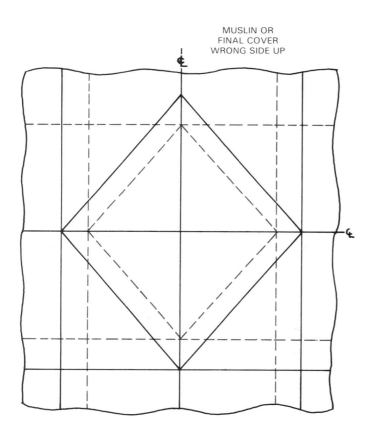

Fig. 10-19. Enlarged grid pattern for diamond tuft. Top covering is larger over tufting to accommodate bulge of padding.

d. Draw in the diamond pattern as in Fig. 10-18.

3. Using a marking pen, reproduce the pattern on the back of the chair. It is necessary only to mark the button positions but you can draw in the lines, too. Keep the points of the lowest part of the diamond pattern about 3 in. (76 mm) above the seat. Be sure the pattern is carefully centered. Check that the lines of button positions are running straight. Pin the pattern to the chair before marking.

TUFTING METHODS

Tufting falls into two basic methods:
1. Tufting by making individual pockets.
2. Tufting a single, integrated, padded surface.

Most upholsterers prefer the second method since it is faster and less painstaking. Both methods will be shown.

Either way, the pattern must be transferred to a part of the upholstering material. When tufting by building individual pockets, the pattern is placed on a piece of muslin which becomes the underside of the casing. When tufting on a single padded surface, usually foam, the pattern is traced on the foam pad itself.

TUFTING INDIVIDUAL POCKETS

In this type of tufting, you will work directly on the muslin or burlap which is covering the back or seat of the furniture piece.

1. Locate and mark the center of the top and bottom (or front and back).
2. Establish position of the pattern on the surface. As a general guide, the bottom of the design, (that is, the first row of buttons) is 1 to 3 in. (25-76 mm) further away from the edge of the surface than the distance between the first and second horizontal line.
3. Draw the pattern of the pockets, working outward from the center.
4. Locate and mark the position of each button.
5. Lay out the same pattern (but enlarge it) on a piece of muslin big enough to cover the back or seat. The pattern area must be larger than that in the previous steps because it must hold the padding for the tufts. Usually an additional 2 in. (51 mm) on each dimension of the diamond or square should be enough, Fig. 10-19.

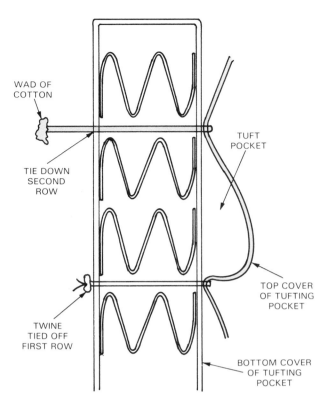

Fig. 10-20. Cross-sectional view of tufting pockets being formed. First two rows are tied in place at points where buttons are to be located. In next step, V shaped pockets formed by tying will be stuffed with padding.

Fig. 10-21. Partial view of pockets tacked and partially stuffed. Note how excess material is pleated by folding under.

Tacking and stuffing

1. Lay the piece of muslin over the design on the piece of furniture. Line up the first row and, using strong stitching twine, tack the muslin down at the location of each button on the first row. Take the twine all the way through to the springs and/or webbing. Use a knot to secure each tack. Place a wad of cotton under the twine to prevent the knot from pulling through.
2. Tack the button positions on the second row, Fig. 10-20. This forms the pockets for the first row of

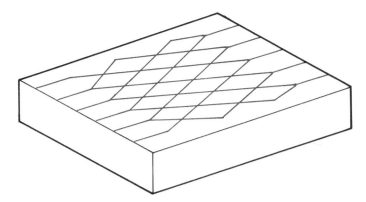

Fig. 10-22. Draw tufting pattern on foam pad trimmed to size for chair back. Cutting lines are shown in color.

half diamonds and the lower half of the second row which will be full diamonds.
3. Stuff the row of half diamonds first.
4. When stuffing of the first row is finished, immediately tack the covering down to the tack rail.
5. Pack the second row of tufts with stuffing. This will form the bottom half of the first row of diamond-shaped tufts. You may have to fold some of the material under in pleats, Fig. 10-21. Tack down the next row of button positions and stuff the top half of the tuft pockets. Then stuff the lower half of the next row of tufts. Continuing in the same manner, complete tacking and stuffing the entire back.
6. Pull loose edges of the muslin tight and tack them down to their tack rails. Be sure edges are adequately padded.

Installing top cover

1. Lay a thin layer of padding over the entire tufted surface. This step is optional, being preferred by many upholsterers because it softens and improves the appearance of the tufting.
2. Position final cover. Line up the button positions with the tacked button positions underneath.
3. Tie off the bottom row of buttons.
4. Pin tack adjacent edge of final cover to its tack rail.
5. Position and tie buttons for rest of tufted area.
6. Pull edges tight and pin tack them.
7. Check covering for appearance and adjust, if necessary. Permanently tack all edges.

TUFTING A COMPLETELY PADDED SURFACE

For the beginner, tufting a surface already padded is much easier than tufting pockets. The job is made even simpler with the use of foamed materials.

The foamed rubber or foamed plastic is prepared in the regular way described in Chapter 8, *Installing Padding.* Then, to prepare the pad for tufting, use the following procedure:

1. Lay out the tufting pattern lines on the foamed pad, Fig. 10-22.

2. With a sharp knife, cut along the diagonal lines from button position to button position. Make the cuts about 1/2 in. deep.

3. It may be desirable to cut or drill plugs at the button positions as shown in Fig. 10-23. This will accentuate the tufted appearance.

4. Position the pad on the piece of furniture.

5. Position the marked final cover over the pad and attach the buttons.

6. Pin tack, adjust, and permanently tack final cover to tack rails.

TUFTING VINYL PLASTICS

Tufting is often done using vinyl plastics such as Naugahyde. This material should present no special problem for the upholsterer. Many of these materials are capable of two-way stretch. Figs. 10-24 through 10-26 show how it is done.

REVIEW QUESTIONS — CHAPTER 10

1. Channeling, sometimes called _____ or _____ is a series of padded _____ usually as part of the design on the backs and sides of chairs or sofas.

2. What is tufting?

3. Describe how the width of a channel is determined.

4. In laying out channels on the final cover, why is the channel width allowance wider than for the underside?

5. Are channels padded before or after the top and bottom are stitched together?

6. What precaution should be observed in laying out a tapered channel or napped and/or patterned cover fabric?

7. Why is a grid pattern used in laying out a tufting pattern?

8. What are the two basic methods of tufting?

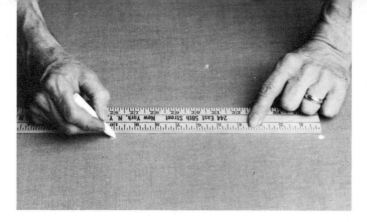

Fig. 10-24. Button positions are marked off on the vinyl plastic material using chalk and ruler. Work on the wrong side of the fabric. (Uniroyal Coated Fabrics Dept.)

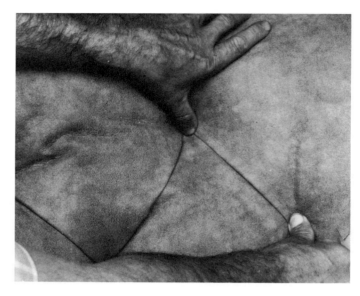

Fig. 10-25. Stretch and fold the fabric between button points for smooth-fitting pockets. Folds should face downward on backs so they will not be dirt catchers.

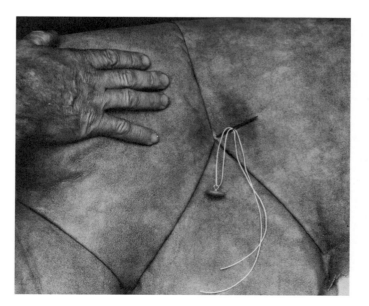

Fig. 10-26. Buttons will help to preserve folds. Be sure to use heavy twine to hold button in place.

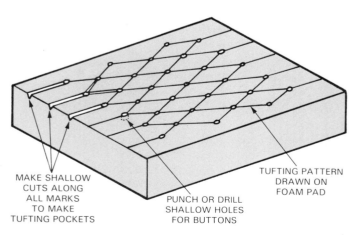

MAKE SHALLOW CUTS ALONG ALL MARKS TO MAKE TUFTING POCKETS

PUNCH OR DRILL SHALLOW HOLES FOR BUTTONS

TUFTING PATTERN DRAWN ON FOAM PAD

Fig. 10-23. Make shallow cuts with sharp utility knife along all pattern lines so upholstery cover will sink into them and foam will fill pockets in the cover.

Section 3
PROJECTS IN UPHOLSTERING

Small upholstered frames require practically the same skills of the upholsterer as do larger pieces such as a chair or sofa. Thus, nearly all of the techniques can be applied on a small scale until they are mastered. From this section you will be able to develop skill in designing frames, selecting woods, installing webbing, padding, and springs. Because of the small size, few materials are used. This economy may encourage you to complete additional projects using different designs, techniques and materials.

Chapter 11
MAKING SMALL UPHOLSTERY FRAMES

Books, magazines and catalogs are excellent sources of ideas for small upholstery frames. You can select a frame you like and redesign it to satisfy your taste and need. You might prefer to create a furniture frame entirely of your own design.

STOOL DESIGN

Fig. 11-1 shows a simple, yet interesting, stool. Designed especially for use in the kitchen, it is stable enough and high enough to allow you to reach most storage areas. As you can see from Fig. 11-2, there are only four parts.

The stool can be assembled by several methods:

1. Since upholstery materials will cover its top, you can assemble the stool with screws through the top into the legs and braces. Two screws into each component are enough.
2. You can also assemble the components with finishing nails and glue. However, this method produces a weaker frame than the first method. Set the nails below the wood surfaces.

Fig. 11-2. Parts of kitchen stool. Assembly will require only six wood screws.

3. Another method is to drill pocket cuts into the top, inside edges of the legs and the brace to receive screws. Pocket cuts can be drilled with a forstner bit and drill press or a portable drill. Parts can be held with a clamped fixture during drilling. Pocket

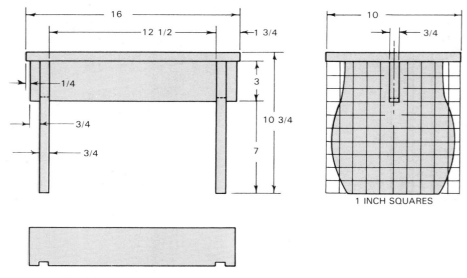

Fig. 11-1. Plans for simple kitchen stool. It will receive a padded top.

Fig. 11-3. Drilling setup for making pocket cuts in stool leg to receive screws. Simple jig makes drilling operation easier.

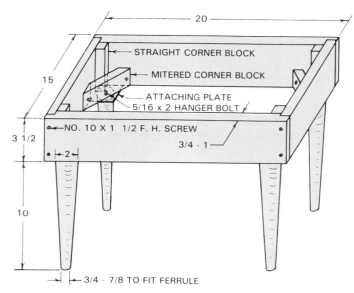

Fig. 11-4. This stool design has a framed base with turned legs.

cuts are preferred since they produce a professional appearance. See Fig. 11-3.

WOOD TO USE

Medium hard hardwoods are recommended for most upholstery frames. Bear in mind these desirable characteristics before making selection:
1. Ease in driving tacks and nails.
2. Ability of the wood to hold tacks and nails firmly without cracking.
3. Ability of the wood to bear considerable stress and strain.
4. Economy.
5. Availability.

Close, straight grained woods, such as soft maple, poplar and gum, are the best for furniture frame parts hidden by upholstery. More expensive and attractive woods such as walnut, cherry, birch and mahogany, although excellent for frames, are usually used only for exposed parts such as turned legs, ends of arms and feet.

Hard maple and oak are considered too hard to use where tacks and nails are driven. Basswood and white pine lack sufficient strength for most frames. Because western cedar and redwood split easily and are relatively weak, they should be avoided.

Lumber used for frames should be well seasoned to prevent shrinkage. Even better is lumber kiln dried to 7 or 8 percent moisture content. Hidden frame lumber should be reasonably free of large knots to assure adequate strength.

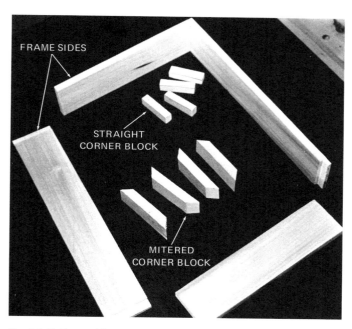

Fig. 11-5. Parts of framed base. Glue blocks are used to reinforce the corners and legs.

FRAMED WOOD BASE

You can select or create a design for a framed wood base in a size and shape to harmonize with existing or intended decor. Square and rectangular shapes are popular because they are easy to construct.

Framed wood bases also offer a chance to use numerous upholstery techniques. Webbing can be used to support both nonspring and coil spring materials. Another method is to stretch sinuous springs between frames to form an upholstery base for a seat or back.

Fig. 11-4 illustrates a typical framed wood base design. Fig. 11-5 shows its components.

ASSEMBLY

A framed wood base may be assembled with screws and glue. Side and end components can be strengthened by use of rabbet and butt joints. Glue blocks should be carefully cut for an accurate fit.

To prepare the side and end components for assembly, drill two holes in each end of adjacent pieces to receive flat head screws, Fig. 11-6. Then glue up each joint, Fig. 11-7, and install the screws, as in Fig. 11-8.

Install glue blocks. You can attach the straight glue blocks with finish nails and glue. Then fasten the mitered corner blocks with screws and glue. See Fig. 11-9.

Construct or select legs. You can purchase ready-made feet or legs for the framed wood base or make them yourself. Turned, square-tapered and square-straight shaped legs are functional and popular for upholstery frames.

Fig. 11-6. Holes for flat head screws are being drilled with a portable electric drill and a screw-mate bit.

Fig. 11-8. Install wood screws in joint before glue sets.

Fig. 11-7. Apply glue before assembling joint. Glued joints are stronger than screws alone.

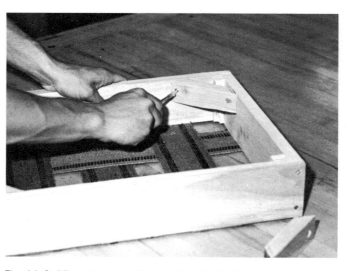

Fig. 11-9. Mitered corner block is installed with glue and screws also. In addition to strengthening the corner, the corner block provides a better base for anchor plates.

142

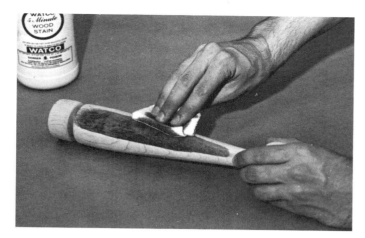

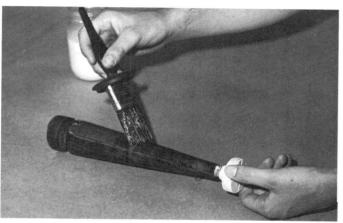

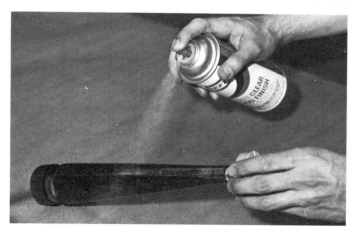

Fig. 11-10. Applying finish to turned leg. Top. Stain is applied with cloth pad. Center. Clear finish may be brushed on. Bottom. If preferred, clear finish can be sprayed from a pressurized can.

Fig. 11-11. Use a hand screw to hold leg during drilling. Note that hole is drilled before waste stock is removed from ends.

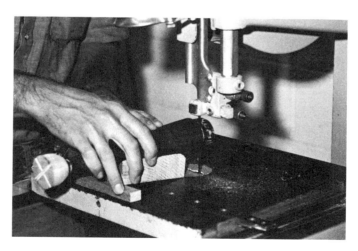

Fig. 11-12. Using bandsaw to remove waste stock from turned legs. Jig for holding leg consists of a V block and piece of scrap wood.

Turned legs can be partially prepared for assembly before waste ends are removed. The waste ends can be used to steady or hold the legs while you apply finish, Fig. 11-10. Refer to Chapter 5 for finishing methods.

Drill a hole to receive the hanger bolt. Select a drill the same size as the core diameter of the hanger bolt. Wrap a piece of tape around the bit to indicate the depth of cut. (Be sure to allow for waste stock which will later be cut off.) Fasten the waste end of the leg to a hand screw clamp and drill the hole, Fig. 11-11.

Remove the waste ends from the leg as shown in Fig. 11-12. Support the leg with a V block held against a miter gauge or in a clamp. Cut off the waste ends with a band saw or backsaw.

Put in a hanger bolt. Protect the leg with a cloth and clamp it in a vise. Turn two nuts onto the machine thread of the hanger bolt. The top nut acts as a lock nut to prevent the second nut from turning when pressure is applied with a wrench. Turn the hanger bolt into the leg as shown in Fig. 11-13.

Fig. 11-13. Use wrench and double nut arrangement to turn hanger bolt into leg.

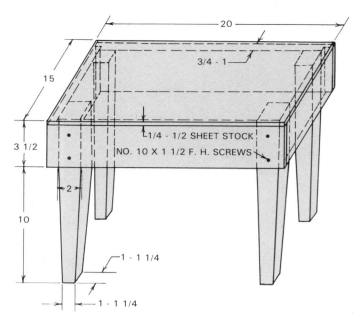

Fig. 11-15. Alternative leg design for framed wood base. With this design no glue blocks are needed.

Fig. 11-14. Use light tap with mallet to seat glide.

Install a glide. Clamp the installed hanger bolt (with nuts still in place) into a vise. Place a glide over the small end of the leg and tap it down tight with a mallet, Fig. 11-14.

Legs are installed upon completion of upholstering. The method is shown in Chapter 13, page 160.

SOLID WOOD BASE

Construction of a solid wood base is similar to the processes used to build a framed wood base. Fig. 11-15 shows a simple drawing for such a stool. Fig. 11-16 shows parts ready for assembly. Assemble with glue and screws. Follow steps illustrated in Figs. 11-6, 11-7 and 11-8.

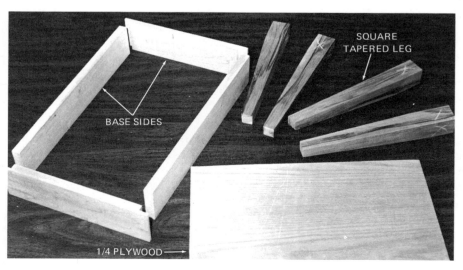

Fig. 11-16. Parts of solid wood base are ready to be assembled.

Then fasten solid wood, plywood, particle board or hardboard to the top side of the frame with screws or nails and glue. This forms an excellent base for your choice of nonspring upholstery materials. Sheet foam, rubberized hair and loose-fill materials are a few from which you may choose.

Square-tapered legs can be fastened into each corner of the frame with screws and glue, eliminating the need for glue blocks. You might want to fasten the legs with attaching plates and hanger bolts. This method is shown in Chapter 13, Fig. 13-21 and Fig. 13-22.

REVIEW QUESTIONS — CHAPTER 11

1. Name at least two sources of design ideas for constructing your own upholstery frames.
2. What kinds of woods are best for furniture frames where the frame is hidden by upholstery coverings? Why?
3. Frame woods should be _____ _____ to prevent shrinkage.
4. Why are glue blocks used? Why can they be eliminated when square-tapered legs are used?

Chapter 12
UPHOLSTERING SMALL FRAMES WITHOUT SPRINGS

Not all upholstering involves a large project such as an overstuffed chair or sofa. Most of the principles of upholstery can be learned on small projects. This chapter will show methods used to upholster slip seats and small pieces of furniture where no springs are used. The frames for some of these projects can be constructed from procedures shown and discussed in Chapter 11. The slip seat is popular for dining and occasional chairs. The process for stripping and finishing these pieces of furniture is shown in Chapters 4 and 5.

PADDED STOOL

Stools can be used for many purposes around the home, Fig. 12-1. They are small enough so that they can be easily pushed out of the way or stored when not in use.

Fiber mat, a relatively rigid material, can be used as padding. Vinyl plastic, such as Naugahyde, is a very durable and easily maintained material. It makes a good covering material.

Fig. 12-1. Simple padded stool. This frame is easy to build and easy to upholster.

FASTENING FIBER MAT

With upholsterers' shears or tin snips, cut a piece of fiber mat about 1 in. (25 mm) narrower and 1 in. shorter than the stool top. Position the fiber mat on top of the stool. Using an upholstery hammer, drive a No. 3 or 4 upholstery tack through each corner of the fiber mat into the stool top, Fig. 12-2.

Fig. 12-2. Attach fiber mat to stool top with No. 3 upholstery tacks.

ATTACHING COVERING

Cut a piece of vinyl plastic slightly larger than the top. Position the vinyl plastic over the padding on the stool top.

Using the upholstery hammer, fasten the middle of each side with three No. 3 or No. 4 upholstery tacks. Stay back about 3/8 in. (9.5 mm) from each edge of the top. Start each tack with the magnetic (split) end of the hammer and finish driving with the other end. Draw the material taut with your fingers, Fig. 12-3.

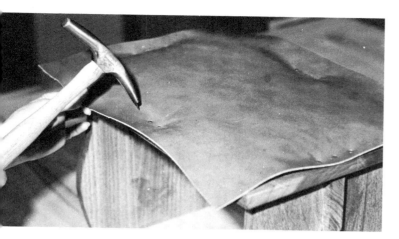

Fig. 12-3. Final covering should be attached at centers of each side first to avoid pull marks or crooked cover.

Fig. 12-5. Trim off excess cover with straightedge and knife. Be careful not to damage wood finish.

Fig. 12-4. Continue tacking cover, working from center to corners of each side.

Fig. 12-6. Installing gimp. Drive in first decorative tack only partway.

Fasten each side, working from the center toward the corners. Space the upholstery tacks about 3/4 in. (19 mm) apart. Pull the material firmly with your fingers to avoid wrinkles, Fig. 12-4. To avoid pull marks, drive the tacks about an inch (25 mm) behind where you are pulling.

Using a metal straightedge and a sharp knife, trim each side about 1/4 in. (6 mm) back from each edge of the top. See Fig. 12-5.

INSTALLING GIMP

Install gimp to cover tacks and the raw edges of plastic vinyl. Measure the distance to be covered and cut a piece of plastic gimp. Allow 2 in. (51 mm) extra to make the corner folds. Select metalene nails with heads that best match the covering color.

Begin at a corner. Drive a metalene nail only part way into the wood so that it can be easily removed later, Fig. 12-6.

Stretch the gimp to the next corner and fold it to turn the corner, Fig. 12-7. Drive a metalene nail through the

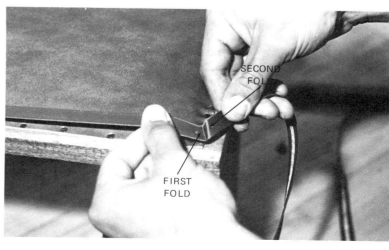

Fig. 12-7. Turning corners with gimp. Fold gimp back at about 45 deg. angle. Then fold forward at right angle to previous run.

fold into the wood, Fig. 12-8.

Fasten the gimp at the next two corners, Fig. 12-9. Upon reaching the beginning corner, stretch the plastic gimp taut and cut it to length, Fig. 12-10. Fold the end under at a 45 deg. angle. Remove the beginning tack and reset it through the 45 deg. fold into the first corner, Fig. 12-11.

Complete installation of gimp by driving a metalene nail through the center of each side. Then drive other metalene nails 1 1/2 to 2 in. (38 to 51 mm) apart, Fig. 12-12.

OTHER TYPES OF PADDED SEATS

Padded seats are in demand wherever furniture is used. Chairs, ottomans, vanity benches, hassocks and stools can be designed and constructed with a few materials and tools.

Fig. 12-10. Cutting gimp to length. Trim it off even with outside edge of gimp at starting point.

Fig. 12-8. Drive metalene nail through fold into wood.

Fig. 12-11. Pull starting tack, fold end of gimp under and drive tack through fold.

Fig. 12-9. Second corner has been turned. Metalene nail will hold fold permanently.

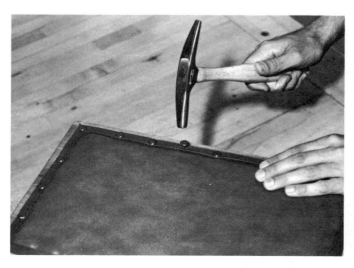

Fig. 12-12. Locate centers, drive in metalene nails. Then fill in with more nails from center to corners.

Upholstering Small Frames Without Springs

Fig. 12-13. Alternate style for padded seat. Heavier frame has padding and upholstery on sides as well as top.

Fig. 12-13 illustrates a padded seat which is easy to build. Construction details for the base or frame are given in Chapter 11.

Padded seats can be built upon:
1. Solid base (wood or plywood).
2. Framed base.

Both types are shown in Fig. 12-14. Framed bases using webbing for support are more comfortable.

FOAM PADDING SOLID BASES

Using upholsterers' shears or tin snips, cut a piece of rubber or plastic foam 1 to 1 1/2 in. (25 to 38 mm) thick to fit the base.

Apply foam rubber cement or contact cement at several locations on the underside of the foam pad, Fig. 12-15. Position the foam pad over the top of the base. Beginning at one end of the base, lightly press the foam pad to the top edge. Carefully press the foam pad in place as you move toward the other end of the base, Fig. 12-16.

Fig. 12-15. Foam padding intended for use over a solid base should be firmly attached with adhesive. Foam adhesive can be brushed or sprayed onto the padding.

Fig. 12-16. Foam pad should be firmly pressed in place on the solid base so that adhesive makes good contact.

SOLID SEAT

FRAMED SEAT
WITH WEBBING

Fig. 12-14. Padded seats may have either solid base or rails and jute webbing.

ADDING COTTON FELT

Unroll a length of cotton felt. Lay a rule beside the cotton felt and tear it to desired dimensions with your fingers. Then separate the cotton felt layers with your hands to get a 1/2 in. (12.5 mm) thickness.

Use a stapler or No. 3 or 4 upholstery tacks to fasten strips of cotton felt to the sides of the base, Fig. 12-17. Then spread a layer of dacron polyester fiberfill batting over the foam pad for an extra soft, cushioning effect, Fig. 12-18.

INSTALLING WEBBING

Webbing is laid on across both dimensions of a frame. Attach all the webbing on one direction before attaching cross webbing. Determine how many strips will be used and the amount of space between strips.

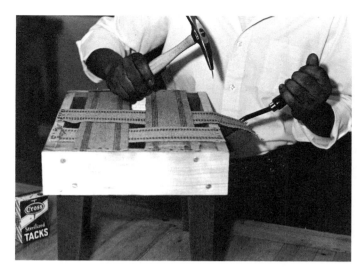

Fig. 12-19. Installing jute webbing. Tack is started with magnetic end of upholstery hammer.

Fig. 12-17. Attaching cotton felt to sides of base. Use stapler or hammer and tacks.

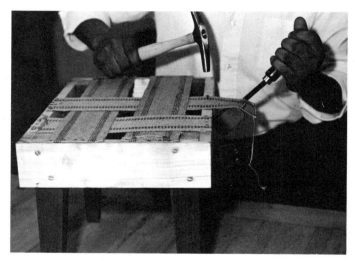

Fig. 12-20. Finish driving tack with other end of upholstery hammer.

Fig. 12-18. Adding dacron fiberfill over foam. Fiberfill gives added resilience to padding materials.

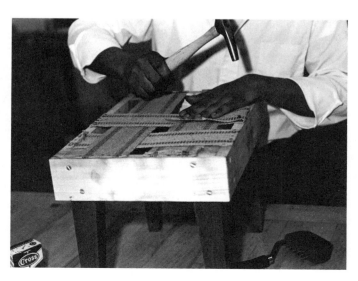

Fig. 12-21. End of webbing is lapped over and tacked to frame.

Then position the first strip and tack the webbing to the frame with No. 10 or 12 tacks. Allow enough webbing to fold back over (about 1 in. or 25 mm). Tack down the folded-over material with two tacks.

Insert the sharp points of the webbing stretcher through the webbing and stretch it taut over the opposite rail. Fasten the webbing to the rail with three tacks, Fig. 12-19. Use the magnetic (split) end of the upholstery hammer to start the tacks. Finish driving with the other end of the hammer, Fig. 12-20.

Cut off the webbing leaving enough material to fold over the top of the tacked end. Fold the end over the top and secure with two tacks, Fig. 12-21. Attach the rest of the webbing using the same method. When attaching cross webbing, weave it over and under the webbing it crosses.

If you wish to cut all webbing pieces at one time, you will have to splice a short length of webbing to each piece so you can use the webbing stretcher. Since the splice is temporary, "pin" the extending section to the webbing with a nail. Push it through the material twice as you would in basting with pins.

ATTACHING RUBBERIZED HAIR MAT

With upholsterers' shears, cut a piece of rubberized hair mat 1 to 1 1/2 in. thick to fit the frame. Lay the mat over the webbing, Fig. 12-22, and staple or tack with No. 3-4 upholstery tacks to the frame, Fig. 12-23.

INSTALLING COTTON FELT

Using fingers, tear layers of cotton felt about 1/2 in. (12.5 mm) thick and to desired dimensions for sides and top of frame.

Attach cotton felt strips to sides of frame with a stapler or upholstery tacks, Fig. 12-24. Then position the top piece over the rubberized hair mat, Fig. 12-25.

Fig. 12-23. On small frames, rubberized mat can be stapled to rails on all sides.

Fig. 12-24. Attaching strips of cotton felt to rails. Use staples or tacks, size No. 3 or 4.

Fig. 12-22. Attaching rubberized hair mat over webbing. On larger frames, it will be stitched to webbing to hold it in place.

Fig. 12-25. Add thin layer of cotton felt over rubberized hair mat.

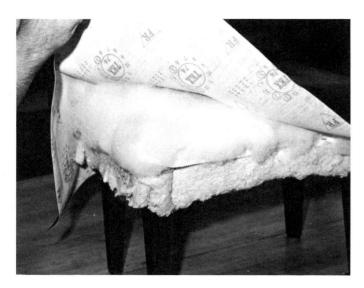

Fig. 12-26. Top covering is cut large enough to wrap under rails.

Fig. 12-27. Tack center of all sides first.

Fig. 12-28. For a better fit, shape and tack corners before completing tacking of sides.

INSTALLING COVERING

Cut a piece of vinyl plastic large enough to lap around the frame and attach on the underside. Position the fabric over the frame, Fig. 12-26. Then turn the frame upside down.

Fasten the middle of each side to the bottom of the frame with three No. 4 or No. 6 upholstery tacks, Fig. 12-27. Draw the material over tightly with your fingers.

Fig. 12-29. Using decorative nails. To assure equal spacing between nails some upholsterers use a spacer made out of cardboard.

Fig. 12-30. Slip seat reupholstering project. Often the chair must be refinished too.

Continue to fasten the cover working from the center toward the corners. Fold each corner, Fig. 12-28, drawing the material firmly to the frame and attach it with upholstery tacks.

Using an upholstery hammer, drive decorative nails through corner folds and along the bottom edge of the frame. Space the nails 1 1/2 to 2 1/2 in. apart. See Fig. 12-29.

REUPHOLSTERING SLIP SEATS

Slip seats, Fig. 12-30, are popular in upholstered furniture, particularly for dining and kitchen chairs, occasional chairs, stools and vanity benches. The slip seat is easily dismounted by removing a few screws, separating the upholstered section from the furniture frame.

Processes employed to strip used upholstery materials from a slip seat are shown in Chapter 4. Refinishing processes are discussed in Chapter 5.

Fig. 12-31. Cutting new piece of foam padding for slip seat. Use slip seat to mark material for cutting.

Fig. 12-32. Use straightedge to measure and mark covering. Work on wrong side of material.

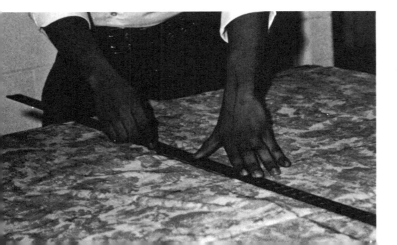

Fig. 12-33. Cutting the material. Use heavy upholstery shears and cut along lay out lines.

ATTACHING FOAM PADDING

Lay the slip seat on a piece of rubber or plastic foam, 1/2 to 1 in. (12.5 to 25 mm) thick, and mark around it with chalk. Cut along the chalk lines with upholstery shears or tin snips, Fig. 12-31.

Using a spray can or brush, apply foam rubber or contact cement at several locations on top surface of slip seat. Beginning at one end of the slip seat, carefully attach the foam pad to the slip seat. Lightly press the foam pad to one edge of the slip seat and gradually move toward the other end, pressing the foam in place.

Tear a layer of cotton felt about 1/2 in. thick to fit the slip seat. Lay it in place over the foam pad.

INSTALLING FABRIC COVERING

With a rule, straightedge and chalk, Fig. 12-32, lay out a piece of fabric large enough to wrap around the slip seat and attach on the underside. All marking should be done on the wrong side of the material. Cut along the chalk line with an upholstery shears, Fig. 12-33.

Position the fabric covering over the slip seat, Fig. 12-34. Then turn the slip seat upside down. Fasten the

Fig. 12-34. Position covering over slip seat. Be careful not to disturb padding materials.

Fig. 12-35. Flip seat upside down and attach covering, working from centers to corners.

Fig. 12-36. Shaping corners of cover. Fold extra material under from each side and tack. If folds are too thick, cut away some of material folded under.

middle of each side with three staples or upholstery tacks. Use No. 4 or 6 tacks. Draw the material over tightly, Fig. 12-35.

Continue to fasten cover, working from the center toward the corners. Fold each corner of the fabric, and draw it neatly across the corner of the slip seat at an angle of 45 deg. Cut away excess material from beneath the flap to reduce fabric thickness. Then draw

the flap tight and staple or tack it to the slip seat. Fasten the other corner flaps in the same way, as shown in Fig. 12-36.

INSTALLING SLIP SEAT

Lay the slip seat cushion on the chair seat frame. Turn the chair over holding the slip seat in place. Support the chair by resting the cushion on an upholstery trestle or a bench top. Insert a wood screw, size No. 8 or 10 and of appropriate length, through the hole in the corner block of the chair frame. Set the screw with a screwdriver. Fasten the other corners in the same way. See Fig. 12-37.

Fig. 12-37. Reattaching slip seat to chair. If screw holes in slip seat are worn, use slightly larger screw of same length.

REVIEW QUESTIONS — CHAPTER 12

1. What size tack should be used to attach the covering for a stool or other small upholstered seat?
2. Describe how to turn a corner with plastic gimp.
3. Why is fiberfill used over a foam pad?
4. If you cut all jute webbing pieces at one time, how can you use the webbing stretcher to stretch it?
5. Explain how to measure and mark a new foam pad for a slip seat.

Chapter 13
UPHOLSTERING SMALL FRAMES WITH SPRINGS

The small framed wood base in Chapter 12 can be used to construct a spring upholstered stool or seat. To make the base, follow the instructions in Chapter 11.

Either coil springs or sinuous springs may be used. Coil springs require more work and skill of the upholsterer but they are usually softer and more comfortable than sinuous springs. For additional information on installation refer to Chapter 6.

COIL SPRING STOOL

The coil spring stool pictured in Fig. 13-1 is a simple piece of furniture that can be used as a footstool or as an extra seat in a den, bedroom or family room. It can be built and upholstered in several hours.

INSTALLING WEBBING

The coil springs will require some type of support. A solid wood support or steel webs are sometimes used but the most popular support is jute webbing.

To attach the webbing use No. 10 or 12 upholstery tacks and stretch the webbing across the base of the seat as shown in Fig. 13-2. Use a stretcher to pull the webbing tight. Tack the ends of the webbing with three tacks, fold over the extra material and install two more tacks.

SEWING SPRINGS TO WEBBING

Select six double coil springs of medium firmness, 8 to 9 in. (203 to 229 mm) high. Cut a piece of stitching twine long enough to fasten each spring to the webbing at four points.

The springs have a top and a bottom. On one end the spring wire is bent toward the center. This end is the top. It should be placed up with the tip bent still further downward to prevent puncturing padding and covering placed over it.

Place one of the springs over a corner intersection of woven webbing. With the curved needle or a double-pointed straight needle, sew the base wire of the spring

Fig. 13-1. This upholstered stool with crowned coil springs is simple enough for the beginner in upholstery to make.

Fig. 13-2. Jute webbing is used to support coil springs. Cut webbing pieces long enough so stretcher may be used or temporarily attach a short strip of webbing with a nail.

to the webbing at four points. Wrap the twine tightly around the spring at each point. Continue sewing the other springs to the webbing in the same way. Fig. 13-3 shows springs in place and sewing is about to begin. With a curved needle you can work from the top pushing it down through the webbing on one side of the spring and up through the webbing on the other side of the coil. Fig. 13-4 shows stitching pattern from the bottom.

TYING SPRINGS

The tops of the springs are tied down firmly to prevent them from falling sideways out of position. They are tied to uniform height so that each spring is kept from expanding to its full height. Before tying, springs usually stand about 1 1/2 in. (38 mm) above "normal" height. Firm springs are often tied at freestanding height. Medium springs are generally tied 1 in. below normal height and soft springs 2 in. (51 mm) below.

Two-way tie
The two-way (four knot) tie is often used to fasten round seats. Each row of springs is tied lengthwise and crosswise with separate pieces of spring twine.

Measure the distance across the frame lengthwise and crosswise. Double each measurement and allow 12 in. (about 305 mm) extra for knots. With scissors, cut pieces of spring twine to run lengthwise and crosswise for each row of springs.

Fastening springs lengthwise
Drive two No. 12 tacks into the frame opposite the center of each row of springs at each end. Space the tacks 1/2 in. (13 mm) apart and drive them only halfway into the frame.

Fig. 13-3. Place coil springs over intersections of jute webbing for best results. Loose coils should be removed during stitching operations giving the upholsterer more working room.

Fig. 13-4. Stitching coil springs to webbing, bottom view. Pull twine taut to hold spring securely.

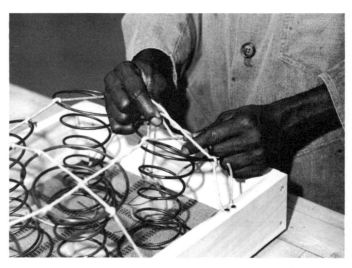

Fig. 13-5. Cross tying is being completed. In crowned tie, outside edges of coils are tilted downward toward seat rail.

Form a clove hitch knot at one end of spring twine piece. Loop the knot around two of the partially driven tacks. Then drive the tacks tightly into the frame against the knot.

Push down the edge of the first spring (nearest the double tack) to the desired height for a round seat. Pull the spring twine tightly around the top coil and make a clove spring knot or an overhand knot. Then pull the twine taut to the opposite side of the spring and tie another knot. Tie the other springs in the same way.

Tying springs crosswise
Drive two No. 12 tacks into the frame opposite the center of each row of springs at each side. Then fasten the twine crosswise following the same steps as for tying lengthwise. See Fig. 13-5.

ATTACHING BURLAP OVER SPRINGS

With a tape, rule or string, measure the distance lengthwise and crosswise over the contour of springs between the frame's edges. Add two inches each way to allow for folds. Cut a piece of burlap to these dimensions.

Fold under about an inch of the burlap along one side. Then lay the folded edge over the frame's edge. Drive three No. 3 tacks near the center of the frame through the fold, Fig. 13-6. Fold under about an inch of the opposite edge of burlap. Pull the burlap firmly over the springs and fasten it with three tacks near the center of the frame. Space the tacks about 1 to 1 1/2 in. (25 to 38 mm) apart. Fasten the other edges of burlap in the same way.

Continue fastening each edge. Work from the center toward each end. This helps prevent wrinkles in the material. Then stitch the burlap to the tops of springs with a curved or double-pointed straight needle and sewing twine.

ATTACHING EDGE ROLL

Edge roll should be attached to the top edge of the frame. It produces a soft, rounded edge which will improve the appearance of the final cover. It also keeps the cover from rubbing against the hard edge of the frame. Measure the distance around the frame and cut enough edge roll to cover.

Mark the corners on the edge roll and cut a 90 deg. notch at each corner. Attach the edge roll with tacks.

If preferred cut edge roll for each side separately. Cut ends at a 45 deg. angle before attaching them.

ATTACHING RUBBERIZED HAIR PAD

Measure and lay out a piece of rubberized hair pad large enough to cover the springs up to the frame's edges, Fig. 13-7. Then cut along the chalk lines with an upholstery shears. With a stapler or No. 4 tacks, fasten the hair pad to the frame.

Fig. 13-7. Padding of rubberized hair is installed over burlap. Edge roll has also been tacked to rails.

Fig. 13-8. Layout lines are marked on reverse side of fabric using straightedge and chalk.

INSTALLING COTTON FELT

Measure and tear off a piece of cotton felt large enough to cover the rubberized hair pad. Spread the cotton felt pad over the hair pad. The felt will give the seat a smooth, cushioning effect.

FINAL COVERING

Lay out final covering pieces on the underneath side of the upholstery fabric. The top piece of fabric should be large enough to cover the padding and attach to the upper side of frame, Fig. 13-8. Allow an inch extra width for side panels (boxing) to cover padding and to attach beneath frame. Ends of these panels should be sewed together to form one piece. Welting should be 1 1/2 to 2 in. (38 to 51 mm) wide, long enough to go around the frame. Cut out all pieces along the layout lines, Fig. 13-9.

Fig. 13-6. Fasten burlap over coil springs using tacks or staples.

Fig. 13-9. Panels of fabric are cut out along chalked lines.

ATTACHING TOP FABRIC

Position the fabric over padding, Fig. 13-10. Then turn frame upside down holding the fabric so that it does not shift. Fasten the middle of each side to top edges of frame with three staples or upholstery tacks. Draw the material over tightly with your fingers before fastening. Continue to fasten the top cover. Work outward from the center of each side toward the corners, Fig. 13-11.

Pull each corner of the fabric down firmly at a 45 deg. angle to complete attachment. This creates a small crease or fold on either side of the corners.

Sew the corner folds with a blind stitch. Use the curved needle and stitching thread, Fig. 13-12. This stitch draws material tightly together, yet is almost invisible.

FASTENING SIDE PANELS

In the next operation, you will install welting and the side panels. Prepare the welting if you have not already done so. Chapter 8, especially Fig. 8-12, will describe the proper techniques. It involves sewing the welting cord inside a long narrow strip of the upholstery material. See Fig. 13-13.

Fig. 13-12. Blind stitch corners to flatten folds. Blind stitch technique is shown in Fig. 13-18.

Fig. 13-13. Making welting. Keep seam as close to welt cord as possible.

Fig. 13-10. Attaching top cover. Position fabric over padding.

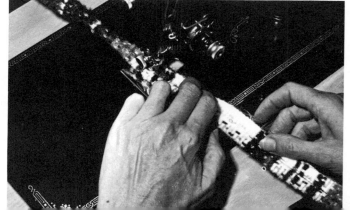
Fig. 13-11. Use stapling gun or tacks. Staple center of each side first; then fasten rest of cover working from centers to corners.

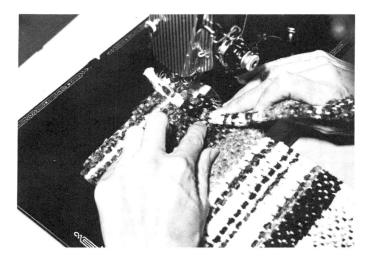

Fig. 13-14. Welting is attached to side panel of top cover before it is attached to frame of stool.

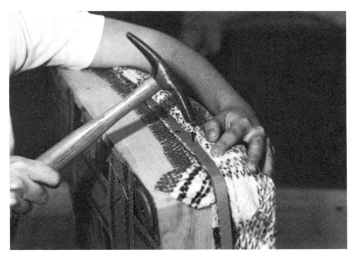

Fig. 13-15. Blind tack side panels to stool. Material is laid wrong side out. Cover will be folded down over tacking strip.

Fig. 13-16. Stapling light padding to bare frame. Extra resilience will improve finished upholstering job.

Now stitch the welt edge to the side panel. Lay the welt strip on the folded edge of the side panel and stitch the two together with a sewing machine, Fig. 13-14.

Attach the side panel with blind tacking strip. Cut a piece of blind tacking strip long enough to go around the frame.

1. Position the welt edge of the side panel, underside out, along the top edge of frame. The welt should be toward the bottom of the frame. Lay the blind tacking strip over the welt edge.
2. Drive No. 4 or No. 6 tacks through the blind tacking strip into the frame. Space the tacks 1 to 1 1/2 in. apart, Fig. 13-15.

Next, install cotton felt padding. Measure and tear pieces of cotton felt to fit the sides. Fasten felt padding over the sides of the frame. Use staples or tacks, Fig. 13-16. Pull the side panels down over the padding.

With the upholstery shears, cut the end of the side panel to length. Allow about 1 in. extra length for folding, Fig. 13-17.

Fold under about 1/2 in. of the end of each of the side panels. Then with curved needle and stitching thread, blind stitch the side panel ends together. See Fig. 13-18.

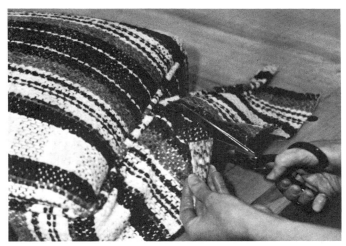

Fig. 13-17. Trim off extra material where ends of side panels meet.

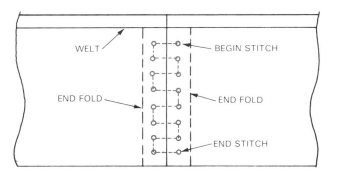

Fig. 13-18. Blind stitch pattern. Alternate curved needle between horizontal and vertical stitches.

Fig. 13-27. Use No. 3 tacks to attach burlap over sinuous springs.

the tacks 1 to 1 1/2 in. apart, Fig. 13-27.

Attach edge roll, padding, covering, legs and cambric dust cover, as described for coil spring construction.

REVIEW QUESTIONS — CHAPTER 13

1. What are the advantages of the coil spring compared to sinuous spring?
2. How would you proceed to attach edge roll to the small frame?
3. Why is a thin layer of cotton felt added on top of the rubberized hair pad?
4. Describe or demonstrate how to attach the side panels to the stool.
5. Discuss the advantages of installing sinuous springs.
6. Compare the padding of sinuous springs with padding of coil springs.

Section 4
RELATED INFORMATION

Offerings in this section are intended to expand your knowledge of upholstering. The discussion of careers opens up additional opportunities for those who look to upholstery as a new livelihood. Sources of additional information are suggested.

Finally, a dictionary of terms defines words which are part of the upholsterer's vocabulary. While such words are usually described where they occur in the text, their appearance in the "dictionary" provides an easily used method of recall.

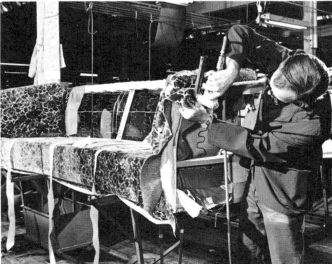

Chapter 14
CAREERS IN UPHOLSTERING INDUSTRIES

Career opportunities in upholstery are found in two distinct areas:

1. Several thousand large firms which manufacture furniture and employ large numbers of people.
2. Many thousands of small upholstery shops which

Fig. 14-1. Large furniture factories employ many people and have huge facilities.   (Flexsteel Industries, Inc.)

employ three to ten persons each.

Most large, prominent upholstering industries are located in southern and midwestern states. These industries employ designers, drafters, engineers, buyers (of materials such as cloth, wood, metal, finishes), salespersons, secretaries, computer technicians, product development specialists, mill workers, springers, upholsterers, sewers, photographers, packers, truck drivers and others.

Retail outlets employ buyers, salespersons, stockpersons, secretaries and clerks. Some will employ spot finishers who repair finishes damaged in transport. There are nearly 2,000 manufacturers sharing the upholstered furniture market.

Fig. 14-1 is an aerial view of a large midwestern furniture plant. This plant employs 750 personnel. It has 725,000 sq. ft. of space with 600,000 sq. ft. being devoted to upholstered furniture and 125,000 sq. ft. being used as production space for the company's metal division. Over 700 upholstered furniture units are manufactured here daily. The metal division manufactures spring units for all the company's nine upholstering divisions.

Obviously, not all persons employed in a furniture manufacturing enterprise are directly involved in construction or upholstering processes. However, for many of them, a knowledge of the processes is helpful.

UPHOLSTERY INDUSTRY

The upholstering industry and those industries related to it produce many of the furniture pieces we use and enjoy in our homes and at work. These products are manufactured to meet almost every need and to fit into almost any decor and life-style. See Fig. 14-2.

COMBINING MATERIALS AND SKILLS

Manufacturers build their reputations and attain success through satisfied customers. Durable upholstered furniture is as much the result of careful work as it is the result of using good materials. Figs. 14-3 through

Fig. 14-2. Upholstery is manufactured for many purposes and to fit the varied life-styles of many people.   (American of Martinsville)

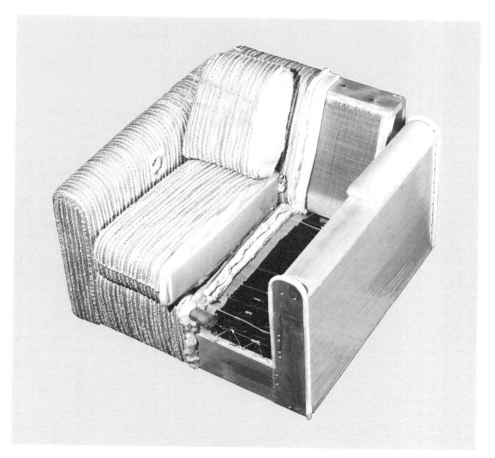

Fig. 14-3. Many different materials and parts go into manufacture of furniture. Many skills are required.
(Thomasville Furniture Industries, Inc.)

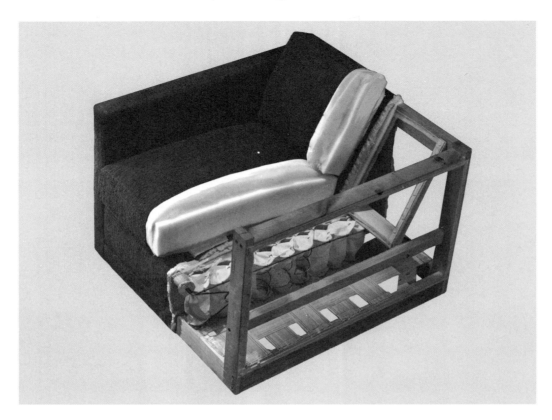

Fig. 14-4. Manufacturers are proud of their products and try to instill pride in their workers. Cutaway like this is used to demonstrate furniture quality to buyer.

Fig. 14-5. Cutaway of sofa shows frame, springing, padding and final cover. Each component represents a type of job opportunity in the upholstering industry.   (Bassett Furniture Industries, Inc.)

Fig. 14-6. Workers keypunch information onto data processing cards.   (Flexsteel Industries, Inc.)

14-5 illustrate the many parts and variety of materials that go into a chair or couch. Each step of construction requires the skills of well-trained workers.

OFFICE PERSONNEL

Successful companies depend upon efficient employees who are skilled in record keeping, typing, shorthand, accounting, public relations and selling. Designers, drafters and engineers must work together to create new designs and patterns for production of beautiful furniture, engineered to give years of trouble-free pleasure and comfort.

Efficiency in manufacturing is often improved by the use of data processing equipment, Fig. 14-6, to help control inventory, sales and shipping. The efforts of all these people result in better service and communication between furniture manufacturers and their customers. See Fig. 14-7.

FABRIC QUALITY CONTROL

Special testing carried on by technicians insures that all fabrics meet or exceed the standards of the National

Fig. 14-7. Computer operator receives computer information readout from data punched in by keypunch operator.

167

Fig. 14-8. Incoming fabrics are being checked for weaving flaws and color consistency.   (Flexsteel Industries, Inc.)

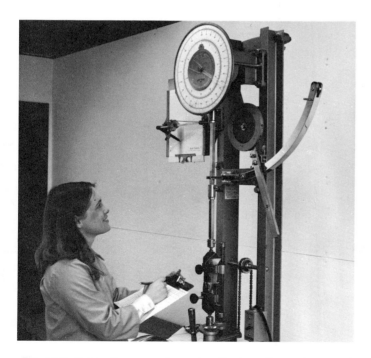

Fig. 14-9. Seam slippage and yarn tensile strength are also tested.

Fig. 14-10. Technician uses fade-ometer to determine color fastness and fading.

All incoming fabrics must pass these tests before they can be used as final coverings. Since the testing program is continuous, the manufacturer can control the durability and quality of its upholstery fabrics.

Association of Furniture Manufacturers and Southern Furniture Manufacturer's Assoc.

These tests evaluate:
1. Weaving flaws and color consistency. This is a sight inspection, Fig. 14-8.
2. Tensile strength, Fig. 14-9.
3. Colorfastness, Fig. 14-10.
4. Resistance to abrasion and wear, Fig. 14-11.

MAKING FURNITURE FRAMES

Wood parts for furniture frames are either made by a subsidiary division of the upholstery firm or are purchased by contract from another company. Specifications are generally rigid.

Fig. 14-11. Fabrics in foreground are undergoing test for pilling and fuzzing. Technician is preparing to test for abrasion and wear on a Wyzenbeck testing machine.   (Flexsteel Industries, Inc.)

Parts for furniture frames are usually assembled by skilled workers at the plant where they are to be upholstered, Fig. 14-12. Joints are often double doweled for greater strength, speed and ease of assembly. Workers apply glue to joints and attach special clamps and fixtures to hold the assembly until the glue dries. Assembled furniture frames which will have exposed parts are sent to the finishing department to receive the specified stains, sealers and top coatings, Fig. 14-13. Assembled furniture frames which are ready for upholstering are stored until needed, Fig. 14-14.

MAKING SPRINGS

Some upholstery industries purchase ready-made springs and other metal assemblies used with furniture

Fig. 14-12. Furniture manufacturing often makes heavy use of the doweled joint for strength and rapid assembly.   (Kathy Myers, WIU)

Fig. 14-14. Assembled furniture frames, ready for upholstering, are placed in temporary storage.   (Kathy Myers, WIU)

Fig. 14-13. Frames are sent through finishing department so "show wood" can be stained, sealed and varnished before upholstering. This unit has just come through an automatic spray unit.   (American of Martinsville)

frames. Other upholstery industries have metalworking departments capable of producing springs, action mechanisms for recliner chairs, and other metal parts. Experienced machinists and metal workers operate equipment to cut, form, weld and do other finishing operations. See Fig. 14-15, Fig. 14-16 and Fig. 14-17.

CUTTING PADDING

Special machine knives, operated by other workers, cut polyurethane and rubber foam padding components to specific sizes. Various parts of fine furniture, incorporating padding and covering, are pre-upholstered to save time during final upholstering processes. Fig. 14-18 shows a cutting table operation. Fig. 14-19 pictures the fabric being fastened to a furniture part.

Fig. 14-17. Spray finishing is final operation on spring unit. Spring travels along continuous chain through finishing booth. Waterfall in background helps remove airborne dust particles.
(Kathy Myers, WIU)

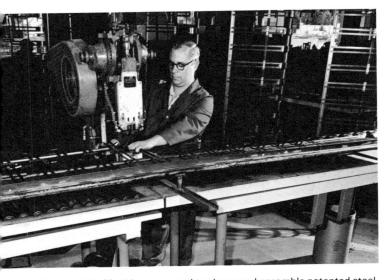

Fig. 14-15. Machines are used to shape and assemble patented steel spring units.   (Flexsteel Industries, Inc.)

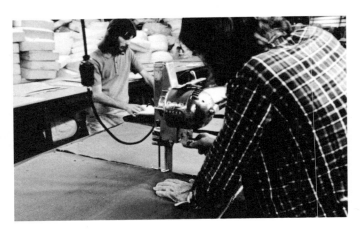

Fig. 14-18. Cutting foam padding. Cutter is using special power knife.   (Flexsteel Industries, Inc.)

Fig. 14-16. This machine operator is forming sheet metal for a patented spring mechanism.

Fig. 14-19. Skilled worker staples upholstery fabric over padding. Single components are often upholstered before assembly.

Fig. 14-20. Final covering fabrics are placed in storage until used. (Kathy Myers, WIU)

Fig. 14-21. Hand cutting operations are still a part of the industry. (Thomasville Industries, Inc.)

Fig. 14-22. Many pieces of upholstery are cut in one cutting operation with a power knife. Vinyl fabric is being cut here. (Ted Stenerson, WIU, and Howell Div. of Burd, Inc.)

Fig. 14-23. Power cutter is following chalked pattern lines made with perforated paper patterns. (Flexsteel Industies, Inc.)

CUTTING FABRICS

Large upholstery industries generally stock hundreds of fabric selections for final coverings. Buyers purchase fabrics from numerous suppliers or directly from mills. The large rolls of material are stored in stock rooms until needed, Fig. 14-20.

Inspectors go over every roll carefully as it comes into the plant checking for flaws. If major imperfections are discovered, the roll is rejected. Minor flaws are marked with a red tag so that the cutting room can cut around them.

Hand cutting

In small shops, fabric components are frequently cut out by hand. Rigid pattern pieces are laid on the material and traced with chalk. The cutter uses large upholstery shears to cut out the fabric a piece at a time. Even when machine cutting is employed, hand cutting is necessary for making repairs and for cutting quilted fabrics. See Fig. 14-21.

Machine cutting

In large plants, layers of fabrics are generally stacked together on long work tables. The cutter lays out the pattern on the top layer. Then machine knives are used to cut many layers of fabrics at once, Fig. 14-22. Component shapes are sometimes marked around prepared templates. In another method a worker forces chalk dust through perforations made in paper patterns. Fig. 14-23 shows this method.

Machine cutting operations are usually directed by skilled workers. Computer-controlled cutting is a recent development. See Fig. 14-24.

SPRING ASSEMBLY

Other skilled workers attach springs to the previously assembled and finished frames. The spring units may be assembled coil by coil or strip by strip as with the units shown in Fig. 14-25 and Fig. 14-26. Along with the springs the worker may install patented platforms such as the one displayed in Fig. 14-27.

Sinuous springs, preferred when a low profile is wanted, are installed by hand. They may be used in furniture backs, seats or in combination with other kinds of springs.

Single coil springs are attached to wire, wood or flat metal strips. See Fig. 14-28. Some companies have their own spring designs, called patented springs,

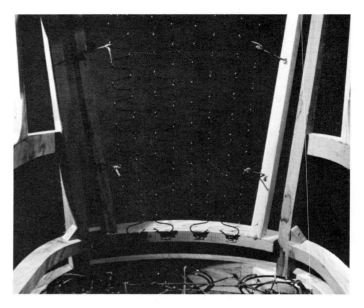

Fig. 14-26. Sinuous springs are installed by hand. Seat in this unit has coil springs.

Fig. 14-24. Computer is controlling cutting operations. No pattern is needed.

Fig. 14-25. Factory installation of coil springs requires some skill and is a hand operation. Here springs are being tied. (Thomasville Industries, Inc.)

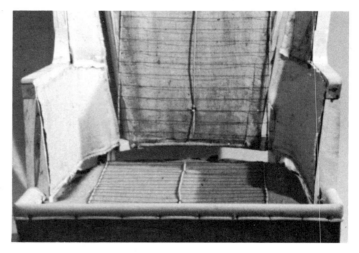

Fig. 14-27. Spring installation has been completed. Worker has also installed burlap over springs and a patented wire platform to distribute weight more evenly over springs. This chair is ready for padding.

Fig. 14-28. Single coil assembly is being attached to furniture frame. Supply bins for spring parts are located under the frame.

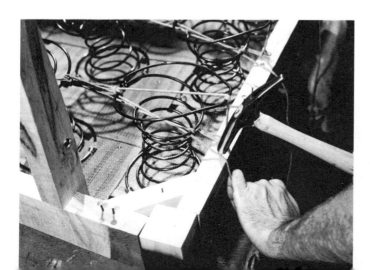

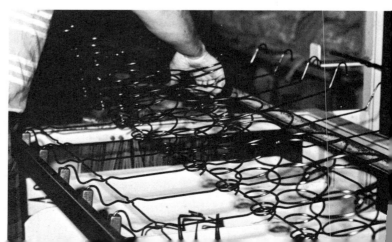

Fig. 14-29. Flexsteel spring unit is preassembled before being installed in furniture frame.   (Flexsteel Industries, Inc.)

which are used instead of coil springs. Fig. 14-29 shows such a unit. Sometimes the unit is preassembled before it is installed in the frame.

SEWING

Fabric intended for covering components is efficiently and swiftly sewn together by skilled sewing machine operators, Fig. 14-30. Extra incentive pay is often awarded to workers for the quantity of work accomplished. In large factories machine operators work on an assembly line, Fig. 14-31.

Beautiful prints are sometimes outline-quilted using lockstitch with continuous filament nylon thread. This requires special skill from machine operators who generally develop their own technique in sewing quilted designs. See Fig. 14-32.

Fig. 14-30. Power sewing machine operator sews together parts of final covers.   (Thomasville Industries, Inc.)

Fig. 14-32. Quilted designs are sewn in with power sewing machine.

Fig. 14-31. Automatically controlled conveyor transports materials to skilled machine operators.   (Flexsteel Industries, Inc.)

Fig. 14-33. With speed and skill, upholsterer tacks final covering to frame.   (Flexsteel Industries, Inc.)

INSTALLING FINAL COVERS

After springs and padding materials are added to the frame, installation of final covers begins. Both hand and portable machines are used.

Larger upholstering plants tend to use production methods and techniques more fully then smaller plants. Frames are placed on continuous, moving belt or chain lines. Skilled workers perform a variety of processes of installation as furniture reaches their stations. Every detail in the upholstery processes receives careful attention from expert upholsterers. See Figs. 14-33 through 14-36.

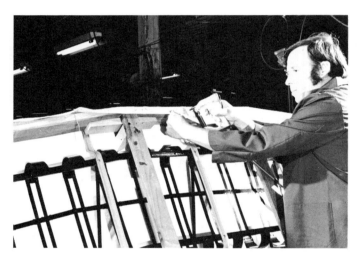

Fig. 14-34. Furniture frame receives muslin covering in preparation for final covering.

Fig. 14-36. Bucket seats with sculptured foam padding move down assembly line to receive final coverings.   (Howell Div. of Burd, Inc.)

Fig. 14-35. Team of upholsterers attach upholstery fabric as furniture frame moves slowly down assembly line.   (Flexsteel Industries, Inc.)

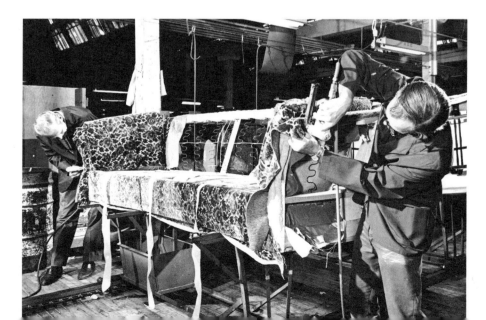

COVERING FOAM CUSHIONS

Special equipment, consisting of adjustable metal boxes operated by a skilled worker, compresses the foam or spring cushion reducing its thickness and width. Then the cushion cover is carefully slipped over the compressed cushion. Compression is then released and the metal plates of the compressor are pulled or pushed from the covered cushion, Fig. 14-37.

INSTALLING SPECIAL HARDWARE

Hide-a-bed springs, action seating mechanisms and other hardware are added to upholstered furniture to improve versatility and usefulness. Installation is usually near or may even follow completion of upholstery processes, Fig. 14-38.

Fig. 14-37. This assembly line upholsterer is stuffing foam cushions into cushion covers. (Flexsteel Industries, Inc.)

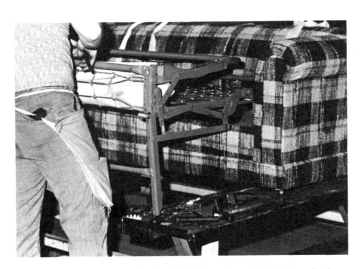

Fig. 14-38. Fold-out bed unit is being installed in hide-a-bed. (Kathy Myers, WIU)

FINAL INSPECTION

Careful inspection of furniture during all upholstering processes is important to assure quality of materials and work. Quality control may require additional work to correct small problems. See Fig. 14-39.

WRAPPING FOR SHIPMENT

Completed furniture must be protected to prevent damage. One method of protection is with the "shrink wrap." This method employs special equipment which creates a vacuum around furniture and forces plastic sheeting tightly around it, Fig. 14-40.

Fig. 14-39. Final inspection of upholstered furniture may show need for simple adjustments or repairs. This upholsterer is adjusting padding with needle-like tool called a stuffing regulator. (Flexsteel Industries, Inc.)

Fig. 14-40. Furniture pieces are vacuum wrapped before storage or shipping.

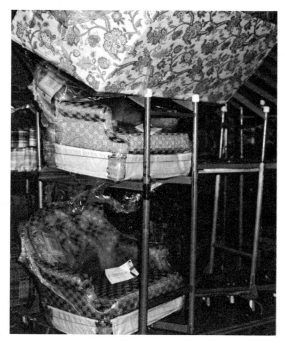

Fig. 14-41. Furniture is stored on portable trucks until it can be shipped. (Kathy Myers, WIU)

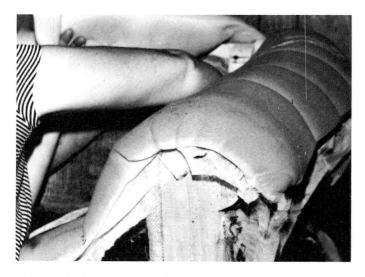

Fig. 14-42. The work of upholstery shops is to strip and reupholster used furniture thus restoring it to many more years of usefulness. This upholsterer is attaching new foam padding to the arm of an overstuffed chair. (The Wrenn House)

STORING AND SHIPPING

Completed furniture is generally wrapped, boxed or crated, then stored, Fig. 14-41, until ready for shipment. Shipment is usually by truck.

FURNITURE REUPHOLSTERY AND REPAIR

Those working at reupholstering and repairing used furniture offer a very useful and needed service in extending the life of good upholstered pieces, Fig. 14-42. Quality of work is important for success.

Whereas the skilled worker in a furniture factory works mainly at one process, the persons who repair and reupholster work at all the processes from stripping, to respringing, to padding, to installing new coverings. Some may specialize in refinishing or repairing of damaged finishes.

EMPLOYMENT OPPORTUNITIES

According to the OCCUPATIONAL OUTLOOK HANDBOOK, over half of the people working as upholsterers are employed at small upholstery shops. A few work for furniture stores and businesses such as hotels which maintain their own furniture. About one in three upholsterers is self-employed. This is a much higher proportion than in most other trades.

The most common way to enter the upholstery trade is to start as a helper in an upholstery shop. Beginners are assigned the job of stripping away old covers and padding. As they gain experience they will be assigned more complex tasks such as attaching webbing and springs, sewing on fabric and trimming. It usually requires three years of full time employment for a beginner to become a skilled worker.

REVIEW QUESTIONS — CHAPTER 14

1. Small upholstery shops usually employ from _____ _____ to _____ people.
2. List types of workers employed by industries which manufacture upholstered furniture.
3. Retail outlets (stores) employ (check all answers that are correct):
   a. Buyers.
   b. Clerks.
   c. Drafters.
   d. Engineers.
   e. Salespersons.
   f. Secretaries.
   g. Spot finishers.
   h. Stock persons.
   i. All of the above.
4. Technicians employed by furniture factories test upholstery fabrics. What tests are made?
5. What methods of cutting fabrics are used by furniture companies?
6. What happens in final inspection and quality control?

DICTIONARY OF TERMS

A

ABRASIVE: Material used to wear away other material, smooth stock surfaces, or polish finishes.

ADHESIVE: Substance used to bond materials together. A variety of natural and synthetic materials are made into cement, paste or glue.

AIR TRANSFORMER: Device used with spray finishing equipment to regulate air pressure and pulsations of the compressor, and to remove dirt and moisture from compressed air.

ALKYD RESIN: Synthetic material widely used as a vehicle in varnishes and enamels to increase durability.

ALLIGATORING: Cracks formed in a finished surface resulting in a mottled pattern caused by unequal expansion and contraction of separate coats of finish.

ALUMINUM OXIDE: (Al_2O_3) An efficient abrasive made by fusing bauxite ore in an electric furnace. It is used to make abrasive paper, cloth, and grinding wheels.

ANILINE DYES: Oily synthetic coloring agents produced chemically from coal tar. Used in coloring fabrics or wood as permanent stain.

ARRIS: The sharp edge formed by the meeting of two surfaces.

ATTACHING PLATE: A metal plate designed for fastening a leg to a seat or table with a hanger bolt.

ATOMIZATION: The process of reducing paint or liquids to minute particles, forming a fine mist for spraying.

B

BANDING: Strip of fabric often used around spring-edge and platform seats. The top edge is usually hand sewn to the edge wire and the bottom edge is fastened to the frame.

BLEACHING: Lightening effect in the color of wood produced by application of a chemical solution.

BLEEDING: The transfer of color from one finish coat to another. For example, varnish applied over an unsealed oil stain dissolves part of its color resulting in discoloration of the varnish coat.

BLIND: Work which is hidden or out of sight. Frequently used in stitching, tacking and doweling.

BLUSHING: Whitish cast formed in a finish. Often occurs in clear spraying lacquer which dries too fast as it is applied. Particularly on humid days, water vapor in the air is condensed and trapped with the finish. Retarding thinner is usually added to lacquer mixture as a preventative.

BOILED LINSEED OIL: Certain metallic driers are added to raw linseel oil, then heat treated and aged for use in the manufacture of varnish and enamel.

BORAX: Used on wood as a second coat water solution to neutralize oxalic acid bleach. Helps prevent pink shades on maple or oak.

BRUSH CLEANER: Water solution of one or more phosphates in which brushes are soaked to soften and remove varnish. Remover is effective and safe for bristles.

BURLAP: Coarse cloth, usually woven with jute or hemp fibers. It is used over springs in upholstery.

BURN IN: Process of repairing damaged finished furniture. Stick shellac, in colors to match finished surface, is melted into damaged area, then polished.

BUTTONING: Use of covered buttons to hold final covering in place and produce a low relief decorative effect.

C

CAMBRIC: Generally black or white sized cotton fabric

used as dust cover on bottom of upholstered furniture. It also prevents particles of padding from falling to the floor.

CATALYST: Substance which starts and aids in the control of a chemical action.

CHAMFER: Sloped edge formed by cutting at a slanted angle across one arris of a square edge.

CHANNELING: Tubes or channels are sewn, usually straight up and down in fabric. These are filled with stuffing materials and sewn shut, resulting in rounded ridges with depressions between them.

COIL SPRINGS: Coils formed by spirals of wire which supply the major resiliency in upholstered furniture.

COLONIAL FURNITURE: The kind of furniture first made and used in the American colonies.

COMPATIBILITY: Term used in finishing to denote ability of mediums to mix together harmoniously.

COMPONENT: Integral part which fits harmoniously with other parts to become a useful object.

COMPUTER-CONTROLLED: Directed by calculations performed with an automatic electronic machine.

CONTACT CEMENT: Cement which, when properly used, bonds two surfaces or edges together upon contact.

CONTEMPORARY FURNITURE: (also Modern) Modern day furniture made with characteristic smooth, trim lines and simple construction.

COTTON MAT (FELT): Combed cotton formed into a soft, flexible mat. It is used over rubberized hair and other upholstery materials to produce a cushioning effect.

CRYSTALLINE FINISH: A novelty finish similar to enamel or paint which, upon drying, forms a mass of wrinkles or crystals.

CUSHION SPRINGS: Springs made especially for comfort and strength in seating.

D

DACRON POLYESTER FIBERFILL: Soft, resilient padding made with plastic materials and used over other padding as a substitute for cotton mat.

DATA PROCESSING: Method of information and process analysis and control. Information is key punched into cards. Punched cards are then used in a computer for information and process analysis and control. See Computer-Controlled.

DECKING: Fabric used as substitute for expensive covering under cushions or other platforms hidden from view. Denim is generally used.

DENATURED ALCOHOL: Combination of wood and grain alcohol.

DENIM: Strong, twilled cotton fabric of excellent wearing quality. Sometimes used as decking under loose cushions.

DESIGN: Plan or scheme in which ideas and thinking are incorporated as direction for creating with materials and tools.

DOWEL: Cylinder of wood, usually birch, manufactured in a variety of diameters by a standard length of 36 inches. It is often used to strengthen joints.

DOWEL PEG: A short dowel made especially for wood joints.

DOWEL POINT: Metal cylinder with a flange and a sharp center point. It is used to mark the location of a mating hole for a dowel joint.

DOWN: Soft, under feathers of ducks and geese.

DRIER: Catalyst added to finishing material to speed curing and drying time.

DRYING: Process causing finish to harden by evaporation of solvents or by chemical (oxidation) action.

DULL FINISH: Finish without gloss obtained by rubbing or by chemical action of flattening agents.

DURABILITY: Ability to resist and withstand use, abrasion, weather, or other stresses.

DUST COVER: See Cambric.

E

EARLY AMERICAN FURNITURE: The type of furniture made and used as industry developed during the period of the American Revolution.

EARTH PIGMENTS: Coloring matter mined from the earth such as ochre, sienna and umber.

EDGE ROLL: Fabric tube filled with fibrous padding materials to roughly round or triangular cross sections. It is used to soften frame, platform and spring edges. It is sometimes made by hand but is available ready-made. Ready-made edge roll is often paper core with burlap covering.

EDGE WIRE: Heavy gage (generally 8 or 9 ga.) wire, especially made for spring edges.

EDGE WIRE CLIPS: Clips stamped from strip steel used to fasten edge wire to springs.

EMULSION: Suspension of tiny particles of water in oil, or oil in water, with the aid of an emulsifier.

EMULSION PAINT: An oil, resin, varnish or lacquer which is emulsified so that it can be mixed with water.

ENAMEL: Finishing material creating a hard, durable, waterproof finish. It is made by adding pigments to varnish to give it color and opacity.

EXCELSIOR: Shredded wood made of basswood or poplar and sometimes used as foundation padding in less expensive furniture.

EXPOSED WOOD (SHOW WOOD): Furniture parts which are finished and intentionally left exposed during upholstery processes.

EXTENDER: Material used as a filler in paint or glue to provide body and increase coverage.

F

FEATHERING: Lightly brushing thin coat of finish, using only tips of bristles, to yield a blending action.

FIBER MAT: Processed fibers of the sisal plant formed into a mat for padding.

FILLER: Material used to repair defects in wood. Examples are plastic wood, wood putty, water putty and stick shellac.

FLATTENING AGENT: Substance used in paints, varnish and lacquers to reduce gloss in finish and give it a rubbed appearance.

FLOW (finishing): Quality of a material to spread or move evenly into a uniform and level coating.

FLUTING: Concave (inside curve) band formed in an edge, cylinder, molding or surface.

FOAM CEMENT: Specially made adhesive to stick foam cushion padding to seat material.

FOAM PLASTIC: Soft, cushioning material used as padding in upholstery. It is produced from polyurethane plastic.

FOAM RUBBER: Soft, cellular and highly resilient material providing cushioning effect useful in upholstery. It is produced from rubber latex.

FRENCH POLISH: This term refers to a type of glossy surface produced as a result of using certain finishing materials. The ingredients include white shellac, boiled linseed oil, and denatured alcohol.

FRENCH PROVINCIAL FURNITURE: The kind built and used during the reigns of Louis XIV to XVI. It has simple, curved lines and is devoid of ornate carvings and gildings.

FURNITURE NAILS: Decorative nails made of brass or steel used to attach gimp or outer covering to furniture.

G

GATHER: Forming folds in fabric by drawing it along a thread or drawstring.

GAGE: Diameter or thickness of material such as wire used in springs and sheet metal used for fastening plates.

GIMP: Thin, narrow, decorative material used to cover tacks or staples around edges of covering material.

GIMP TACKS: Tacks with small, round heads used to fasten cloth gimp or tack covering invisibly around exposed portions of furniture frames.

GLIDE: Metal or plastic fastener with large, smooth surface used on bottom of furniture feet as an aid in moving furniture about.

GLOSS: Finished surface with high luster and good light reflecting qualities.

GLUE BLOCKS: Small pieces of wood attached with glue or metal fasteners to strengthen joints.

GLUE INJECTION: Method of tightening loose joint. Drill small hole, about 3/32 in. diameter into loose joint. Force liquid glue through hole into joint with glue syringe. Tighten joint with clamps.

H

HAIR: Curled hair from hogs, cattle or horses used as stuffing.

HAND RUB: Using cloth pad or felt with rottenstone or pumice and oil to smooth top coat finish by hand.

HANGER BOLT: Threaded fastener used to attach leg to table with an attaching plate.

HARMONY: Design term implying that characteristics of parts in an object are in conformity or agreement.

HELICAL SPRING: Short, lightweight coil springs with a hook at either end often used to anchor sinuous springs to furniture frames.

HINGE: Piece of hardware used to fit parts together so that one can swing free of another as a door or window.

HOG RING: Upholstery fastener resembling hog ring. It is used to install burlap, seat covers and other upholstery materials.

HOLIDAY: Spot or place missed during finish application.

I

INNERSPRING: Coil springs individually sewn in muslin or burlap pockets and fastened together in strips or ready-made units. These are used in furniture seats, backs, cushions, arms and mattresses. Also called Marshall unit.

INSPECTION: Method of quality control. Skilled workers carefully inspect products during all upholstering processes to assure quality control of materials and work.

INTERCHANGEABILITY: Parts or devices made to dimensions of close tolerances, often by mass production, which will fit into more than one assembly.

J

JUTE: Plant from which processed fibers are made into burlap and webbing. Plant grows in India.

K

KAPOK (SILK FLOSS): Silky fibers grown in seed pods of a tree called "ceiba pentandra." The tree grows best in Java. Kapok is excellent padding for pillows.

L

LAC: Natural resin used to make shellac. It is exuded from an Indian insect which lives on sap from certain trees.

LACQUER: Hard, durable finishing material made of nitrocellulose. Drying occurs by evaporation of its solvents.

LAG SCREW: Heavy, round shanked wood screw with a square head.

LAMINATE: Product made by bonding thin layers (plies or laminations) of material together with an adhesive.

LEATHER: Made from hides and skins of domestic animals. It is used for final covering on truly fine upholstery.

LEVELING (finishing): Formation of a smooth film,

free of brush marks, on a finished surface.

LINSEED OIL: Valuable vegetable oil obtained by processing flax seeds. This oil, in its boiled form, is used alone as an excellent finish. It is also extensively used in oil base paints and finishes.

LOW PROFILE SPRINGS: Springs which provide spring action slightly above or even with rail level. Sinuous, rubber webbing, and strap and helical springs are examples.

M

MARSHALL UNIT: See Innerspring.

MASS PRODUCTION: Production of parts or products in quantity, often for wide distribution.

MATERIAL: Supplies needed such as webbing, burlap, springs and nails, to construct a part or product.

MESH: Openings formed by crossing or weaving a series of parallel threads or wires as in a sieve.

METALENE NAILS: Decorative nails, generally made of steel, often used to install vinyl gimp trim.

MINERAL SPIRITS: Petroleum distillate used as a solvent in oil base paint and varnish as a substitute for turpentine.

MODERN FURNITURE: See Contemporary Furniture.

MOSS: A padding material sometimes called Spanish Moss, refined from an air plant which lodges on trees in southern United States, particularly Louisiana and Florida.

MUSLIN: Lightweight cotton cloth sometimes used as first covering over padding materials.

N

NAPHTHA: Volatile petroleum solvent used as a thinner to reduce enamel, oil-base paint and varnish.

NATURAL RESINS: Gums and resins, used in finishes, which are obtained from trees or from fossilized vegetable matter.

O

OIL STAIN: Stain having an oil base. It is of two classifications, penetrating or pigmented.

ORANGE PEEL (finishing): Spraying defect resembling the texture of an orange peel caused by improper mixture or application of finish.

OXIDIZE (finishing): Chemical reaction caused by materials uniting with oxygen. This is part of the curing and drying process of such finishes as varnish, enamel, and oil-base paint.

P

PADDING: Soft, resilient materials installed over springs or used as foundation for an upholstering piece.

PAINT: Common term referring to all protective coatings. More specifically, it is a mixture containing pig-

ment and vehicle which can be spread in a thin film on surfaces.

PANEL: Preupholstered section of covering material used to cover exposed tacks, folds or frame, as on the front of overstuffed arms.

PASTE WOOD FILLER: Material used to fill open grained wood in preparation for other finish. It consists of ground silicon (silex), linseed oil, thinner, drier, and coloring.

PICTORIAL SKETCH: A method of sketching resulting in a view of an object which appears approximately as it would by eye.

PIGMENT: Powdered substances which provide color and body for finishing materials.

PILLOW SPRINGS: Light gage wire springs made for arms and backs of furniture.

PINTACKING: See slip tack.

PLAN OF PROCEDURE: Necessary operations, listed in a logical sequence for making a product.

PLASTIC COATING: Application of certain synthetic finishes such as polyurethane varnish.

PLASTIC WOOD: Manufactured, doughlike material used to repair cracks, holes and defects in wood.

PLYWOOD: Manufactured product made with cross-banded layers (plies) of veneer or solid center stock bonded together with glue. An odd number (3, 5, 7 etc.) of plies is used.

PNEUMATIC: Related to, or operated with air pressure.

PRETACKED STRIPS: Tacking strips with tacks inserted 1 or 1 1/2 in. apart. Heads of tacks are covered with hardboard or steel strip. It is used for blind tacking leather or vinyl covering instead of blind stitching as with cloth fabric.

PROCESS: Planned operation performed in the development or fabrication of a problem or product.

PROPORTION: The ratio of the dimensions of a piece.

PULL: Device used as a handle to open a drawer or door.

PUMICE: An organic substance made by pulverizing lava rock. It is used as a fine abrasive to smooth the final coat of certain finishes.

Q

QUALITY CONTROL: Inspection and supervision of material and work quality during all upholstering processes to strive for excellence in finished products.

QUILTING: Decorative stitching around designs or prints through cover fabric with thin layer of padding and muslin backing.

R

REDUCE (finishing): To lower the viscosity (thickness) of a finishing material with a thinner or solvent.

REGULATOR: Needle-like tool used to pierce through muslin cover and move stuffing materials beneath to lessen irregularities.

REMOVER: Solvent for dissolving old paint or other finish film so that it can be removed from wood or metal surfaces.

RESILIENCE: Capability of a material placed under stress to return to its original shape.

RETARDER (finishing): Substance added to a finishing material to prolong its curing and drying time.

RETURN TIE: Short end of spring twine that is tacked to frame and is returned and tied to top edge of spring next to frame.

RIPPING TOOL: Chisel-like tool used to strip upholstery materials from furniture frames.

ROTTENSTONE: Fine rubbing and polishing compound made with decomposed siliceous limestone. It is used to smooth the final coat of certain finishes.

RUB: See Hand Rub.

RUBBER CEMENT: An adhesive especially adaptable to porous materials. It remains flexible, yet holds parts firmly together.

RUBBERIZED HAIR PAD: Curled, refined hog and other animal hair which is formed into rubberized sheet padding.

RUBBING OIL: Mineral oil especially prepared for rubbing top coat finish with pumice or rottenstone.

RUNS (finishing): Abnormal flow of finishing material usually caused by excess application.

S

SAFETY FIRST: Slogan often used around an industrial plant, construction site, or school laboratory. It implies that safety is of utmost importance in considering any task.

SEALER (finishing): Finishing material used to seal the pores of close grain wood. It is also used over stain or filler to prevent bleeding.

SEALER STAIN: Finishing material which combines a sealer and stain together.

SET (finishing): Initial hardening of finishing material prior to drying to complete hardness.

SHEEN: Luster of a rubbed, finished surface.

SHELLAC: Natural finishing material made by dissolving refined lac in denatured alcohol.

SHOW WOOD: See Exposed Wood.

SILENCER: Strip of webbing, cloth or padding material used to help prevent noise in springs from rubbing against frame.

SILICON CARBIDE (SiC): Synthetic compound (bluish black in color) made by fusing coke and silica at high temperatures. It is an extremely hard material used on tools where sharp, durable, cutting edges are needed. It is also crushed and used for abrasive paper and grinding wheels.

SILEX: Hard stone (flint or quartz) which, when finely ground, is used in paints and paste wood filler.

SINUOUS SPRINGS: Wire springs which alternately curve one way and then the other in a winding or zig zag fashion.

SISAL PADDING: See Fiber Mat.

SKEWER: Short wire tool with sharp point on one end and round loop on the other end. It is used to temporarily hold materials in position prior to sewing, tacking or stapling.

SKIVING: Thinning leather edges at an angle to form a taper in preparation for attaching.

SLIP SEAT: Upholstery seat constructed for easy removal from its frame.

SLIP TACK: Tack driven partway into a surface to provide temporary fastening.

SOLID BASE: Upholstery base constructed with flat surface of wood or plywood.

SOLIDS (finishing): Material remaining in a paint after its liquids have evaporated. Solids are usually given by percentage of weight in a paint.

SPANISH MOSS: See Moss.

SPIRIT STAIN: An aniline dye mixed with denatured alcohol to color wood.

SPLAT: Wide, flat, vertical section used in the center of a chair back.

SPLAYED: Pertains to the leg of a chair or table which angles outward in two directions from its seat or top.

SPRAY GUN (finishing): Device which atomizes (forms a fine mist) finishing material so that it can be applied by spraying in thin, uniform coats.

SPRING: Device made in several types, generally of steel wire, which is designed to render resilient support in upholstery seats, cushions, backs or arms.

SPRING BAR: Coil springs mounted on a steel bar support.

SPRING EDGE: Heavy wire, usually 8 - 9 gage, fastened to top edges of coil springs with metal clips or twine lashing to provide uniform action and support.

SPRING AND ROLL EDGING: See Edge Roll.

SPRING TWINE: Twine, generally made of jute, especially made to hold springs in position.

STAIN: Compounds of several types and a variety of colors, used to color material surfaces prior to application of other finishes.

STAPLE: "U" shaped fastener, driven with a stapler, used to install upholstery or a variety of other materials.

STEEL WOOL: An abrasive material made in several grade sizes of thin shavings or shreds of steel. It is packaged in pads and rolls.

STICK SHELLAC: Shellac in stick form used to fill imperfections in wood surfaces around knots and other defects. It is available in a variety of colors.

STRETCHER: Inexpensive fabric attached to expensive covering material to provide a fastening extension which is hidden in completed product.

STRIPPING: Term referring to: (1) removing used fabric or other materials from furniture frame prior to reupholstering or (2) removing unwanted finishing material from wood surfaces and edges prior to refinishing.

STUFFING IRON: Tool used to force loose stuffing

material into corners and crevices which cannot be reached by hand.

SYNTHETIC: Manufactured material made by combining or as a by-product of other materials.

T

T CUSHION: Seat or back cushion shaped like a capital T. Usually found on seats of furniture where arms are shorter than seat section.

T-PIN: Short wire tool with sharp point on one end and T shape on other end. It is used as a small skewer.

TACK RAILS: Parts of the wood upholstery frame whose purpose is to support upholstery fabrics. Stretched materials are tacked or stapled to them.

TAPE: Cloth or flexible steel rule used to measure and lay out upholstery materials.

TAPESTRY: A fabric in which the pattern is woven with colored weft threads. Only heavier weights are used as upholstery coverings.

TEMPERA COLORS: Finishing medium which is mixed with water for application. Pigments or colors are usually mixed with an albuminous vehicle.

TEMPLATE: Piece of cardboard, metal, hardboard, or other material used as a guide to cutting, transfer of pattern, or checking accuracy of work.

TENSILE STRENGTH: Resistance of a material to longitudinal (pulling) stress.

THINNER: Liquid for reducing viscosity (thickness) of a finishing material.

TOP COAT (finishing): Finish used over base or sealer coat.

TOUCH-UP (finishing): Repairing of color defects in finish by blending in shades of new finish with light coats.

TOW: Fiber of the flax plant. Packs easily making firm foundation padding. Less resilient than most padding material.

TRADITIONAL FURNITURE: Furniture created in Europe, particularly during the 18th and 19th centuries. It is named for the rulers who ordered it built or for the craftspeople who originated it. Typical decorations include gilt, fretwork, carvings, claw and ball feet and extravagant fabrics.

TRESTLE: Equipment used to support frames at working height during upholstery processing.

TRIACETATE: Synthetic fibers made by breaking down cellulosic materials (such as wood) with acids.

TRIAL ASSEMBLY: Dry (without glue) assembly of parts to check accuracy and function before final (bonding) assembly.

TUFTING: Use of covered buttons in pattern formation, pulled tightly to hold cover and stuffing in position. The surface is decorated with raised areas (tufts) and well defined, pleated lines.

TUNG OIL: Drying oil (also called Chinawood oil) used in water resistent paints and varnishes. Also used as finish by itself similar to linseed oil and turpentine. It is obtained from the nut of the Tung tree.

TURPENTINE: Volatile solvent used to reduce varnish, enamel and oil base paints. It is manufactured by distilling gum obtained from certain pine trees.

TWEED: A heavy fabric of mixed color in plain, twill or herringbone weave.

TWILL: Type of weave having a characteristic diagonal ribbed pattern.

TWINE: Heavy cord used for various purposes in upholstery. Spring twine is used for tying down heavy upholstery springs. Jute twine is designed for tying down lighter springs. Flax (stitching) twine is used for sewing springs to webbing, fastening buttons and for all kinds of hand sewing.

U

UPHOLSTERY PIN: See Skewer.

UPHOLSTERERS' TACKS: Made of steel with flat heads and used to hold upholstery materials to frames.

UPHOLSTERY COVERED BUTTONS: Used as decoration and to hold final covering and padding materials in position.

V

VARNISH: Durable, water resistant finishing material composed of copal gums or synthetic resins, a vehicle, usually linseed oil or tung oil, and a thinner, often turpentine.

VARNISH STAIN: Generally an interior varnish with pigments added so that both stain and varnish are applied at once. This kind of finish is usually used for coating economically priced furniture.

VEHICLE: The carrying agent (liquid) of a finishing medium.

VELOUR: Soft, tightly woven, smooth fabric with a short, thick pile. Usually made of cotton, wool or mohair.

VELVET: Pile woven fabric in which the pile is short and thick. Usually made of silk or synthetic fiber pile with a cotton back.

VELVETEEN: An imitation velvet made with cotton fibers. May be woven in colors and patterns.

VENEER: Thin sheet of wood, often laminated to core stock to make plywood or paneling. It is cut, sliced, or sawed from a log, cant, or flitch. When united in plywood it is sometimes referred to as a ply.

VENTING: Providing for free passage of air through upholstered furniture.

VINEGAR: An effective spot remover for upholstery fabrics. It should be used in a 10 percent solution with water.

VINYL COVERINGS: Nonwoven fabrics manufactured from plastic usually attached to a knitted backing cloth.

W

WADDING: Thin layer of cotton between soft paper used in the same way as cotton mat.

WARP: The threads which run lengthwise and parallel to finished (selvage) edge of woven yard material.

WASH COATING: An extremely thin coating of sealer, usually shellac or lacquer sealer, applied over stain or paste wood filler to prevent bleeding of stain into succcessive coats of finish.

WATER PUTTY: Dry powder which is mixed with water and used to fill defects in wood surfaces.

WATER STAIN: Colored pigments which are soluble in water, and are used to stain wood and other materials.

WATER WHITE: Clear, transparent as water. A term used to describe an exceptionally clear finishing material.

WEBBING: Used to support padding materials or springs. Jute webbing, a closely woven strap or tape, is made with jute fibers. Other webbing is made of rubber, plastic, wood and steel.

WEBBING PLIERS: Tool with wide jaws used to grip and stretch cut webbing, leather and other materials.

WEBBING STRETCHER: Tool used to stretch webbing taut for fastening to furniture frames.

WEBBING TACKS: Special tacks for fastening webbing to furniture frames.

WEFT: The threads carried by the weaving shuttle and running at right angles to the warp threads and selvage.

WELT: Cord filled fabric strip often sewn along seams in final covering to improve appearance and increase durability.

WELT CORDING: Light cord, usually 3/32 in. or 1/4 in. diameter, sewed inside fabric to make welting (piping). Cording can be made of paper or of textile fibers.

WOOD BENDING: Forming wood by twisting or curving.

WOOD STAIN: Any of the several agents used to color wood.

WOOF: See Weft.

WOOL: Protein-base fiber obtained from sheep. Once used extensively in manufacture of upholstery fabrics, now largely replaced by synthetic fibers.

WORKING DRAWING: An orthographic drawing, drawn to scale, usually with two or more views.

Z

ZEFRAN: Trade name for an acrylic fabric, moderately expensive, which is often used as upholstery material. It has the texture of wool and feels soft and warm to the touch.

ZIG ZAG: See Sinuous.

TECHNIQUES FOR WORKING WITH NONWOVEN FABRICS

Vinyl or plastic upholstery materials are often used on upholstered furniture which will receive heavy use or where durability is wanted for other reasons.

These covering materials are produced in many patterns and textures. The backing may be of spun, woven or knitted materials and are made from either manufactured or natural fibers.

In general, the methods of working plastic coverings are the same as for woven fabrics. There are some variations, however, which are used by such expert craftspersons as Guy Eklund of New York City. These suggestions will assure a more professional job and a more durable one.

(Photographs provided through the courtesy of Uniroyal Coated Fabrics Department)

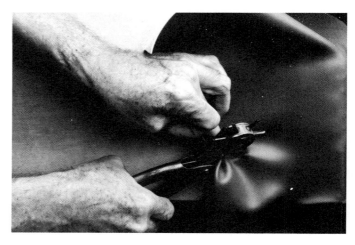

3. Rounding is easier if you use a leather punch to make a neat hole at the corner. Then cut from the edge up to the hole.

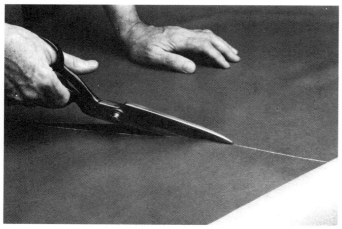

1. Allow an inch extra on all sides of the piece when cutting out the pattern pieces. This will make installation easier.

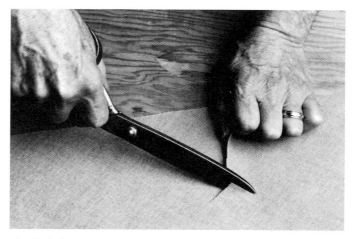

4. Reinforce the fabric at points of stress such as where a seat covering wraps around an arm post. Make the cut as usual, working on the back side.

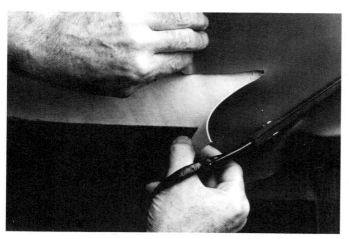

2. To ease the strain on material at corner cuts, and to avoid danger of ripping, you should round off the end of the cut.

5. Iron on a patch of nonwoven heat sensitive fabric over the points of the cut. Use a dry iron at recommended setting.

184

6. When the patch is cool to the touch, go back over the original cut with scissors so that both the fabric and the patch are cut to the same point.

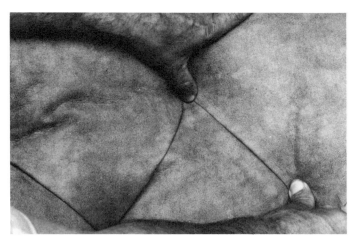

8. Stretch and fold the fabric from button point to button point. Tuck the fold so its opening points downward where it will not trap dust.

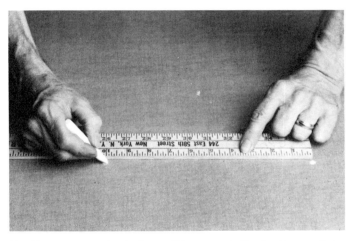

7. To prepare vinyls for tufting, mark the button points on the back side of the fabric.

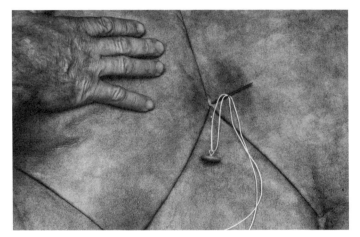

9. Stitch buttons at points where the folds meet. Use heavy thread to secure the buttons.

ACKNOWLEDGEMENTS

The author gratefully acknowledges the contributions of friends, associates and family to this book. Gratitude, appreciation and thanks are extended especially to:

My wife, Lois, and our children, Tom and Jenny Zimmerman, and Dan and Judy Williams, for their help and encouragement; Ted Stenerson and Judy Meyers for their photography; Dr. Wendell Swanson, Dr. Charles Meline and other colleagues of Western Illinois University for their interest and cooperation; Mel Alexander, Gregory Lund, Steve Soderstrom, Mark Stapelton, Aziz Sulieman, Gary Zabilka and the many other students who, in one way or another, contributed to the book's preparation; My editor, Howard "Bud" Smith, whose extensive contributions and additions to the illustrations and manuscript are evident throughout the book.

Further, a book of this nature would be extremely difficult to write and publish without the cooperation of upholstering and related industry. The author and publisher appreciate the assistance of the following firms:

Adjustable Clamp Co., Chicago IL;
Albatross Chemical Co., Inc., Long Island City, NY;
American of Martinsville, Martinsville, VA;
Barrow Fabrics, Inc., Canton, MA;
Basset Furniture Upholstery Division, Newton, NC;
Borden Chemical, Columbus, OH;
The John K. Burch Co., Grand Rapids, MI;
M. L. Campbell, Inc., Kansas City, MO;
Chittenden & Eastman Co., Burlington, IA;
James B. Day Co., Carpentersville, IL;
Deft, Inc., Alliance, OH;
Duo-Fast, Elkhart, IN;
Fastener Corp., Franklin Park, IL;
Flexsteel Industries, Inc., Dubuque, IA;
The Franklin Glue Co., Columbus, OH;
The Geier Mattress Co., Cincinnati, OH;
General Finishes Sales and Service Corp., Milwaukee, WI;
Handy Button Machine Co., Chicago, IL;

Howell, Div. of Burd, Inc., St. Charles, IL;
King Adhesives Corp., St. Louis, MO;
Kroehler Manufacturing Co., Naperville, IL;
La France Fabrics, Division of Riegel Textile Corp., Atlanta, GA;
Lochner Manufacturing Co., Fort Wayne, IN;
Minwax Co., Inc., Clifton, NJ;
George W. Mount, Inc., Greenfield, MA;
C. S. Osborne & Co., Harrison, NJ;
Savogran Co., Norwood, MA;
The Sherwin-Williams Co., Oak Brook, IL;
The Singer Co., Springfield, NJ;
Thomasville Furniture Industries, Inc., Thomasville, NC;
Uniroyal Coated Fabrics Dept., Mishawaka, IN;
Universal Seng, Georgetown, KY;
The Upholstery Supply Co., Brookfield, WI;
Valdese Weavers, Inc. Valdese, NC;
Watco-Dennis Corp., Santa Monica, CA;
The Wrenn House, Macomb, IL.

We acknowledge also, the special assistance of Mr. Tom R. Baldwin, Flexsteel Industries, Inc., Dubuque, IA; Mr. Norton L. Butler, Chittenden & Eastman Co., Burlington, IA; Mr. David Hill, Barrow Fabrics, Inc., Canton, MA; Mr. Raul House, The John Burch Co., Berwyn, IL; Mr. Rex Jones, Kroehler Manufacturing Co., Naperville, IL; Ms. Elizabeth Jordan, Uniroyal Coated Fabrics Dept., Mishawaka, IN; Mr. Henry Loomis, A. Hoenigsberger, Inc., Bridgeview, IL; Mr. Wayne Netzley, Howell, Div. of Burd, St. Charles, IL; Mr. John P. Romano, James B. Day Co., Carpentersville, IL; and of Mr. and Mrs. Charles (Sharon) Wrenn, The Wrenn House, Macomb, IL.

INDEX

Index